IMAGES
of America

CZECHS OF CHICAGOLAND

On the cover: The Legion Tavern in Berwyn was a popular gathering place for the Czechs of Chicagoland. (Courtesy of Frank Magallon.)

IMAGES of America
CZECHS OF CHICAGOLAND

Malynne Sternstein

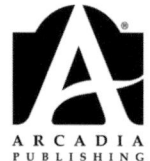

Copyright © 2008 by Malynne Sternstein
ISBN 978-0-7385-5178-4

Published by Arcadia Publishing
Charleston SC, Chicago IL, Portsmouth NH, San Francisco CA

Printed in the United States of America

Library of Congress Catalog Card Number: 2007939007

For all general information contact Arcadia Publishing at:
Telephone 843-853-2070
Fax 843-853-0044
E-mail sales@arcadiapublishing.com
For customer service and orders:
Toll-Free 1-888-313-2665

Visit us on the Internet at www.arcadiapublishing.com

Contents

Acknowledgments		6
Preface		7
Introduction		8
1.	The First Czechs in Chicagoland	11
2.	City at the Tavern of Pilsen	23
3.	California Dreaming and Winter's Days	65
4.	Cicero and Berwyn	95
5.	Czechs in Chicagoland Today	119

ACKNOWLEDGMENTS

With deep gratitude I thank the many Czech Americans who shared their time and memories with me. Their candidness, trust, and fascinating stories were essential to this book and invaluable to me.

In particular I would like to thank Rose and Joseph Pritasil, who are inspirational in the way they have chosen to live their lives and raise their children. Thanks also to Rose Pritasil, Ingrid and Mirek Chybik, MaryAnn Chybik, Rose and John Long, Zdenka Kadlecek, Rosemary Kozelka, Jean Mensik, Vera Wilt, Camille and Frank Mensik, and Angela Bultas. Very special thanks to John Pritasil, whose generosity of spirit and enthusiasm were of constant encouragement. I thank also Marge Stueckemann, Ken Dvorsky, and Paul Nemecek. Special thanks go to Frank Magallon (Strnad on his mother's side), whose impeccably cared-for collection of Berwyn memorabilia is as excellent as the man. To Ray and Matthew Mulac go my deep thanks for sharing their family's story and for being such decent men.

I am indebted to Cary Mentzer, vice president of the Czechoslovak Society of America (CSA), who allowed me to work with latitude in CSA's museum and library. Jean Hruby and Annette Schabowski of Sokol America, Bob Baumruck and the Masaryk School students, Kennan Seda, Dolores Beneš Duy, Evelyn Fergl, Ed Bruna, and Bernice Vendl were all deeply inspirational. And I give tremendous thanks to the staff of the Consulate General of the Czech Republic in Chicago for their incredible support.

I would also like to thank the people of the many institutions who gave so liberally of their energies: June Pachuta Farris of the University of Chicago Library, Morag Walsh and Theresa Yoder of the Chicago Public Library, Julie Bachrach of the Chicago Parks District, and the staff of the Chicago Historical Society. Their professionalism daily adds to my appreciation of responsible scholarship. To Fr. Jim Collins of St. Procopius, one of the very first people to respond to my call for information about the Czechs in Chicagoland, I owe a debt of gratitude.

Melissa Basilone of Arcadia Publishing, for her fastidious and compassionate editorship; Miloš Štehlík, for his inspiration through the years; Norbert Blei, for his sense of humor; and Esther Peters, for her raw smarts, deserve special thanks. Finally, I give my thanks, ad infinitum, to my mother, my sister, my daughter, and my patient and giving husband, for their love and encouragement. They not only made this book possible, they make me possible.

Preface

Let me start by emphasizing that a book about the Czech Chicago was certainly long overdue. Since the mid-19th century, the Czechs or the "Bohemians," as they sometimes called themselves, were leaving their imprint on the fabric of Chicagoland through their work, achievements, culture, and lifestyle. Since the peak during the first decades of the 20th century, the number of Czechs arriving to Chicago from their homeland in the heart of Europe was progressively declining, but for most of the century Chicago and its surroundings have with no contest maintained their central position in the life of the Czech American community.

Landmarks such as the Bohemian National Cemetery or the Thalia House in the Pilsen neighborhood, the statues at the University of Chicago campus or in the vicinity of the Adler Planetarium, and numerous other buildings in Berwyn and in Cicero are the reminders of important moments in the history of Czech Chicago. To most contemporary Chicagoans the name of Cermak evokes nothing more than a relatively lackluster road they are driving through on their way to work or home. But back in Cermak's homeland, the first Democratic mayor of Chicago became over the years a legend, comparable only with the reputation of another colorful, although infamous, Chicago figure of the jazz age. True, other eminent Czechs would later become presidents of foreign countries or state secretary here, but for a long time, there was hardly a more glorious symbol of the opportunities offered by the New World to talented and perseverant outsiders in search of freedom and prosperity than Anton Cermak.

Even less known, but not less important, was the role Chicago played in the establishment of independent and democratic Czechoslovakia at the end of the First World War.

This story needed to be told, and I am glad that the author of the book you are holding in your hands did so with such insight, eloquence, and passion.

Marek Skolil
Consul General of the Czech Republic, Chicago

INTRODUCTION

As late as 1970, Chicago's Czech community has been called the "most ethnically conscious and active city after Prague," despite the fact that it holds few records of firsts for Czechs in the United States. It is not the precedence of Czech churches, businesses, and schools that commends Chicagoland as a citadel of Czech ethnic consciousness and civic and social activity but the quality of that consciousness.

Any study of the Czechs in Chicago and its environs, or in the greater United States for that matter, must take into account the deep social rift that existed among the Czechs as an ethnic group at the very outset of their immigration. The differences within the Czech community made for certain intraethnic conflicts and debates in their newly adopted land, debates that were of necessity underlying in the Czechs' existence as citizens of the Habsburg Empire but that with the freedoms of life in the United States, could, and often did, come to the fore.

As subjects of the Catholic Habsburg Empire, the Czechs were beholden to officially subscribe to the Catholic faith. But once in the United States, Czechs were free to practice whatever religion they pleased. As a rule, this meant that the Czechs of Chicagoland were either Catholic, Protestant, or freethinker. The latter made up the majority of Czechs in the city. Czech freethinkers were often considered atheist and antideist by their Christian compatriots. But the designation does not necessarily denote a lack of faith in a greater power. Indeed, there were several crypto-freethinkers and some outright subscribers to the freethinking movement among Bohemian Catholic priests and Protestant ministers. In addition, among the freethinking Czechs were also subgroups: Czech rationalists, true atheists, secular humanists, and skeptics. The atmosphere of the United States in the mid-19th century was quite conducive to the latter group, whose penchant for questioning authority found fertile soil in such an open-minded climate.

Many of the Czechs who emigrated in the 19th century did so because of religious restrictions in the Austrian-held Bohemian lands. For them and their children, settlement in Chicago meant, finally, the freedom to practice their faith, or to speak plainly, in some cases not to practice any faith. This three-fold religious identity gives the countenance of the Czechs a less unified appearance than many other European ethnic groups, and it did (and perhaps to some extent still does) lead to disputes among the Czechs themselves. But when it came to a sense of national identity the fact of their shared origins unified the Czechs at those points in history when unity was most direly required.

Following in the style of many histories and studies of the Czech experience in the United States, this essay uses the terms *Bohemian* and *Czech* to refer to the Czechs as an ethnic group. Bohemian, strictly speaking, denotes those who live in or come from the area known as Čechy in Czech and Bohemia in English. The Czech lands—as a nation-state and historically as a territory of the Habsburg Empire—are comprised of the regions of Bohemia and Moravia (Morava), but the peoples of those regions have been known collectively as Bohemians in their diaspora. In the United States especially, the early Czech émigrés, whether they came from Bohemia or Moravia, were called and increasingly referred to themselves as Bohemians. This book will use the terms interchangeably for the most part, although the term *Czech* will be favored when any ambiguity might be present.

The story of the Czechs in Chicagoland that follows attempts to operate both as a formal chronology of the history of Czechs as an ethnic group in the Chicago area from the late 1840s and early 1850s up to the present day and as an intimate story of the lives of individual Czechs and Czech families who came to Chicago and its environs to escape political or religious oppression and economic hardship in their native land. The photographs in this study reflect this kind of division, a division that is more often arbitrary than it is actual. The story of the *Czechs in Chicagoland* is told in parallel narratives: through images of well-acknowledged historical value, that is, famous Chicagoans and internationally recognized, news-making events, and also in portraits of the private lives of families who lived through, played an as yet unrecorded part in, and were affected, or passed over, by these events. The hope is that in telling the tale of the Czechs in Chicagoland this way, a sense of the great history of this industrious, humble, and intrepid group is deepened by its relationship to the personal stories of a handful of families who made their way across land and ocean and through time—measured in births, marriages, and deaths—to the great metropolis of the Midwest.

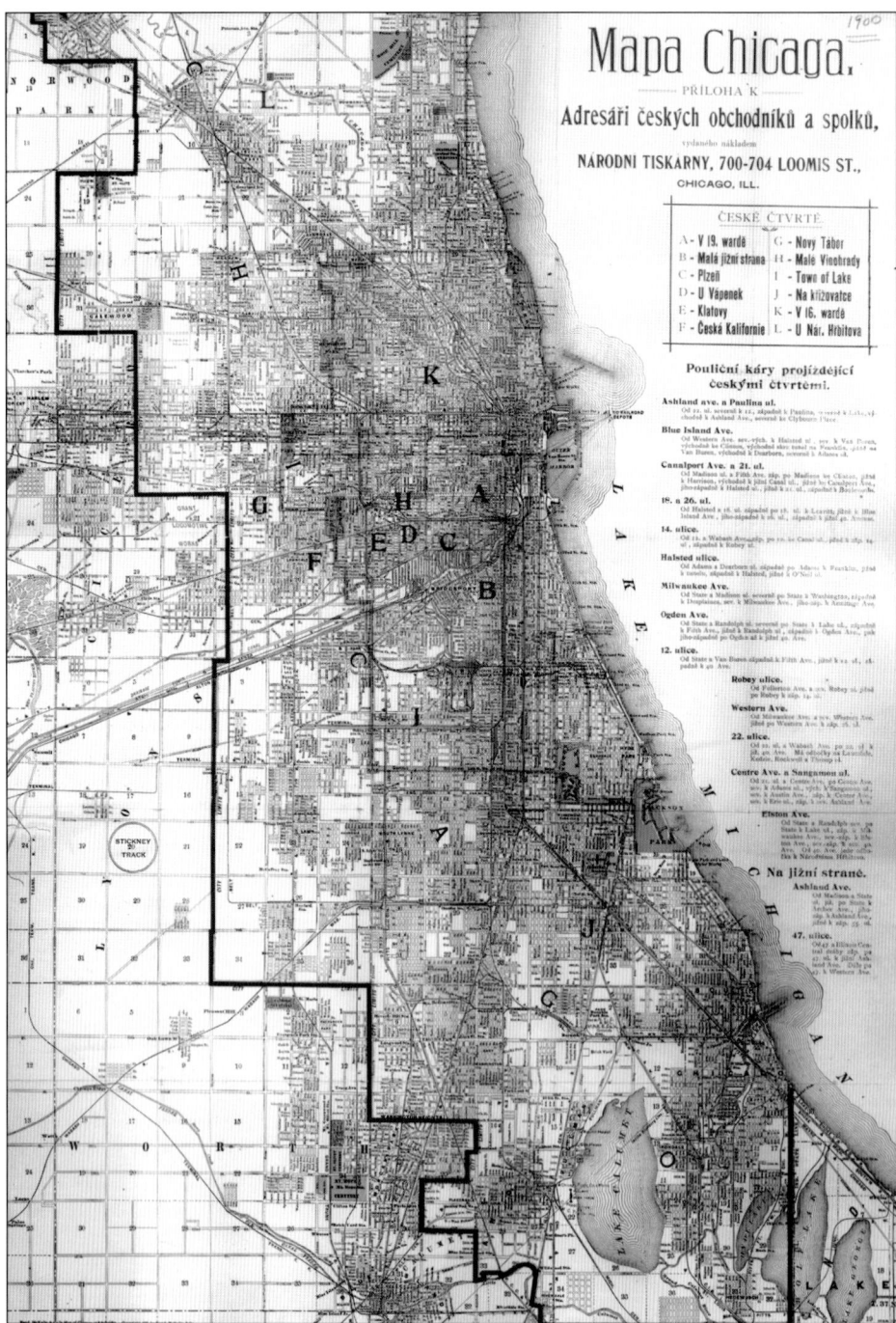

This 1895 Rand McNally map of the city of Chicago was expertly overlaid in 1900 with the neighborhoods, designated A through J, of Czech colonies, with Czech districts as far south as Grand Crossing (Křižovatky) and as far north as the colony around the Bohemian National Cemetery. The map is not only proof of the thriving Czech character of the city but also of the Czech community's sense of its legitimate place in Chicago. (Courtesy Chicago Public Library Special Collections and Preservations Division, CCW 55.)

One

THE FIRST CZECHS IN CHICAGOLAND

There is much dispute about who was the very first Czech to settle in Chicago. Some say he was Moravian physician František Valenta, who arrived in Chicago in 1849, or a working-class Bohemian whose name has been overwritten by history. A Bohemian Jew, Henry Horner (grandfather of Illinois governor Henry Horner) emigrated earlier. Horner had a dry goods business in downtown Chicago and was among the most successful businessmen in the United States.

The first ethnic Czech to come to Chicago may have been Vojtěch Šklíba. Records confirm that Šklíba arrived in Chicago in 1846. He made his living as a saddler and carter and had a flourishing business on Michigan Avenue.

As a rule, the first Czech émigrés to Chicagoland came as single men. Of these, many were political exiles, like Vojtěch Náprtsek, fleeing persecution for participation in the 1848 rebellion against Habsburg rule. These political refugees brought with them values of civil liberty, individual rights, and freedom of speech. They dedicated themselves to Czech national autonomy; indeed, Czech Chicagoans laid one of the symbolic foundation stones— with the inscription "What blood unites, the sea will not sever" ("Co krev pojí, moře nerozdvojí")—for the National Theatre in Prague in the late 1860s.

In 1855, Jan Slavic opened the first Czech tavern in the city on Clark Street near Chicago Avenue. This neighborhood, bounded by Wells Street (then Fifth Avenue) and extending over several streets, was one of the first homes in Chicago to Czech émigrés.

While there were Czechs in Chicago in the 1850s, the first real wave of émigrés came in the 1860s, as economic refugees. Among them was the family of Frederick Nový, born in Chicago in 1863. As a young boy, Nový saved his money for a microscope and, after years of study, became the pioneer of the science of bacteriology.

Once Chicago was connected by rail with New York, it became a destination for larger waves of Czech immigrants, lured by the city's garment factories, docks, and stockyards. Many of these Czechs settled around the municipal cemetery in an area they called Písek, or the Sand(s). When the city decided to convert the cemetery into a park (today's Lincoln Park), they were forced to move. These Czechs and those of downtown Chicago pushed west across the Chicago River to colonize a community they called Praha, which became the first full-fledged Czech neighborhood in Chicagoland.

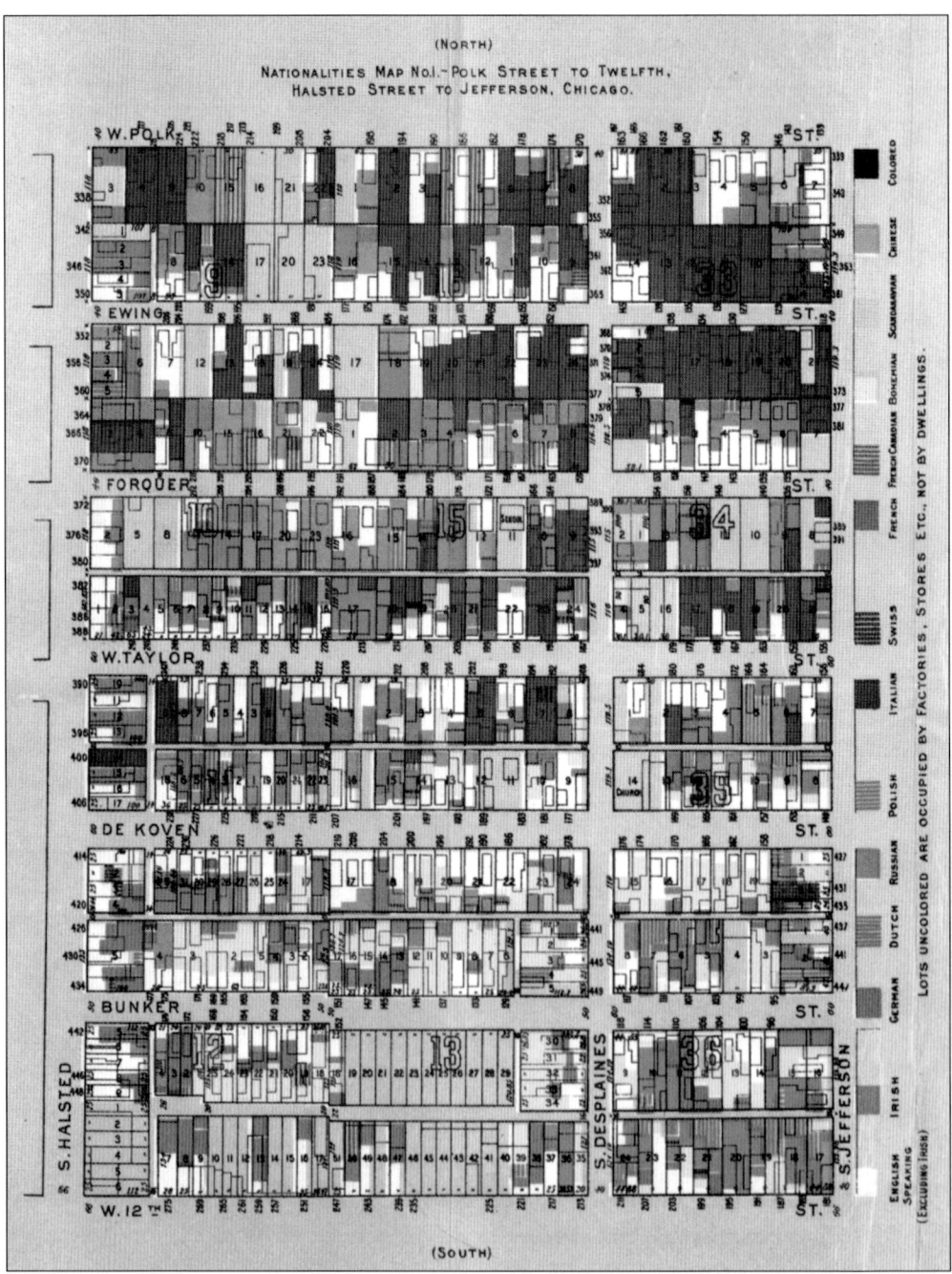

This map by Hull House shows the ethnic makeup of the area around the settlement house founded in 1889 by Jane Addams and Ellen Gates Starr. The Bohemian population is marked by the lightest shade on this map. Hull House was for many immigrants—Czech among them—a haven in the new country for its pioneering educational and social programs. (Courtesy CSA.)

Henry Horner (1818–1878) is considered by some to be the first person of Bohemian heritage to settle in Chicago. A Jew from the village of Ckyn near the German border, Horner came to Chicago in the early 1840s and established the first wholesale business in the city that grew at one point to be the largest of its kind in the United States. Horner's namesake grandson is perhaps best known as the first Jewish governor of Illinois (1933–1940). (Author's collection.)

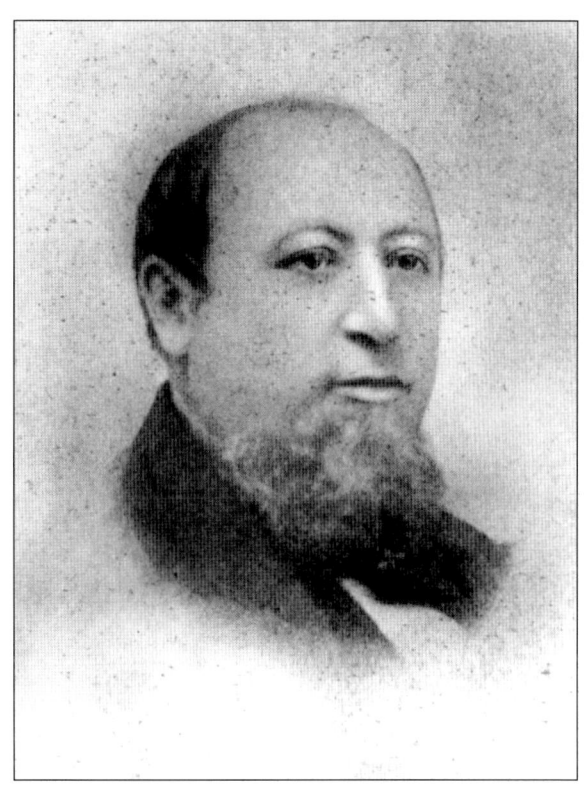

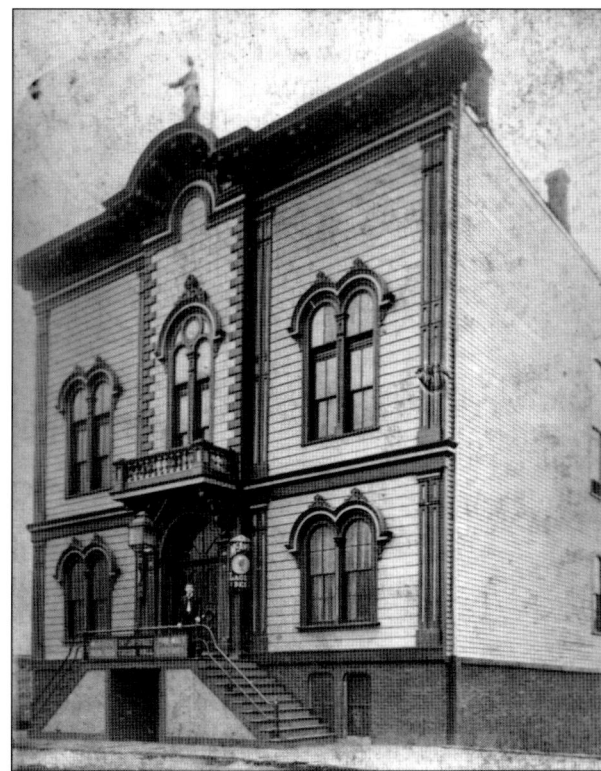

In 1861, the first Czech civic association was established in Chicago on Taylor Street. Called Slovanská Lípa (Slavonic linden tree—the linden being an important symbol of Czech national spirit), it was founded by František Novák. With no hall of its own as yet, the association rented space at German halls for meetings and social get-togethers. (Courtesy CSA.)

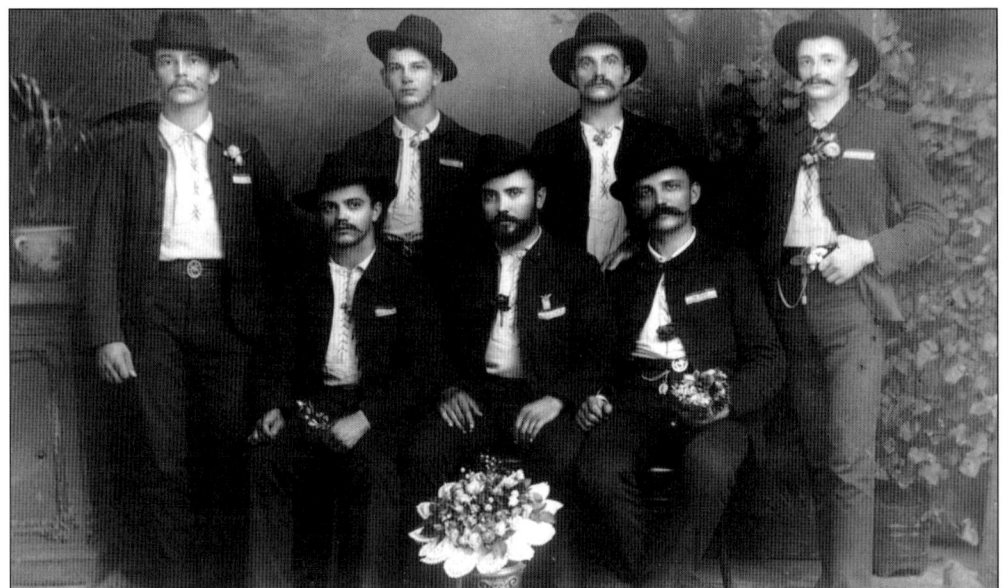

A national Sokol organization—Národní Jednota Sokolská (national union of Sokols)—was established in Chicago in 1878. Sokol leader Karel Štulík was invited from Bohemia to Chicago in the 1880s so that he might teach and train the members of the burgeoning movement. Štulík took to his new environment quickly and became an editor of the Svornost newspaper and, with his medical training from Bohemia, a physician in his community. (Courtesy University of Chicago, Archive of Czechs and Slovaks Abroad.)

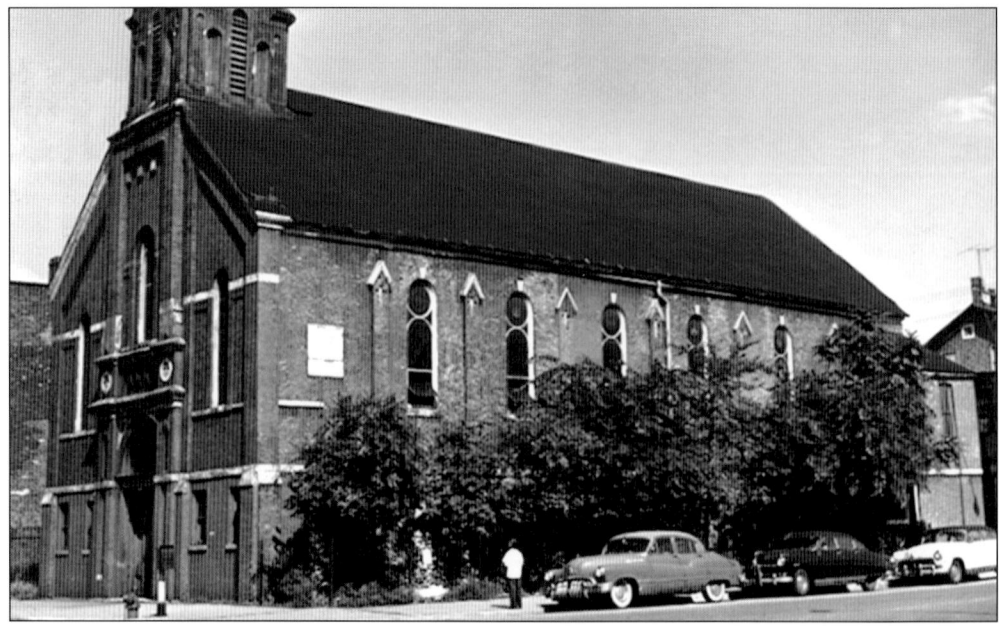

St. Wenceslaus (Svatý Václav), organized in 1863 and located at DeKoven and Des Plaines Streets, was the first Czech church built in Chicago. The building celebrated its last mass on July 10, 1955, after which its congregation was merged with Holy Guardian Angel parish. With the Czech population dwindling in the area and a city plan for an expressway to cut through the heart of Praha, the church was razed in 1955. (Courtesy Chicago History Museum.)

Of the so-called 48'ers, perhaps the most important was Vojtěch Náprstek. Náprstek, a socialist and freethinker, arrived in the United States in 1848 seeking political asylum. In 1857, when the Austrian monarchy granted a blanket amnesty to political dissidents, Náprstek returned to Bohemia. He amassed a sizable collection of Americana (and Czech Americana, specifically) to open a museum of American culture in Prague (it operates to this day). (Author's collection.)

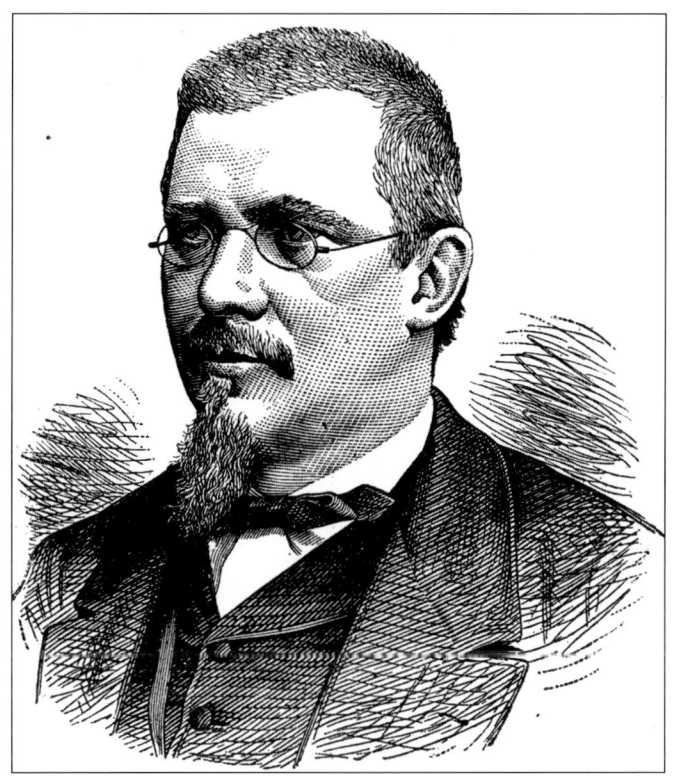

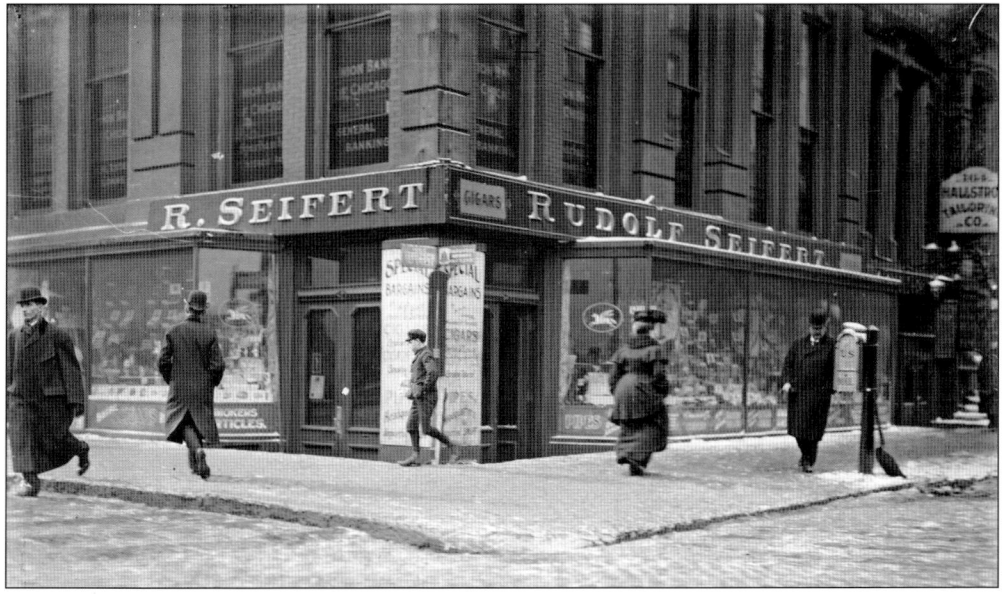

A common industry for many 19th-century Czech émigrés was the cigar business. Czechs were expert at the rolling and packing of quality cigars, and many of their stores, like Rudolf Seifert's depicted here, took up prime locations in the central business district of downtown Chicago. (Courtesy Chicago History Museum.)

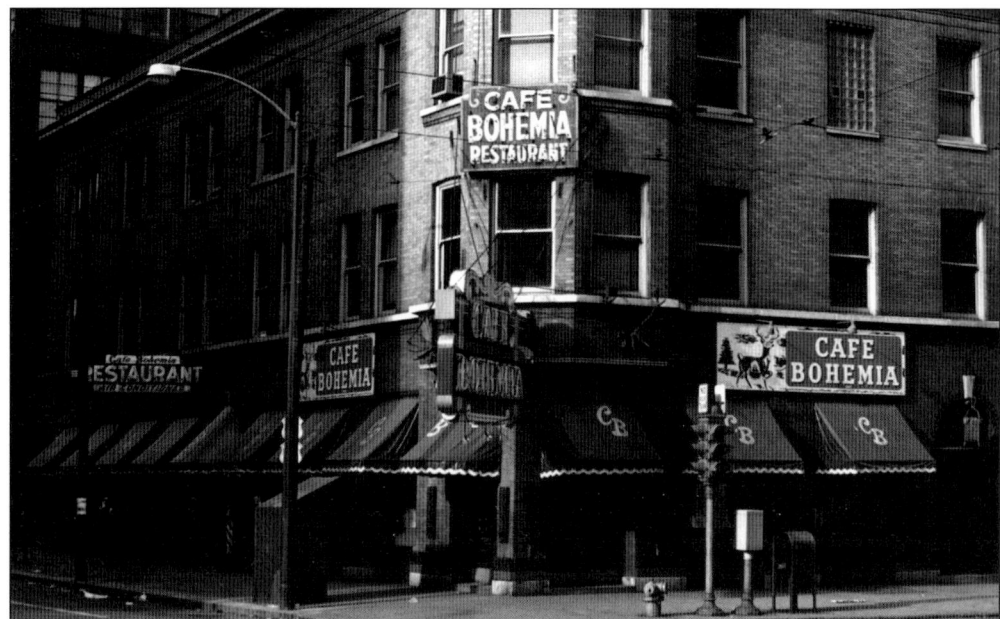

Café Bohemia at Clinton and Adams Streets was established and run by Czechs, although it drew its clientele from all over the city and beyond with its impeccable reputation for its menu of exotic game, including buffalo, elk, moose, bear, and other even more esoteric meats. The restaurant closed not long after this picture was taken, but its reputation is still alive and of legendary proportions today. (Courtesy Chicago History Museum.)

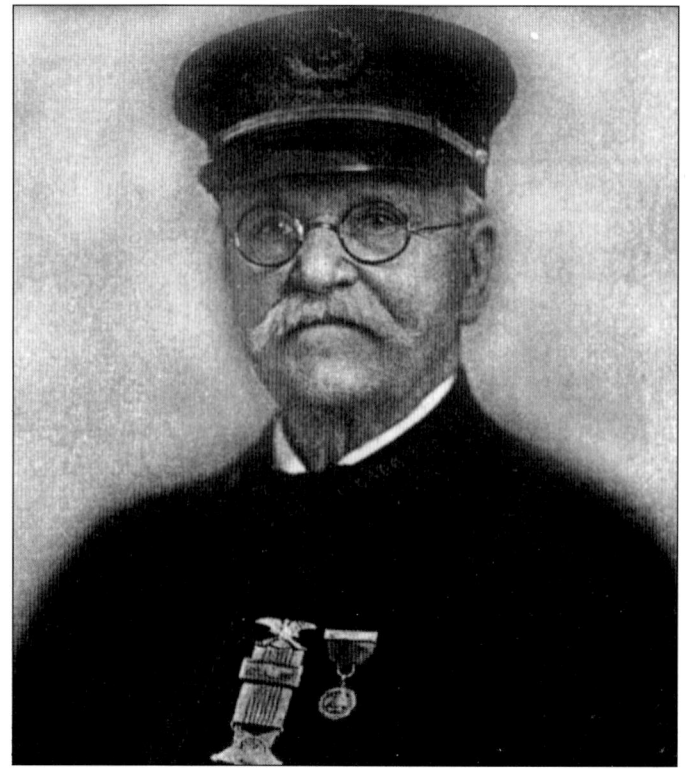

František Stejskal Sr. and Jr. came to the United States in the mid-1850s with one of the first large waves of Czech immigration. František Jr., pictured here, was only 13 years old when he arrived in Chicago in the autumn of 1854. By 1864, František Jr. was a veteran of the Civil War and František Jr. established a bar in the downtown area. In 1892, František Jr. and Jan L. Novák established a bank in Chicago at 675 Loomis Street in the new Czech colony of Pilsen. (Courtesy Paul Nemecek.)

František Boleslav Zdrůbek was an erudite man infused with a dedication to the Czech community and the retention of its Czech identity through the fostering of a cohesive Czech community in Chicago, one with its own newspapers, civic services, and businesses. But Zdrůbek also took ardently to his new homeland and in his many writings it is clear that his desire for the Czechs to become Americans, and model Americans, was a priority that merged with his work to retain the Czech language and customs among his compatriots. (Author's collection.)

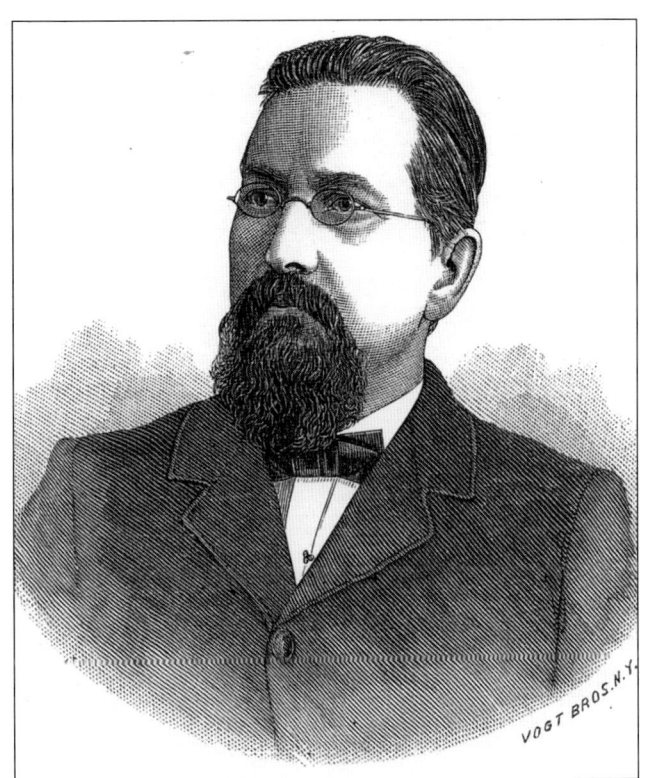

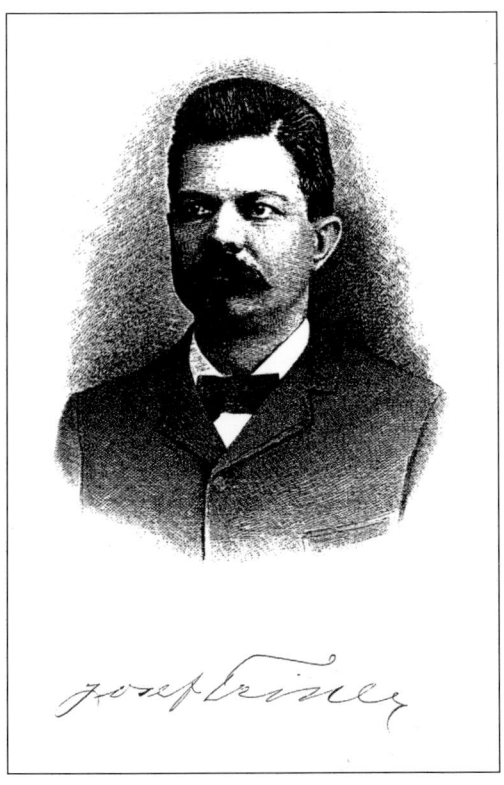

Josef Triner Sr., a leader in the early Czech community, was born in Kaceřov, Bohemia, in 1861. He established a successful business in "healing wine," which he passed down to his son, Josef Jr. In addition to his political activism for the Czechs of Chicagoland, Triner was one of the early members of the Czech-American National Council. (Author's collection.)

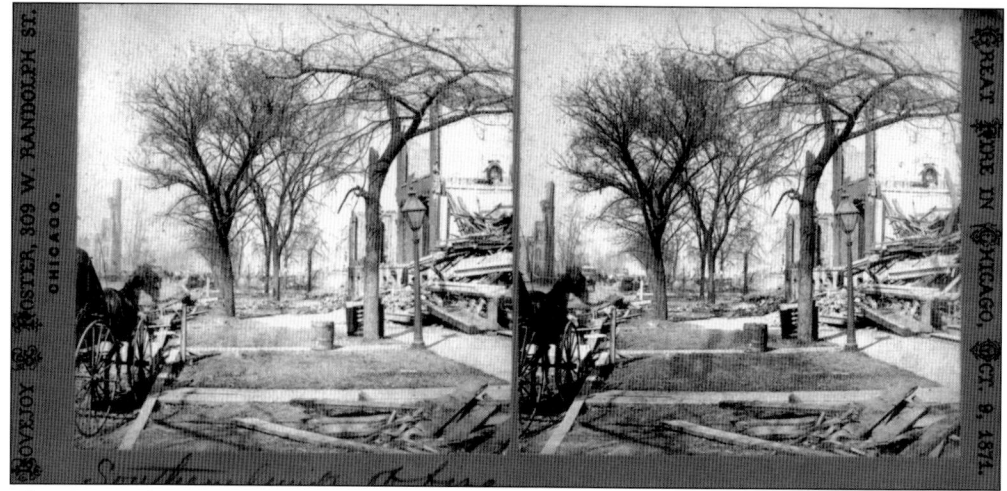

The Great Chicago Fire devastated most of the central and northern portions of the city, but it spared the community west of its legendary point of origin, the O'Leary barn. The Czech community of Praha was located immediately behind this site and, after the flames had been extinguished, both the O'Leary land and the plots of the majority Czech population to its west remained untouched by flames. Property values soared as a result, and many Czechs, spurred by the promise of economic gain, sold their property and moved to the new Czech colony of Pilsen. (Courtesy Chicago Public Library, Special Collections and Preservation Department.)

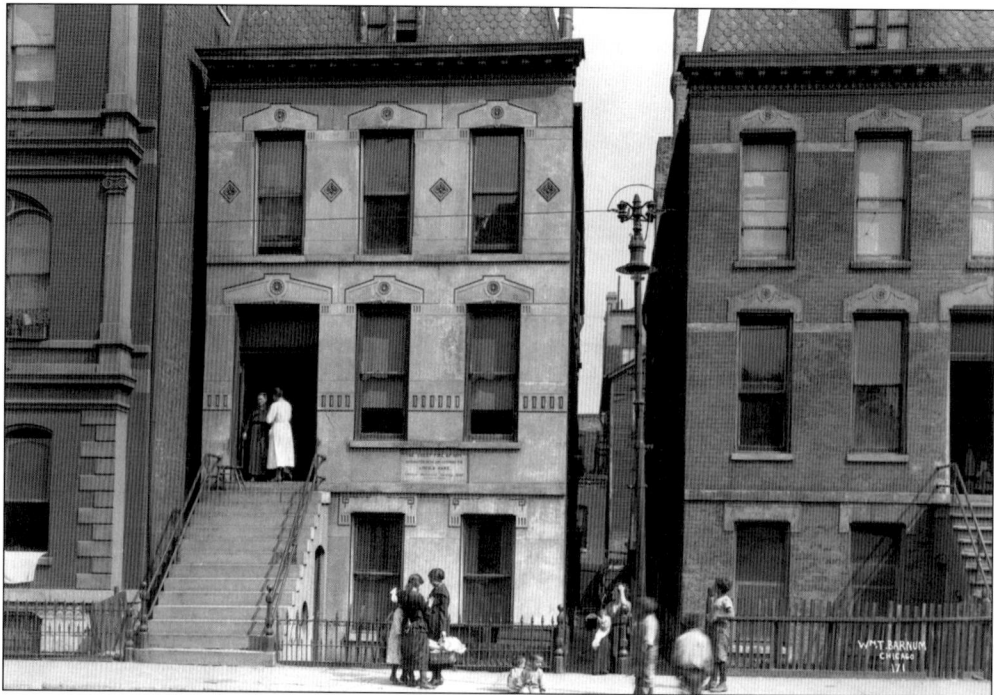

A fashionable roof and stone steps lead to the front door of 137 DeKoven Street. The Czech Kolář family bought the plot from the O'Learys, razed the barn and cottage, and built a fire-code building in 1879. A plaque was added to commemorate the site as the origin of the Great Chicago Fire. In the 1920s, a Czech city alderman, John Toman, introduced a resolution that the home be bought, torn down, and replaced by a fire station. (Courtesy Chicago History Museum.)

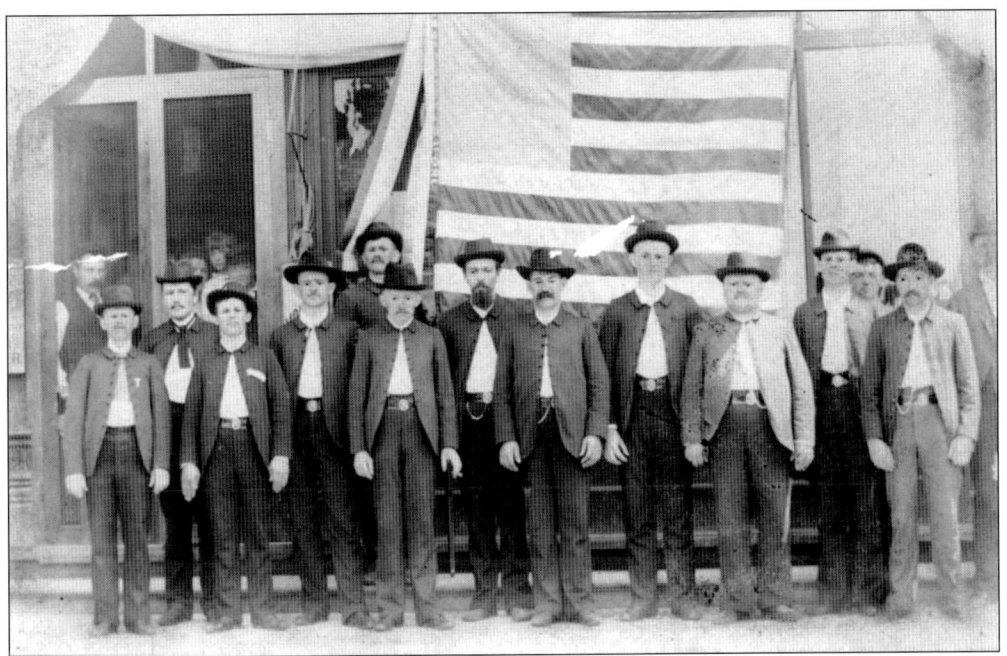

This 1894 picture shows the members of the Sokol Tábor Hall at Karlov and Fourteenth Streets and gives evidence of the early settlement of so-called Merigold or, according to the Czechs, Nový Tábor (new settlement). Sokol Tábor is one of the oldest sustained Sokol lodges in all of Chicago and the United States. (Courtesy CSA.)

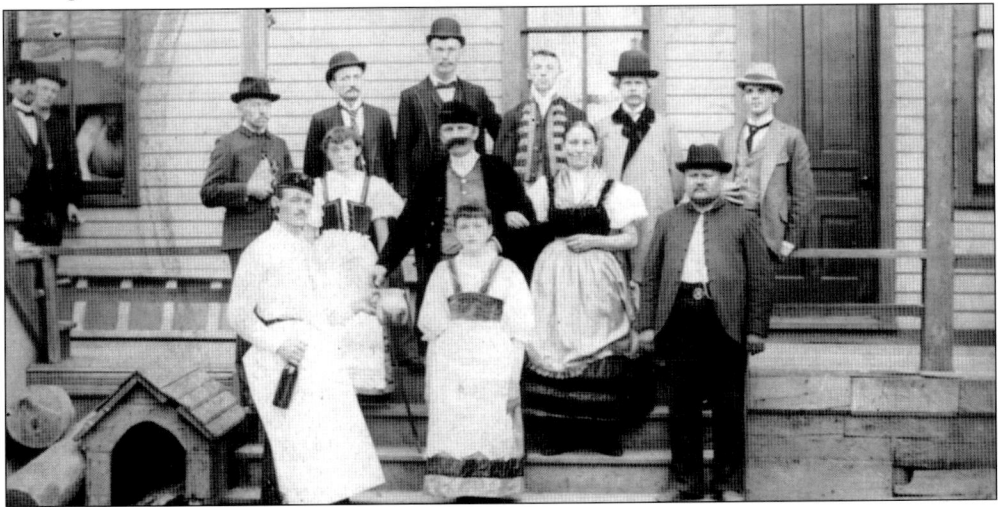

Amateur theater and singing societies like Lyra, Hlahol, and Volnost were a very important part of Czech life. Theater had been an important source of national pride for the Czechs under Hapsburg rule, and its association the growing movement for Czech independence from its Austrian rulers was sewn into the fabric of Czech national consciousness. The practice continued in the New World, and despite one's "day job," if one possessed any talent for the stage, one was welcome and encouraged to participate in the community's productions. In this image, assembled in front of the Sokol hall are members of a stage production from around 1900. (Courtesy Chicago Public Library, Special Collections and Preservations Division, LCCC 1-165.)

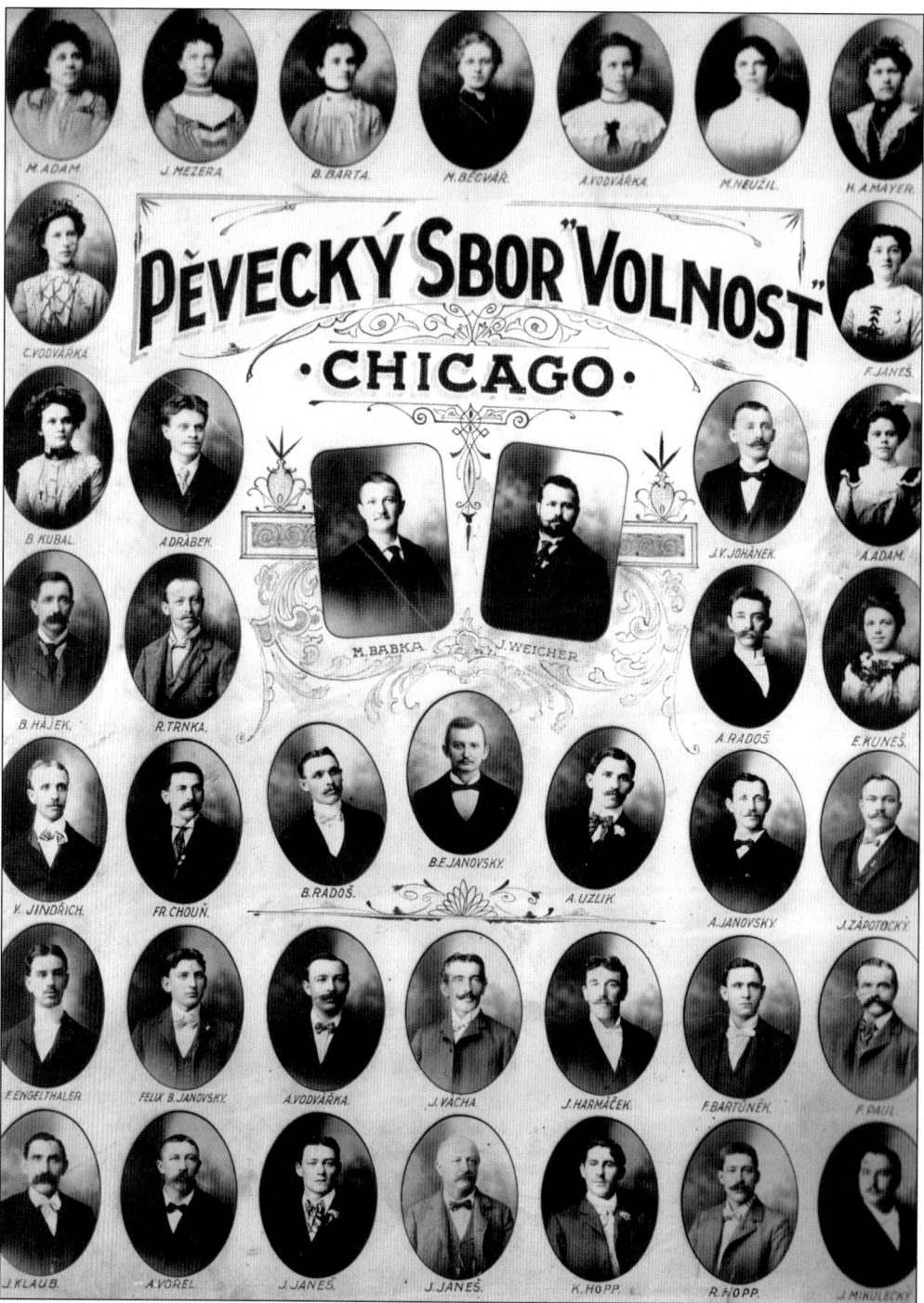

Czechs are famous for their musical gifts and enthusiasm. The *pěvecký sbor*, or singing group, pictured above is one of the earliest formed in Chicago among Czech émigrés. Its name Volnost, or freedom, exuberantly invokes the newfound liberty in their adopted homeland. (Courtesy CSA.)

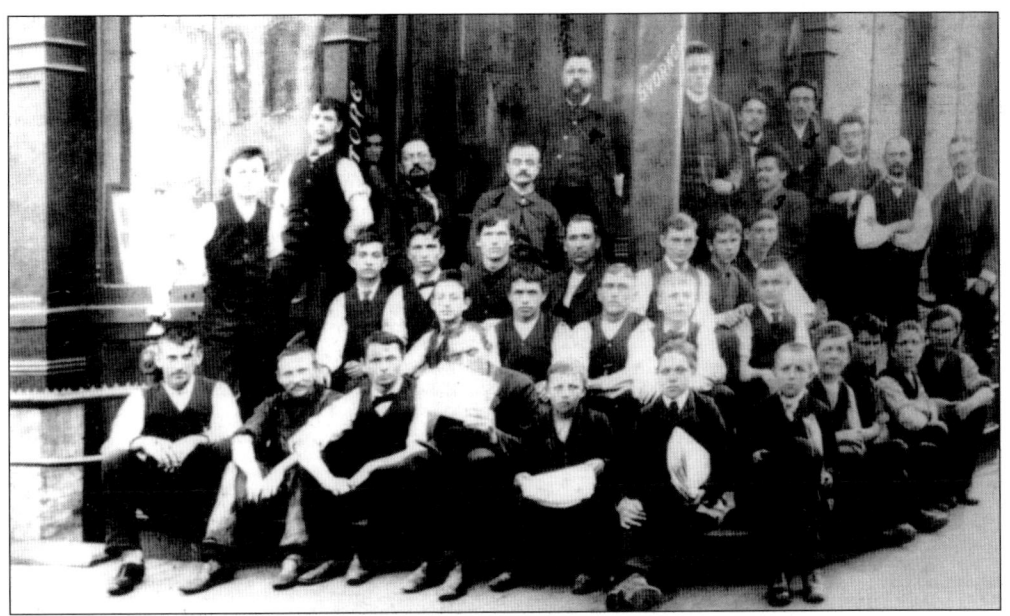

In 1875, the freethinkers (a rationalist and nontheistic sect) had their voice in the *Svornost*, a widely-read labor newspaper. In this photograph, August Geringer (standing, fifth from left) is annotated with a numeral 1 and František Zdrůbek (standing, fourth from left), another leading freethinker, with the numeral 2. The staff of the paper is pictured here in front of Svornost's first offices, which were located on the corner of Twelfth and Clinton Streets in Praha. (Courtesy Paul Nemecek.)

> Jelikož jsem nyní svůj dřívější hostinec tak zvaný
>
> **„Saloon v Plzni"**
>
> čís. 105 Fisk ul.,
>
> zase převzal, měv jej dříve pronajatý, oznamuji to všem svým bývalým přátelům a známým, by mne zase neopomíjeli tak

This 1874 *Chicagsky Vestnik* advertisement for Matěj Škudera's Saloon v Plzně (saloon in Pilsen) on Fisk Street testifies to the fact that the tavern that is often credited with giving the neighborhood its name to this day was in operation well before the 1880s, the time period most historians of the Czechs in the United States refer to as the date the bar opened. The advertisement also makes it clear that the neighborhood that would become Pilsen was already in the 1870s a destination and perhaps home for Czech immigrants. (Courtesy CSA.)

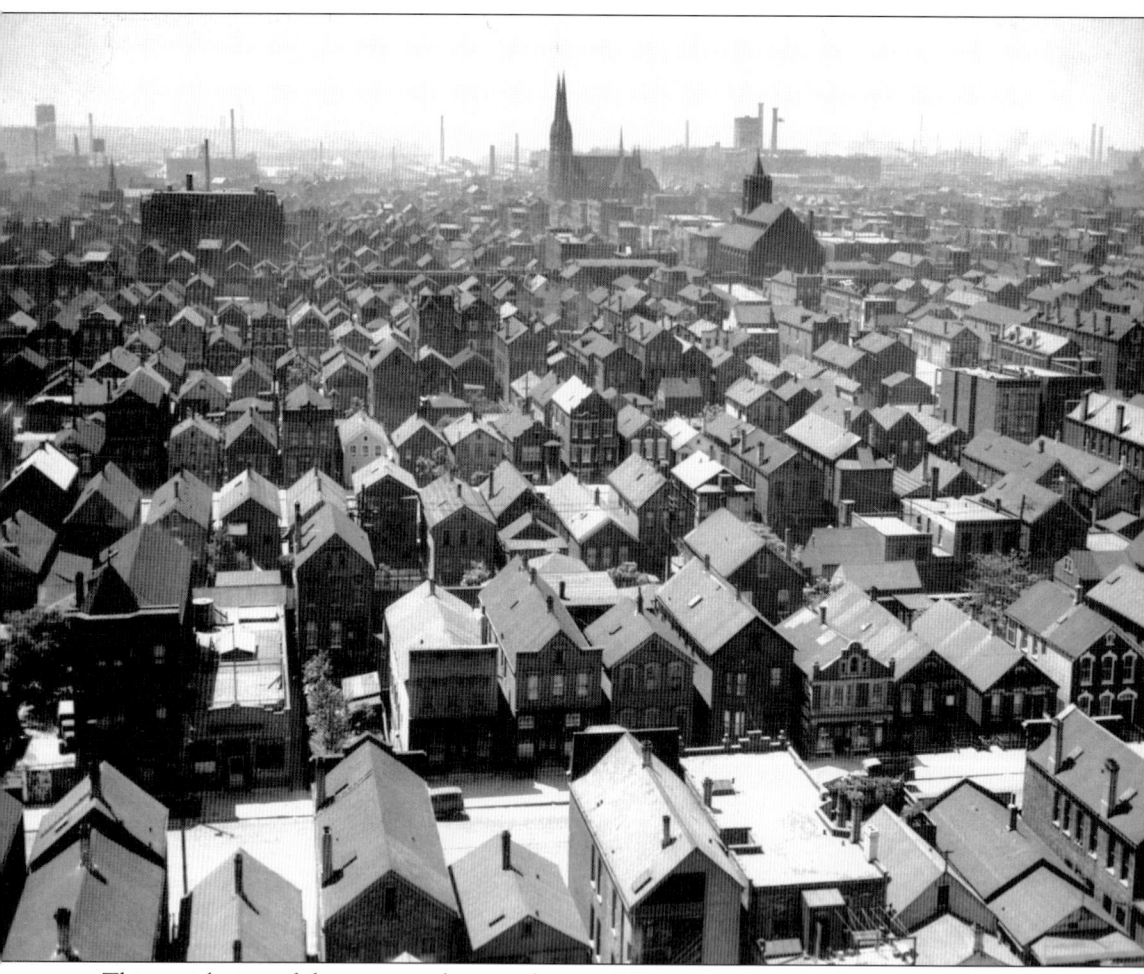

This aerial view of the near southwest side onto Pilsen was taken in the early 1920s and gives a clear picture of how developed the neighborhood was by this time. Homes crowd every block and range from modest two-story wood frame house to taller multiresidence brick structures. (Courtesy Chicago History Museum.)

Two

City at the Tavern of Pilsen

The settlement of Pilsen on the city's southwest side was contemporaneous to the existence of Praha. Evidence exists that Czechs were living in the lower west side as early as 1868. At the end of 1870, František Fučík had established a grocery store on Fisk (now Carpenter) Street and his father-in-law, Bartoloměj Kakuška, had a home on Evans Street (today's Eighteenth Street).

After the 1871 Great Fire, Praha's plot values increased exponentially. Many Czechs decided to sell, as the new fire code mandated they rebuild in brick and stone. Those Czechs who could not afford to remain in Praha began to settle in the Pilsen neighborhood, where they could build affordable wood-frame houses. Although Pilsen was dominantly a working-class neighborhood, it was also one that offered a lively community life, with successful theaters, clubs, churches, schools, and banks.

Pilsen was not an exclusively Czech community (Slovenes, Slovaks, Lithuanians, Germans, and East European Jews were to be found in its midst), but it was overwhelmingly Czech, down to its alias, taken from the tavern, Hostinec u města Plzně, that Matěj Škudera established in the mid-1870s at 103 Fisk Street (today's Carpenter Street and Nineteenth Place), named after the famous brewing town in Bohemia.

Businesses sprung up quickly on Pilsen's Eighteenth Street, with the first Czech hall built as early as 1873. Because of strong religious and philosophical differences (freethinking, Catholic, and Protestant affiliations) in the otherwise unified community, the proliferation of organizations makes it difficult to singularize the Czech experience. The Czech press reflected these differences. In the late 19th and early 20th centuries, the Czechs had many newspapers of various political platforms from which to choose. Being a highly literate group, they could sustain several newspapers at once, and, socially conscious as they were, they gathered around newspapers to voice their deep involvement in the growing labor movement.

The influx of Czech immigrants enlarged from the 1860s to 1900, making Pilsen, the largest Czech enclave in the United States, and Chicago—with at least 10 Czech communities in 1900, home to approximately 75,000–100,000 Czechs—the third-largest Czech city in the world, after Vienna and Prague. But by the early 1900s, expanding to Pilsen's west, a new Czech settlement promised to be even greater than its older siblings. The 1920s and 1930s in Czech California would mark the community's hey-day.

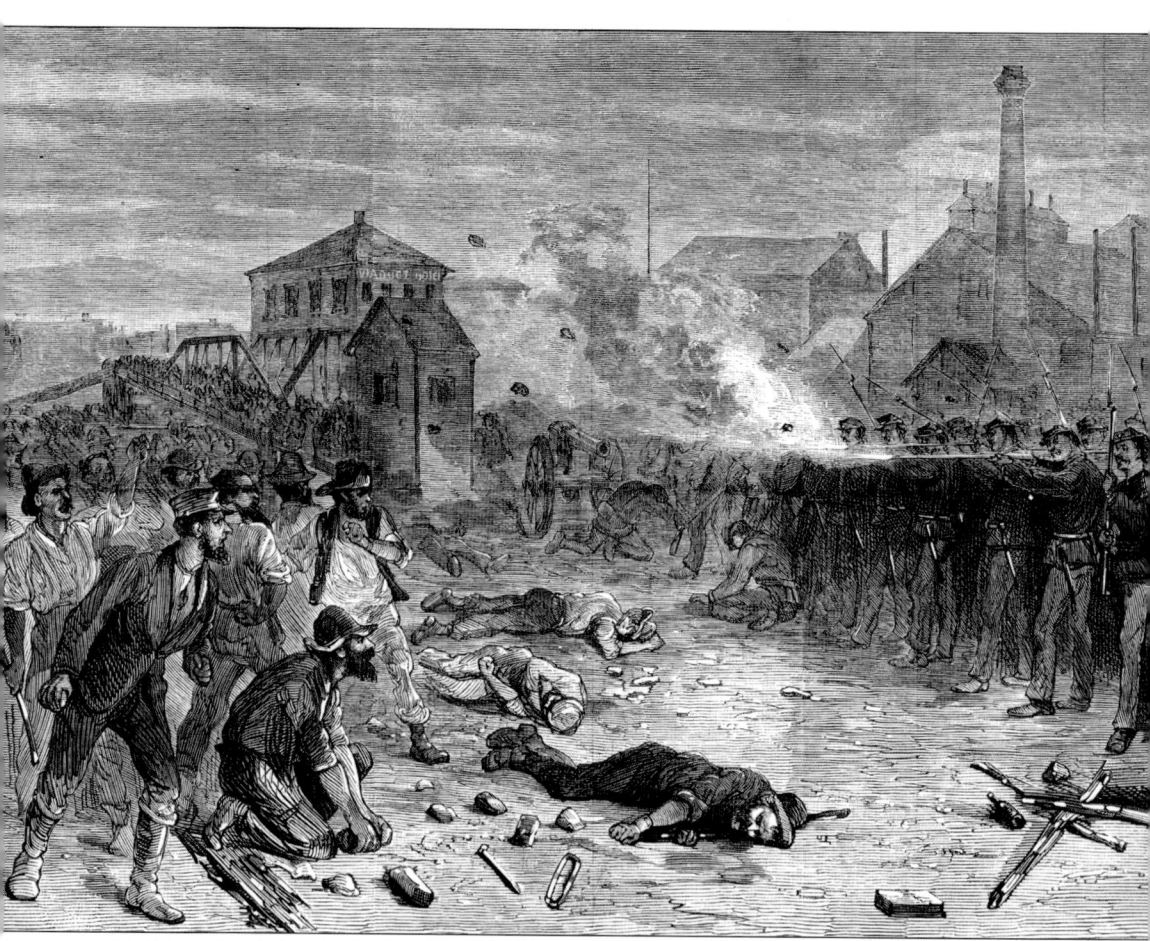

On Thursday, July 26, 1877, an event occurred that would be a major precipitant moment in Chicago history. Emboldened by the long-standing railroad workers' strike, Chicago Czechs protested alongside their German, Polish, Irish, Swedish, and other ethnic brethren for fair working conditions, hours, and wages. Workers of the Pilsen area who had assembled to protest unsafe and unfair working conditions were attacked at the viaduct at Halsted and Sixteenth Streets, by most accounts unprovoked, by federal troops commissioned by the Chicago municipal government to quash protesters. The results were devastating. These troops were fresh from battle with American Indians, namely those who had killed Gen. George Custer in battle, so, war-hardened as they were, the tragic effect may have been inevitable: 30 unarmed men were dead, over 200 persons wounded, and of that number, several were women and children. (Author's collection; illustration by C. and A. T. Sears.)

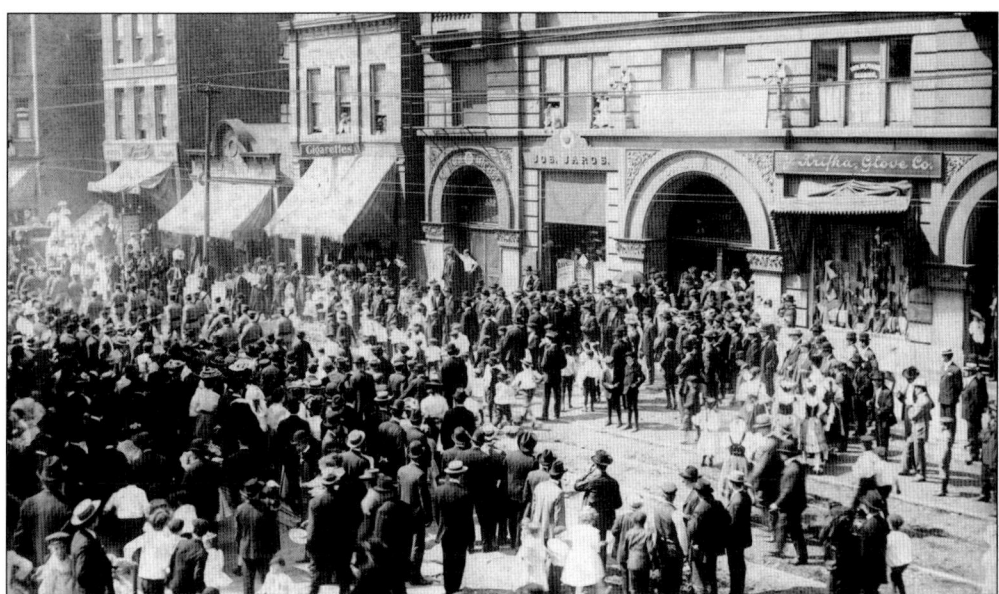

At Eighteenth and Bishop Streets in the center of Pilsen's bustling main street stood the hall of the Česko-Slovanská Podporující Společnost (ČSPS), or Czechoslovak protective society, sometimes translated as the Bohemian Slavic Benevolent Society. The organization for the support of injured workers or for the upkeep of their families, should their primary breadwinner be incapacitated, laid off, or pass away, was also a place where Czech men could meet and socialize. (Courtesy CSA.)

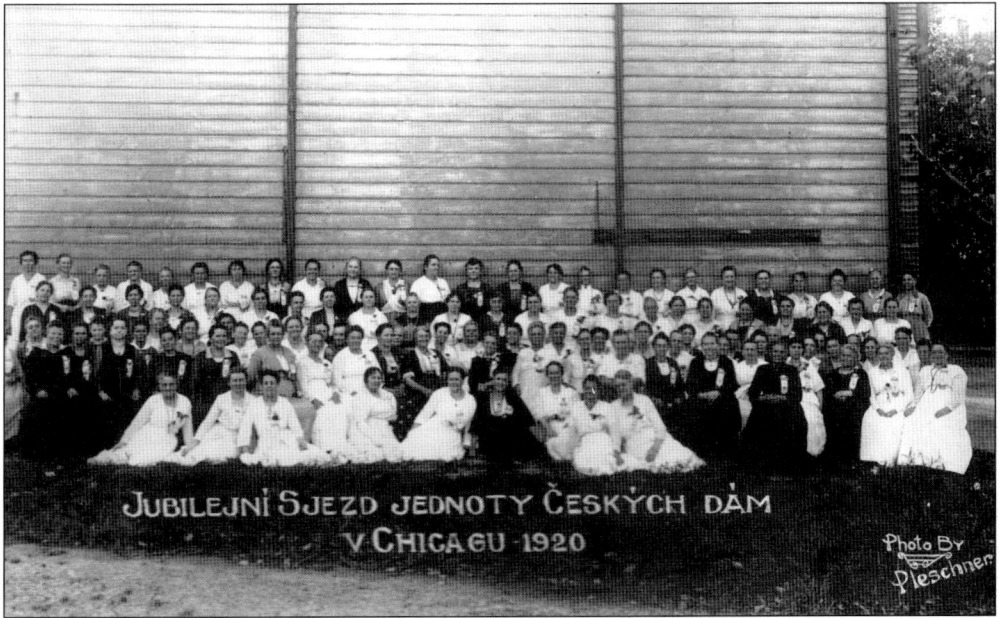

In the early years of the ČSPS, women were not admitted, and so very soon Czech women organized themselves around a national group they called the Jednota Českých Dam (Union of Czech Ladies). By 1920, when this picture was taken, the union had a nationwide membership of approximately 20,000. It collected dues, offered insurance and support (like its male counterpart), and also participated in charitable enterprises. (Courtesy CSA.)

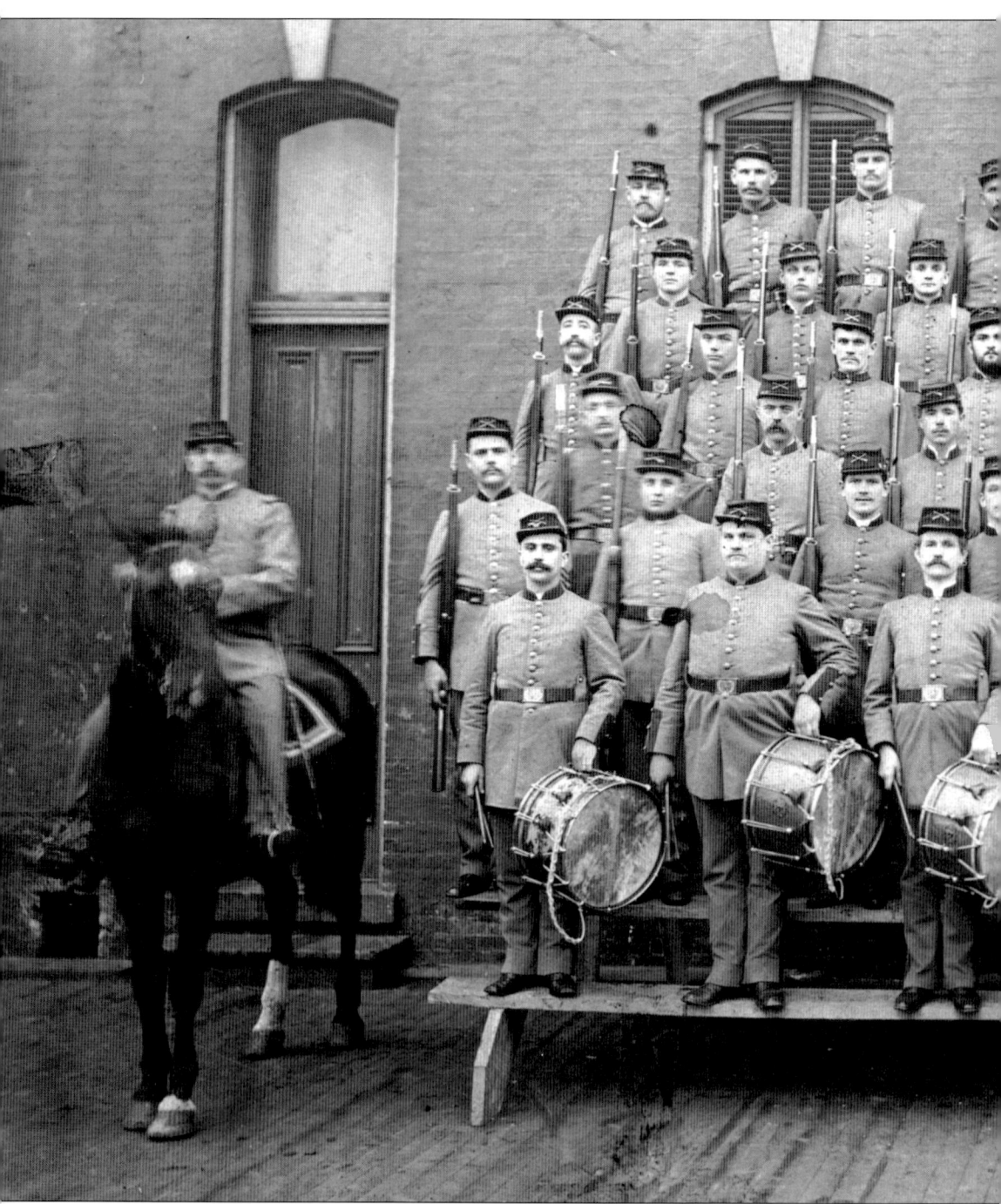

After the Civil War, militias, or gun clubs, were organized by ethnic workers' groups in order to meet the threat of the private armies of employers. The labor struggle in the United States had become increasingly violent in the late 19th century, and wealthy employers habitually hired mercenaries to quash what they saw as rebellious and dangerous unionists. Gun clubs functioned both as community organizations and quasi-military units. They also served as an early test of the United States constitutional right to "keep and bear arms." In 1879, influential industrialists

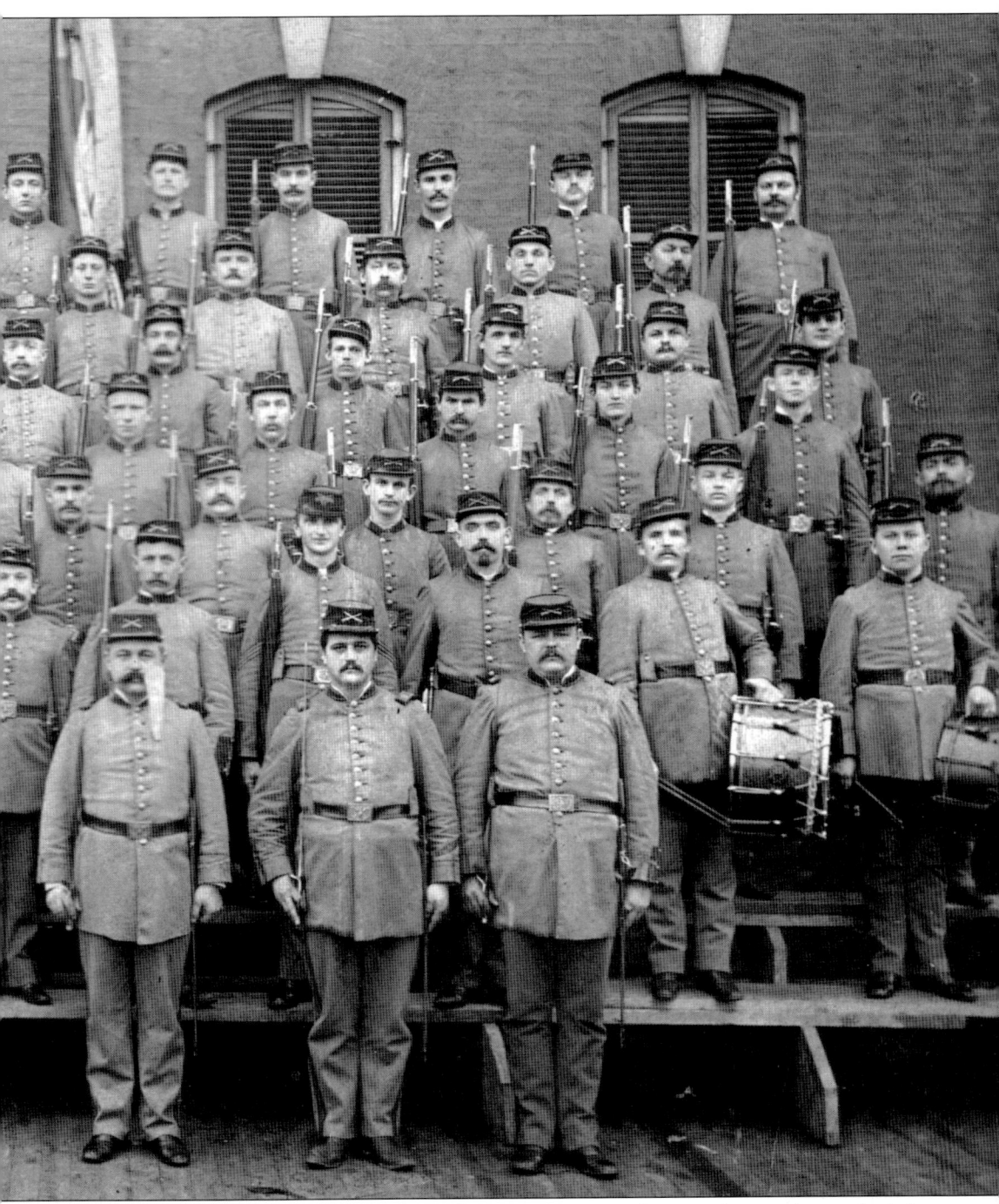

appealed to the U.S. Supreme Court to eradicate such groups. As a result, many were denied their constitutional right to bear arms. Workers' militias, like the Bohemian Sharpshooters picture here, could also be found among the French, Irish (the Fifth Ward Irish Labor Guard), and, to the greatest extent, among German immigrants (the Lehr und Wehr Vereins, or study and strike associations). (Courtesy Ken Dvorsky.)

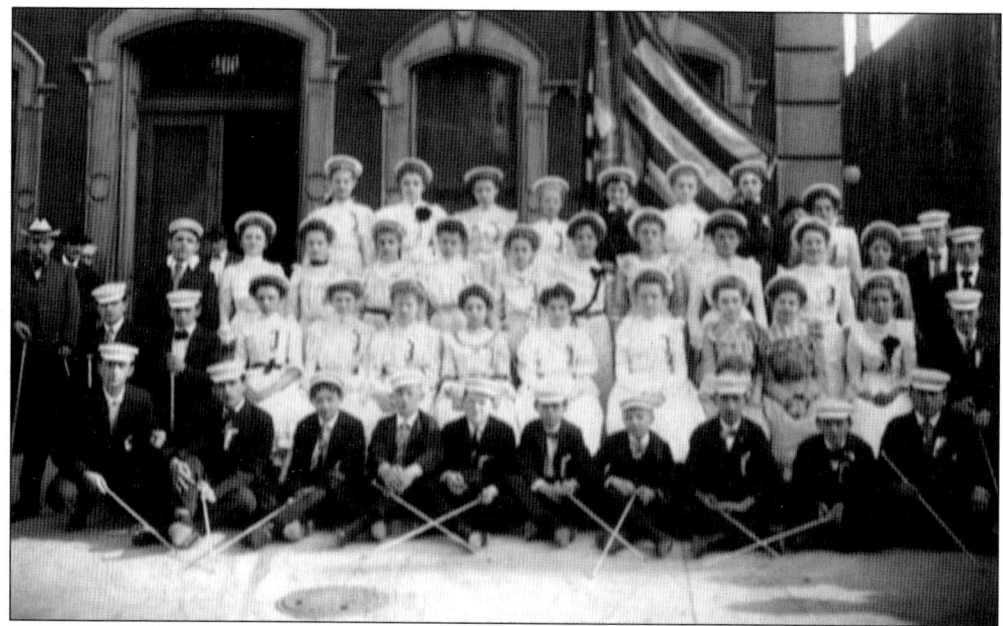

This group portrait is of the sons and daughters of the ČSPS in front of the Czech-English school that operated at Eighteenth Street and Blue Island Avenue in Pilsen. Much as the Czechs were intent on assimilating smoothly into American culture, the desire to retain their native language among their children, most of them here depicted being first generation Czech Americans, was also fervent. (Courtesy CSA.)

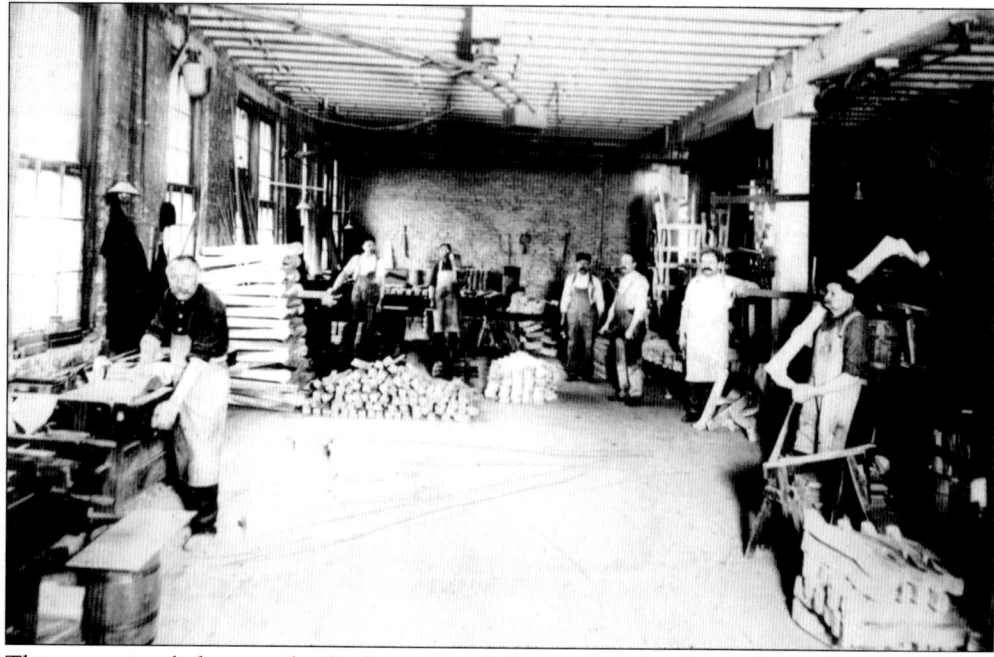

This exceptional photograph affords us a vivid glimpse into the day-to-day working conditions for the Bohemian furniture makers of Chicago in the early 1900s. Czech furniture makers and their unions were also central to the labor reforms of the late 19th and early 20th centuries. (Courtesy CSA.)

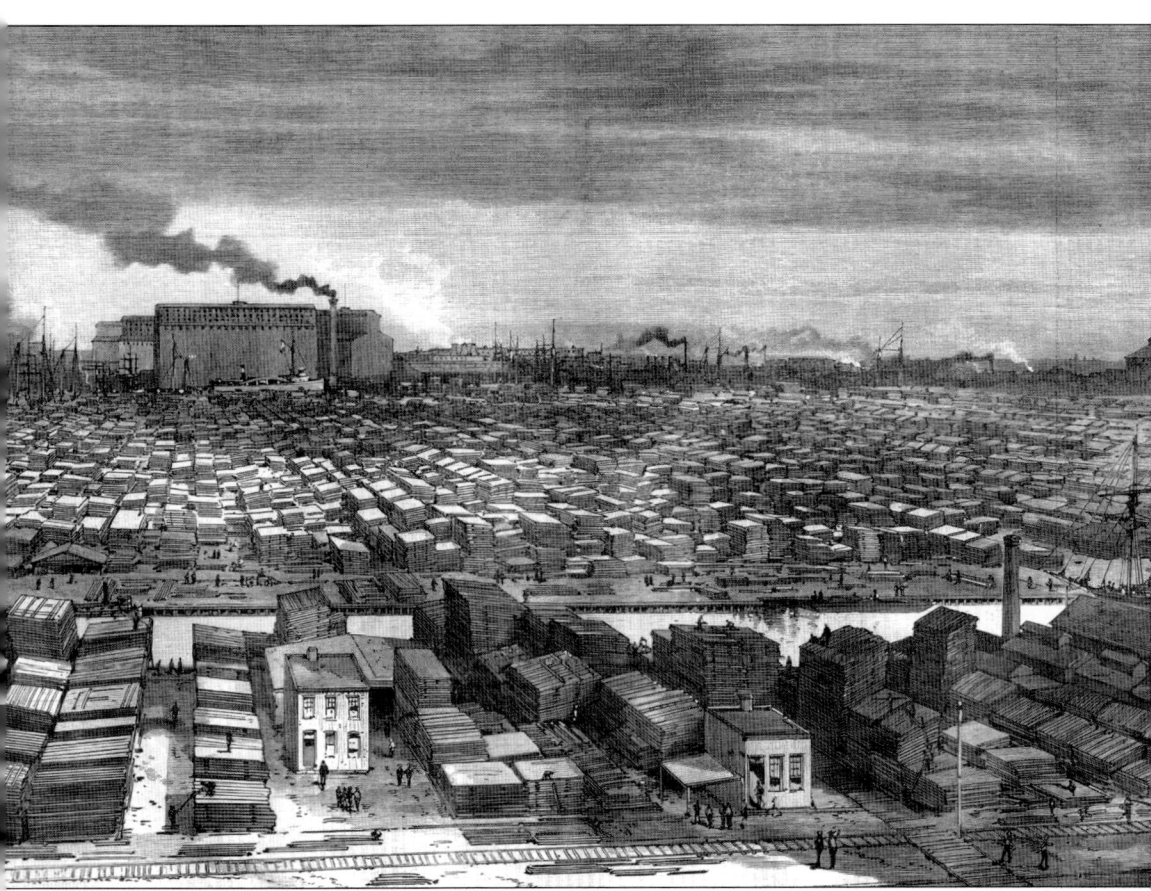

Many of the working-class denizens of Pilsen supported themselves in the growing dockside industries of the south branch of the Chicago River, most especially in the mammoth lumberyards. The work was grueling and arduous. By 1883, when this image was etched for *Harper's Weekly*, Chicago was fast becoming the hub of the lumber trade. The journalist hints at the awful conditions of the yards in the accompanying article and gives a sense of what hard labor the workers—many of them new Czech immigrants— faced: "On the southeastern border of Chicago is another city whose buildings are the blackened piles of lumber, and whose busiest highways are the passages between, just large enough to afford entrance for a wagon. The 'lumber shovers' who unload [the barges of wood] wear a large leather apron extending from the belt to the knees, and leather guards to protect the palms of their hands." (Author's collection; illustration by Charles Graham.)

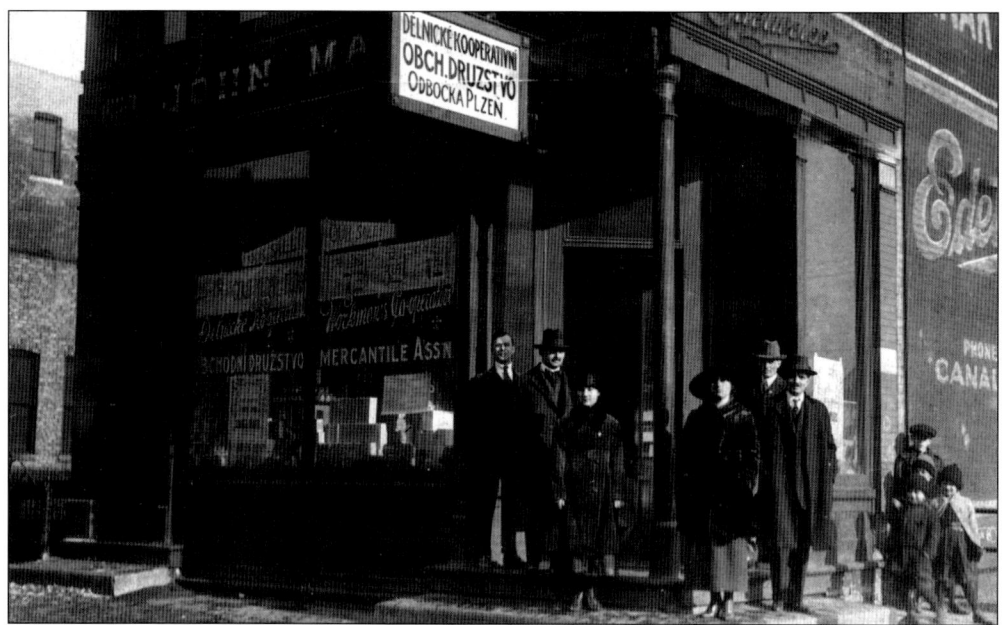

The working-class character of Pilsen is clear in this photograph of the Workmen's Cooperative corner store. The Czech dominance in the neighborhood is also clear from window signs duplicated in both Czech and English and a shingle in Czech only that reads "Workers' Cooperative Collective Store, Pilsen Divigation." (Courtesy University of Chicago, Archive of Czechs and Slovaks Abroad.)

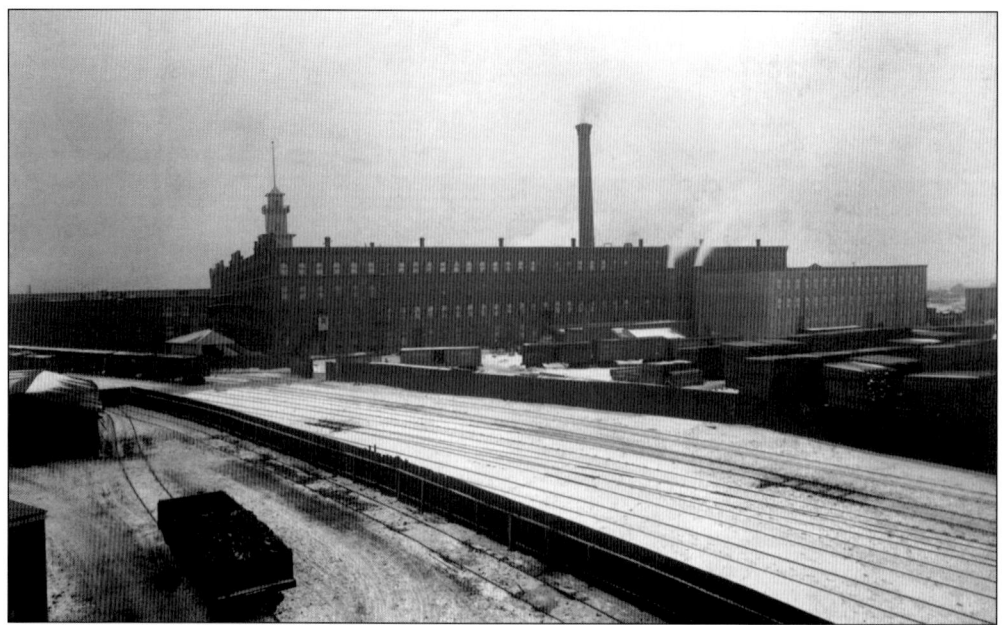

The McCormick Reaper plant on Pilsen's southern edge employed hundreds of Bohemian workers. In the 1880s, it decided, despite growing profit margins, to cut workers' wages. On May 3, 1886, before striking unionists, McCormick opened its gates to nonunion hires. A fight broke out, and police fired on the crowd, leaving four dead and many injured. The incident precipitated the next day's Haymarket incident. (Courtesy Chicago History Museum.)

In 1888, a book with the significant title *Mučennici Nové Doby* (martyrs of the new era) was written by Adolf Hruša and published by the Chicago-based Press of the International Workers' Union (Tiskárna Mezinárodní dělnické jednoty). It is evidence of the empathy Czech immigrants felt with the mainly German-born émigrés connected—most of them falsely—with the violence at Haymarket Square on May 4, 1886. (Courtesy University of Chicago, Archive of Czechs and Slovaks Abroad.)

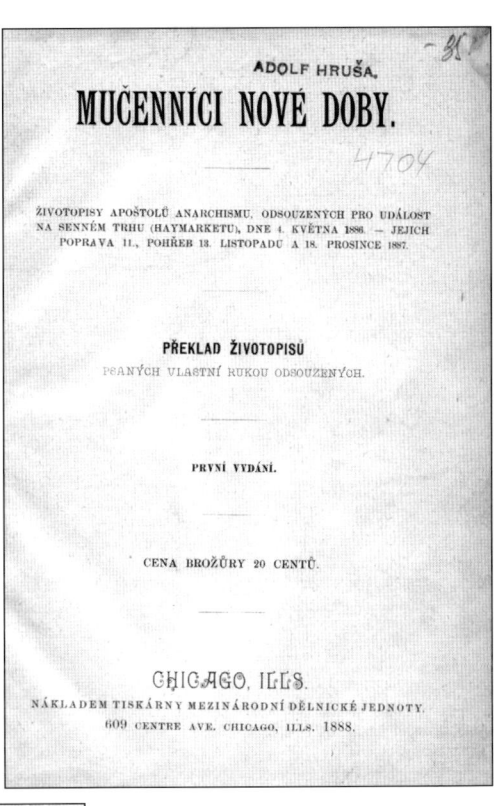

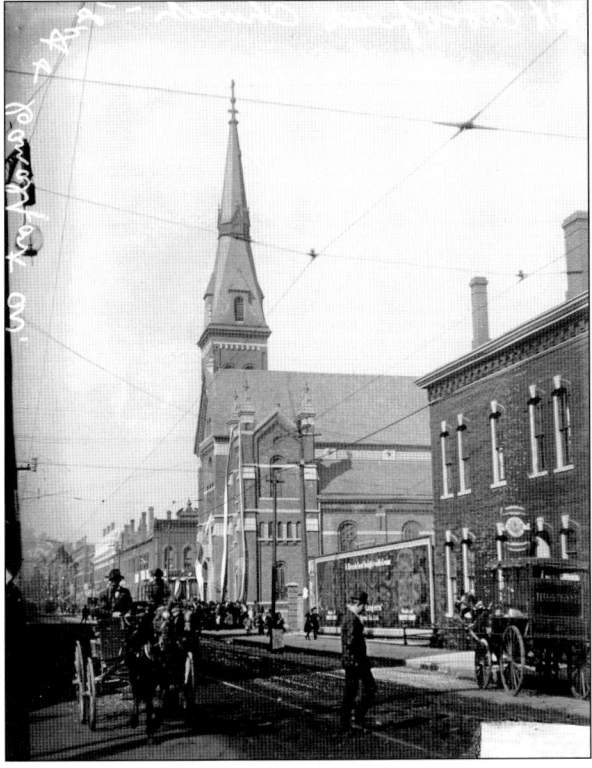

At a Pilsen town meeting, discussions were held to build a Czech Catholic church; a motion was made to name this church after St. Procopius, the first formally canonized Czech saint whose feast day falls on July 4. The nod to U.S. Independence Day attests to the early Czech émigré consciousness of allegiance to native land and adopted homeland. (Courtesy Chicago History Museum.)

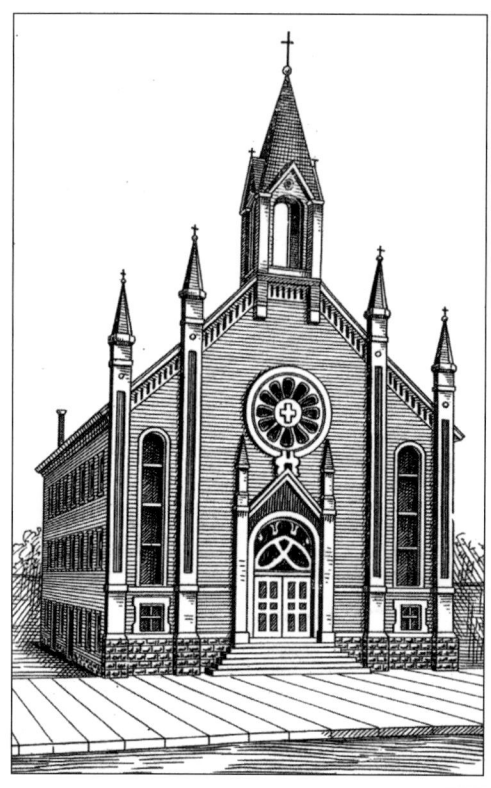

This old frame church was the first incarnation of the first Czech Roman Catholic church in Pilsen, St. Procopius. Prior to its life as a Czech Roman Catholic center, the building belonged to the First Bohemian Methodist Episcopalians. It was sold to the Catholics and moved to Eighteenth and Allport Streets, serving as a site for mass until a permanent brick structure could be raised. (Courtesy St. Procopius, Fr. Jim Collins.)

In 1875, Rev. Vilém Čoka was invited to serve the new congregation of St. Procopius. As a school was to be built as an offspring of the church, Čoka called a town meeting to discuss its nature: should it be nontheistic or Christian. At the time, secularists made up about 70 percent of the city's Czech population, Catholics numbered 25 percent, and Czech Protestants were in the small minority. Despite this, the vote of the public was for a Catholic school. (Courtesy St. Procopius, Fr. Jim Collins.)

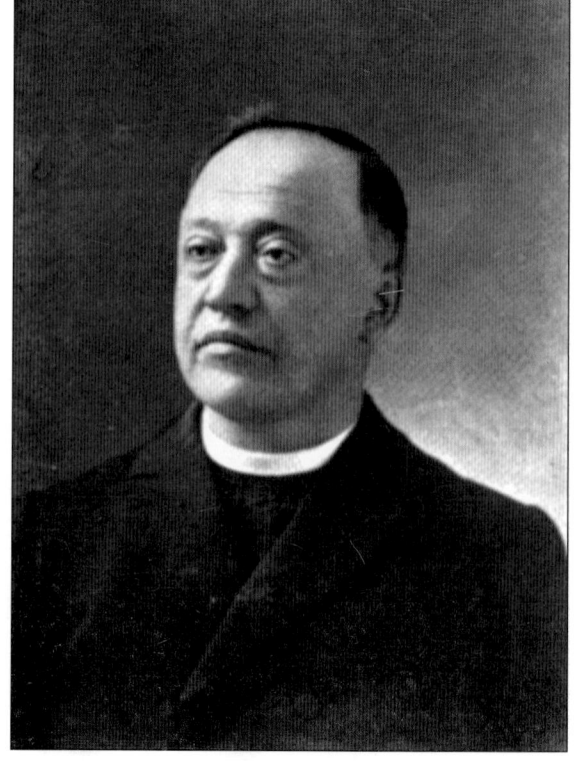

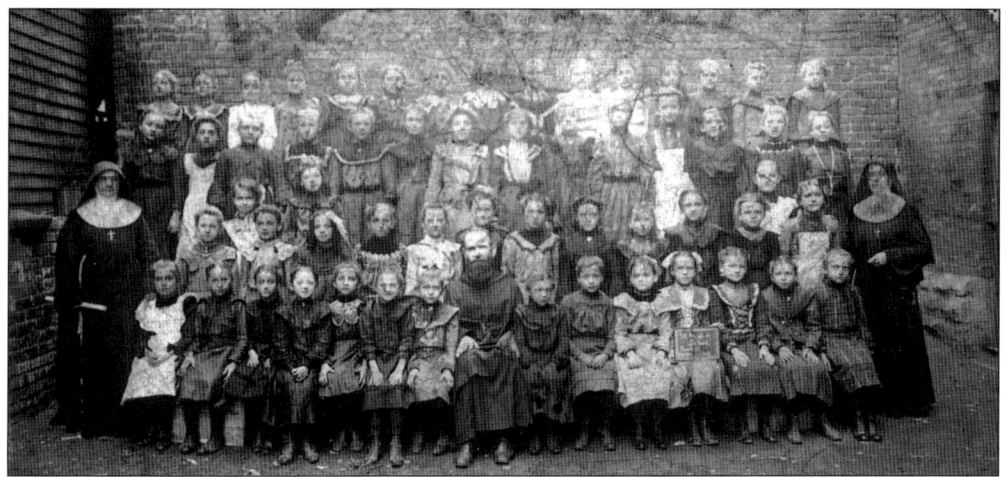

The parish of St. Procopius was growing so fast that Reverend Čoka could not minister the congregation alone. He found a contingent of pastors among the Order of the Benedictines and, in 1885, Fathers Jaeger and Kočárník took over from Čoka. Further construction continued apace: a new school, shown here around 1900, and rectory added to the church's properties. Under the ordinance of the Benedictines, St. Procopius became the largest Czech Catholic congregation in the city. (Courtesy University of Chicago, Archive of Czechs and Slovaks Abroad.)

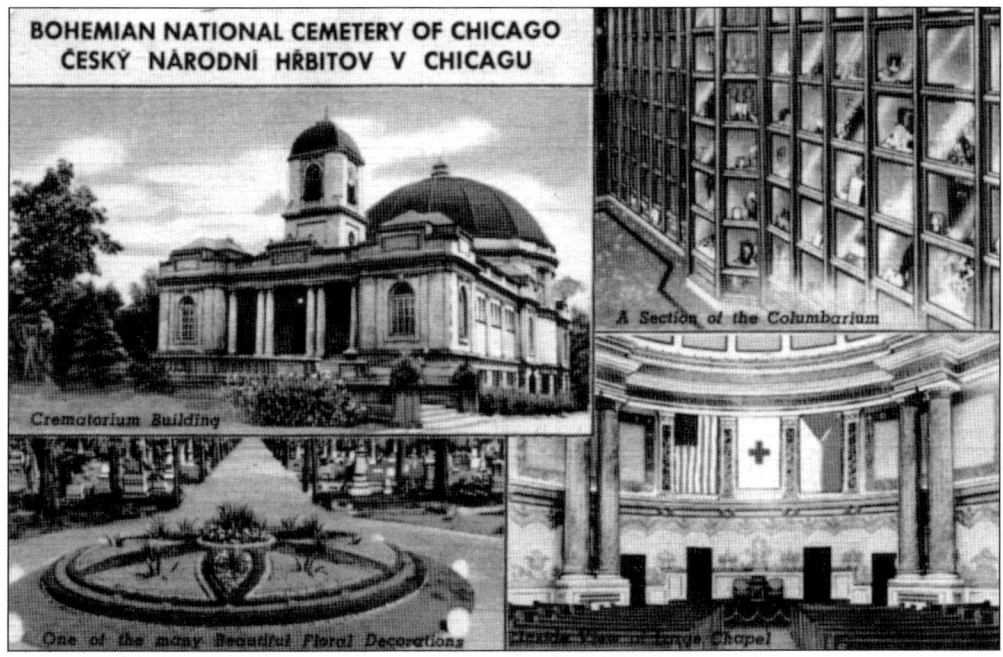

The Bohemian National Cemetery received its state charter in 1877. Legend has it that it opened because a priest refused the burial of a certain Czech women in the Catholic cemetery of St. Adalbert. When the landmark Victorian gatehouse was built, the cemetery's board insisted that both gas and electric sources be installed because of suspicion that electricity was an unreliable and even unsafe utility. (Courtesy CSA.)

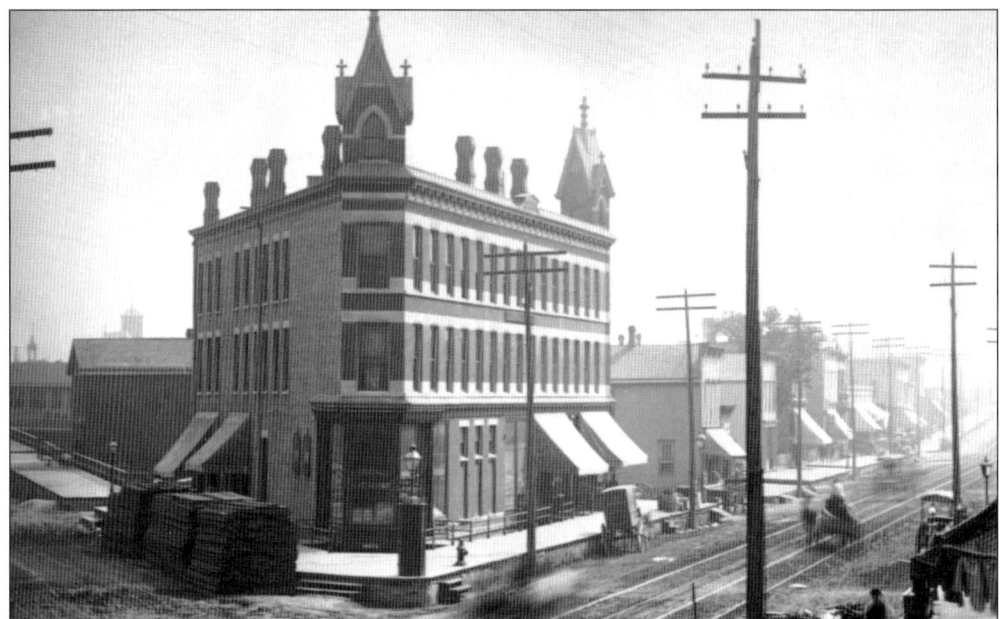

Blue Island Avenue, running diagonally through Pilsen, was a hub of growth for the neighborhood. In this early image one can see just how the neighborhood grew: the conditions of the roads, the accumulated piles of wood planks from the nearby lumberyards, and the pushcarts that would be linked perennially and stereotypically in the minds of other Chicagoans with the city's Czech community. (Courtesy Chicago History Museum.)

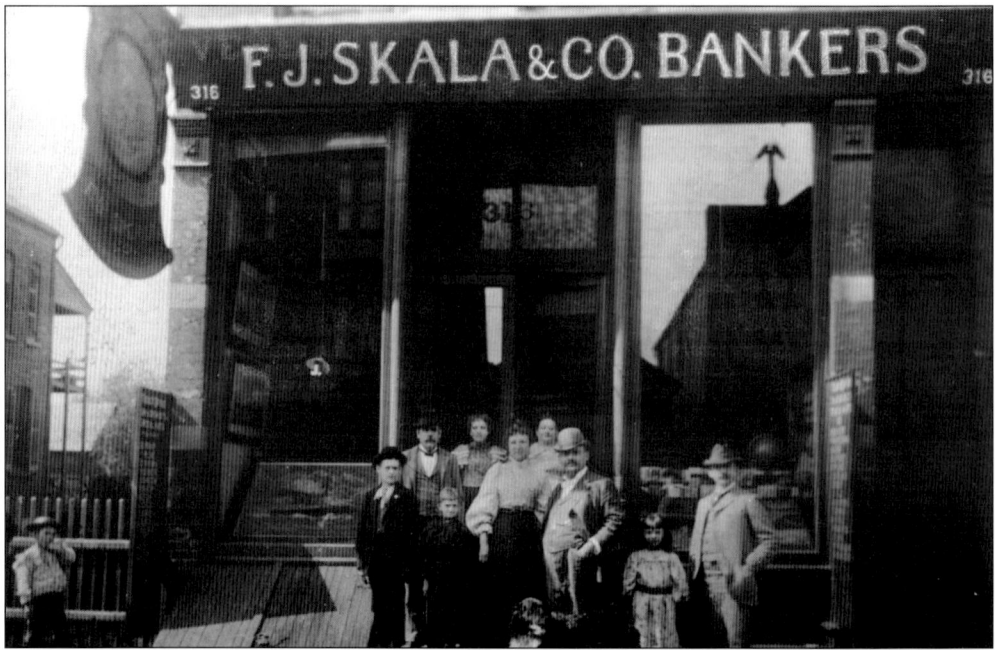

Skala State Bank in Pilsen was one of the oldest Czech banks in the city. It was organized in 1896 by president Frank J. Skala and began its existence, as many banks in the country did, as a ship ticket agency and private bank; by 1919 it was reorganized as a state financial institution. (Courtesy CSA.)

Atlas Brewery's owner and president Karel Vopička played an important role in the Czech National Council (1910–1915) and later the Czech National Alliance (during World War I); he also served as minister plenipotentiary to Romania, Bulgaria, and Serbia from 1913 to 1920. In his position as minister, he made the controversial but astute statement, "Austria wanted war with Serbia, and . . . the death of Archduke Ferdinand was welcomed as a casus belli." (Courtesy CSA.)

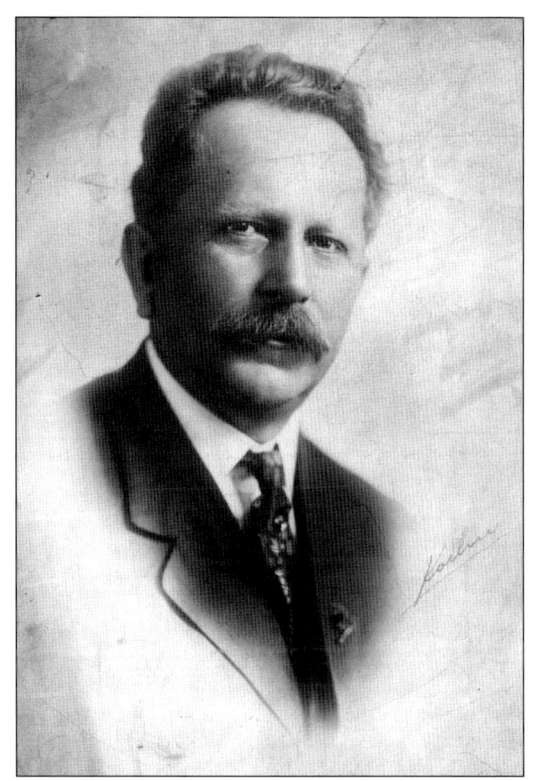

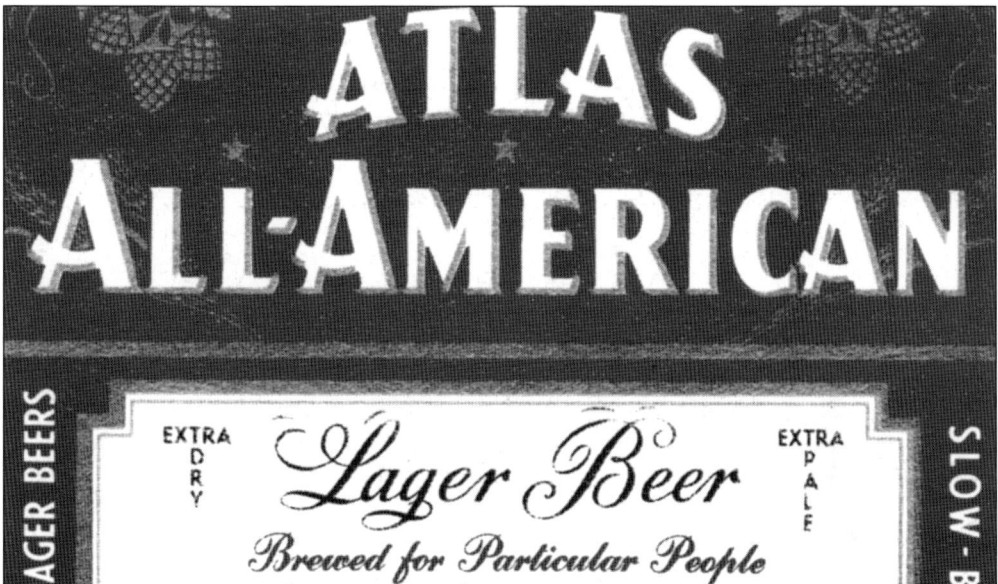

The Atlas Beer label was iconic in the years before and after Prohibition. When the Dry Law was finally lifted in 1933, Atlas's president had posters pasted all over the city on "New Beer's Eve" (April 7, 1933). The posters featured Uncle Sam holding a beer and petitioning patrons who had made their delivery orders for the first legal day to be patient; breweries were so strapped to fulfill orders that even with the hire of hundreds of new workers, the orders were not fulfilled on time. (Courtesy CSA.)

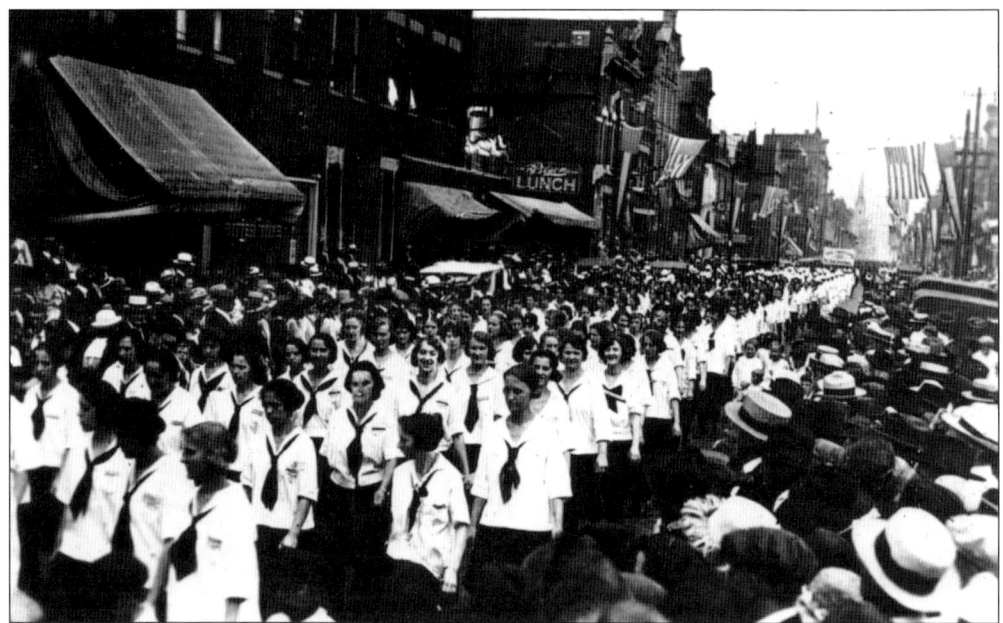

The Sokol lodge named for its neighborhood, Pilsen, was enormously active from its inception through the 1920s and 1930s. Here some of its young members march down Eighteenth Street in the parade during the 1921 Sokol exhibition. Their building at Eighteenth Street and Ashland Avenue still stands today with the hall's name, Plzeňský Sokol, etched into its stone facade. (Courtesy CSA.)

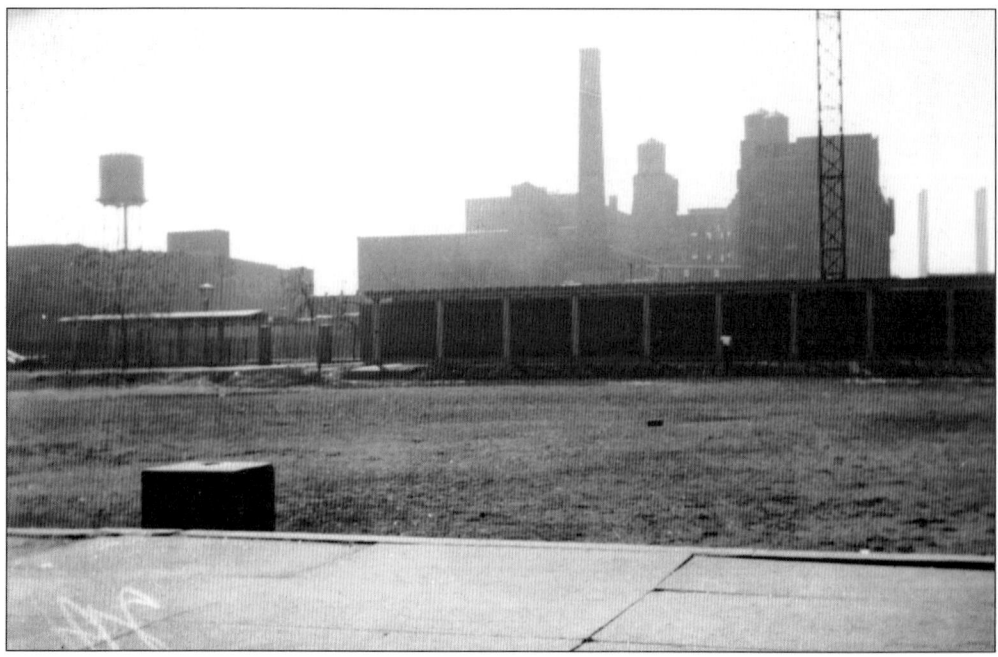

The space that would become Dvořák Park was a central gathering place and recreational area for Czech families. This early image shows clearly impeccably clean conditions of the grounds and the industrial dominated skyline of the Pilsen neighborhood. (By permission and courtesy of the Chicago Park District Special Collections.)

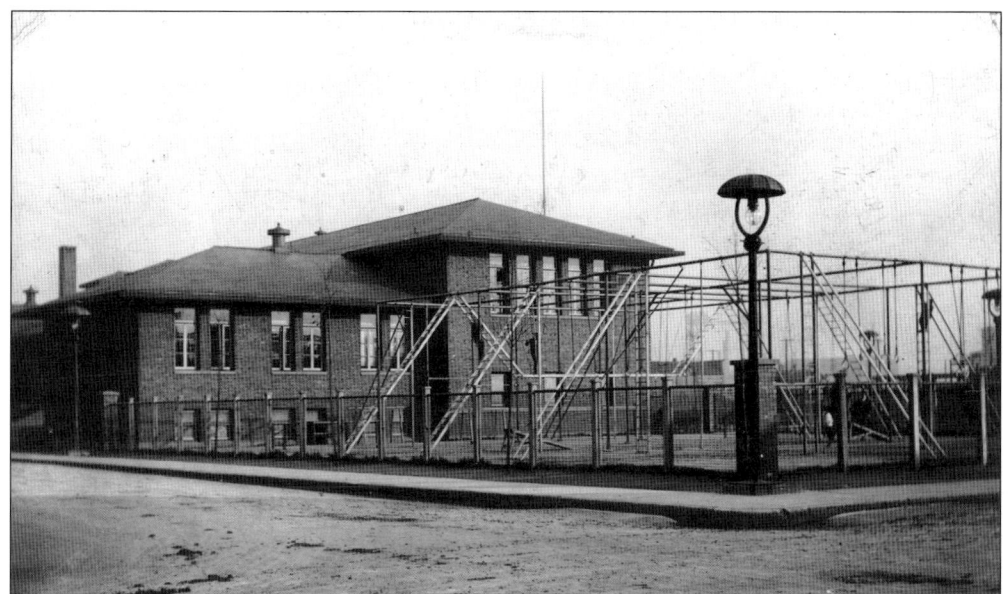

With the celebrated visit of composer Antonín Dvořák to Chicago in 1893, the city officially named the park in his honor and in so doing also honored the Czech denizens of this portion of Chicago. But in this image from before the name change, the park is known by its Czech patrons as Svatopluk Čech Park, after the Czech poet who celebrated and encouraged nationalist spirit, although to the city it was still an unnamed (only numbered) West Park lot. (Courtesy Frank Magallon.)

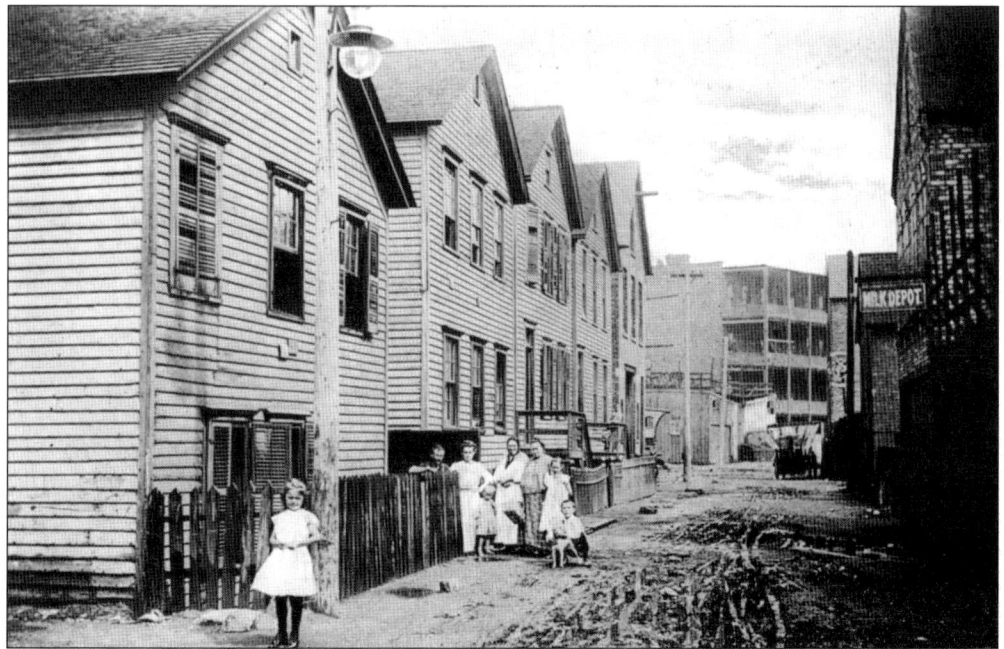

This image of a typical Czech street in Pilsen originates from the 1880s; here Czech families pose for the camera outside their homes in Walker Court, near Eighteenth and Throop Streets. The modest living conditions of the mainly working-class neighborhood of Pilsen are clear from this image. (Author's collection.)

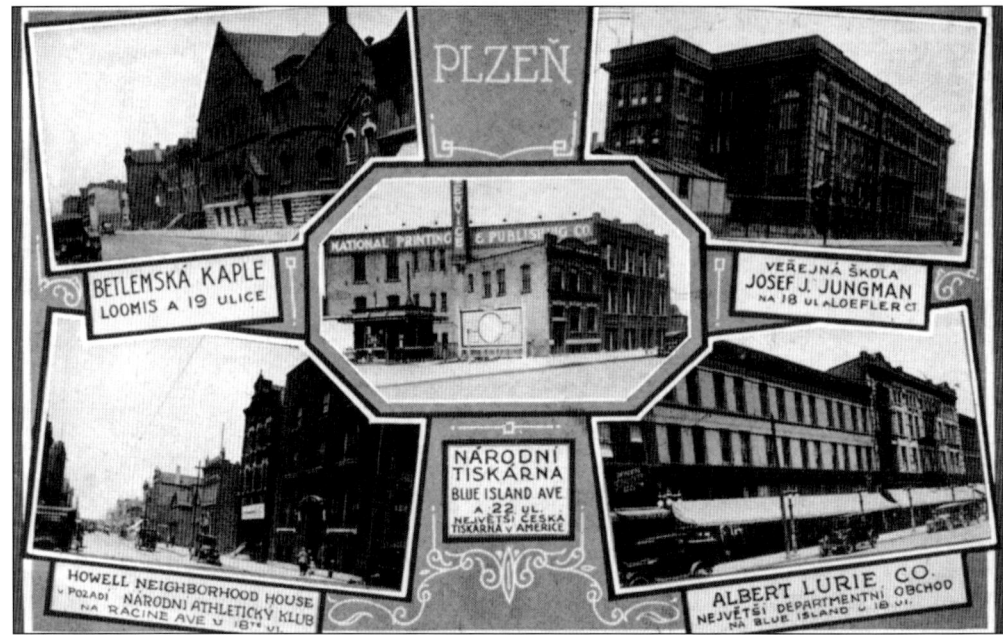

Central to this postcard is the National Printers, publisher of significant works of Czech nationalism. Around it are the Josef Jungman public school, named for the 19th-century Czech national revivalist; the Albert Lurie Company, the largest department store; the Bethlehem Chapel (founded 1890); and the Howell Neighborhood House (established 1905). The latter two institutions profoundly influenced the temperance movement of the second decade of the 20th century. (Courtesy CSA; photograph by E. F. Macha.)

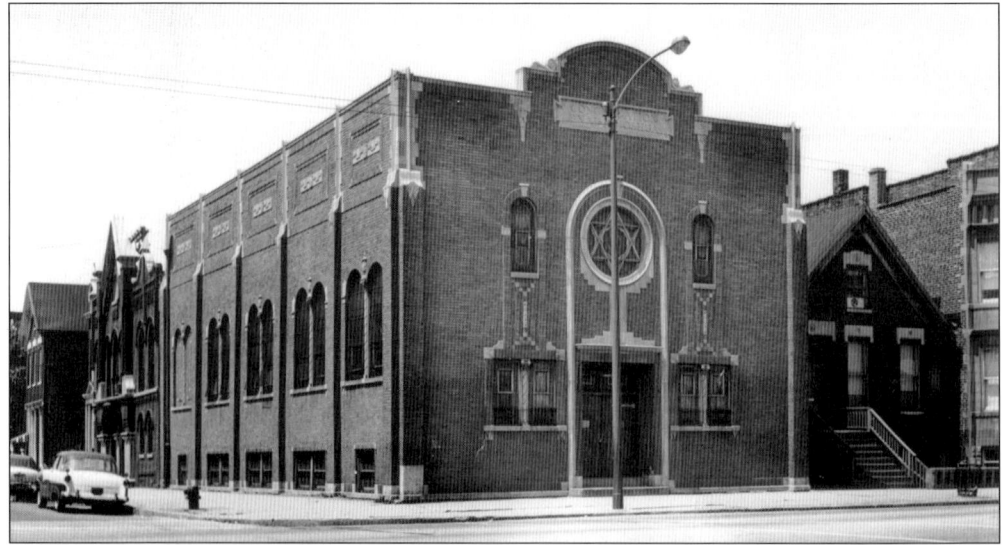

The Reform congregation of B'nai Jehoshua was founded in 1893 by Czech and Slovak Jews. It was one of the few nonorthodox congregations in Chicago. Located at Twentieth Street and Ashland Avenue in Pilsen, its worshippers included Judge Joseph Sabath, his brother and Illinois congressman Adolph Sabath, and the owners of the very popular and successful Leader stores. The temple existed until 1965, at which time the congregation made the decision to merge with Beth Elohim in the suburb of Glenview and sell the Pilsen property. (Courtesy CSA.)

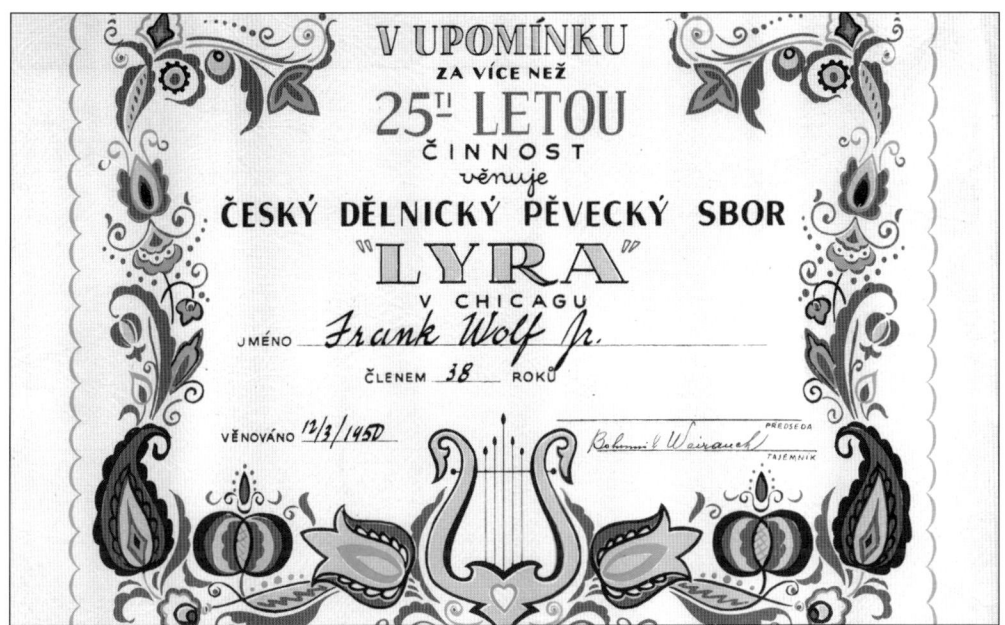

This certificate of membership in the singing group called Lyra marks Frank Wolf's 25 years in the organization. The group, like many Czech organizations built up in Chicago, had close affiliations with labor groups and unions. Lyra was a *Český dělnický pěvecký sbor*, a Czech workers' singing society, which had established itself in 1870 as much as a social union as an artistic one. (Courtesy CSA.)

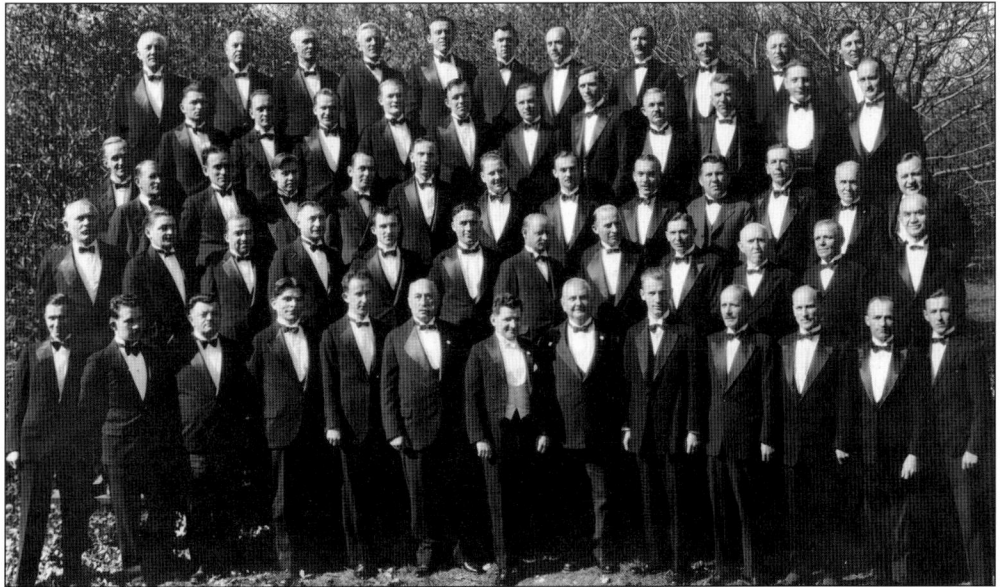

A portrait of the entire membership of the Lyra singing group from the mid-1920s, this photograph was donated to the Czechoslovak Society of America's Library by Joanne Monasco, whose grandfather Frank Hulik is pictured in the top row fourth from the right. In 1928, Lyra went on tour in Prague; the sojourn commemorated the 10th anniversary of a free Czechoslovakia and the singing group's many years of artistic service (the group celebrated its centennial in 1970). (Courtesy CSA.)

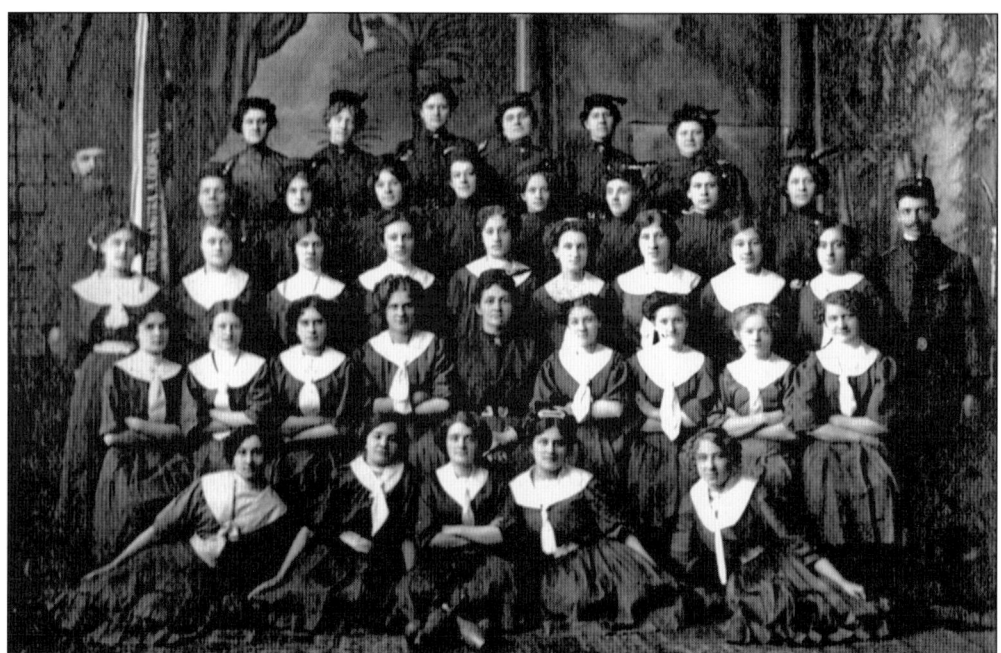

Town of Lake, today's Back of the Yards and New City neighborhoods, was another Czech stronghold in the city and it had its own traditional Czech institutions: taverns, lodges, and community centers. This photograph of female Sokol members from Town of Lake gives a sense of how active women were in the Sokol movement. (Courtesy CSA.)

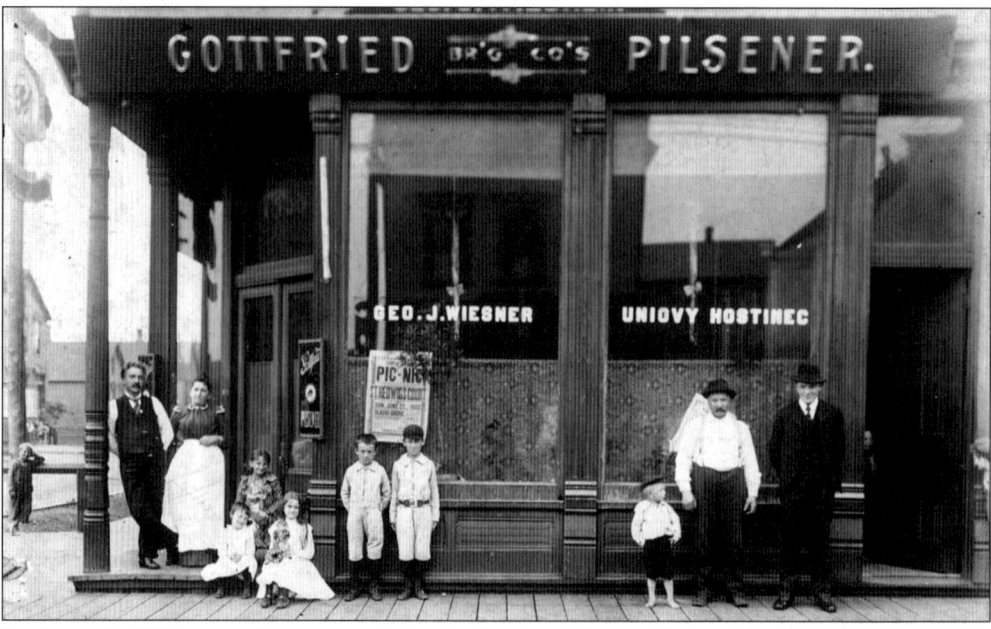

In the early 1900s, a sizable group of Czechs lived in Town of Lake. This area had its hub at Forty-seventh Street and Ashland Avenue and boasted many Czech-owned businesses, such as this tavern operated by Czech Jew George Wiesner. The picture is remarkable for the clarity it gives of the way of life of the time, from the wooden sidewalks to the picnic in Slavie Grove poster. (Courtesy CSA.)

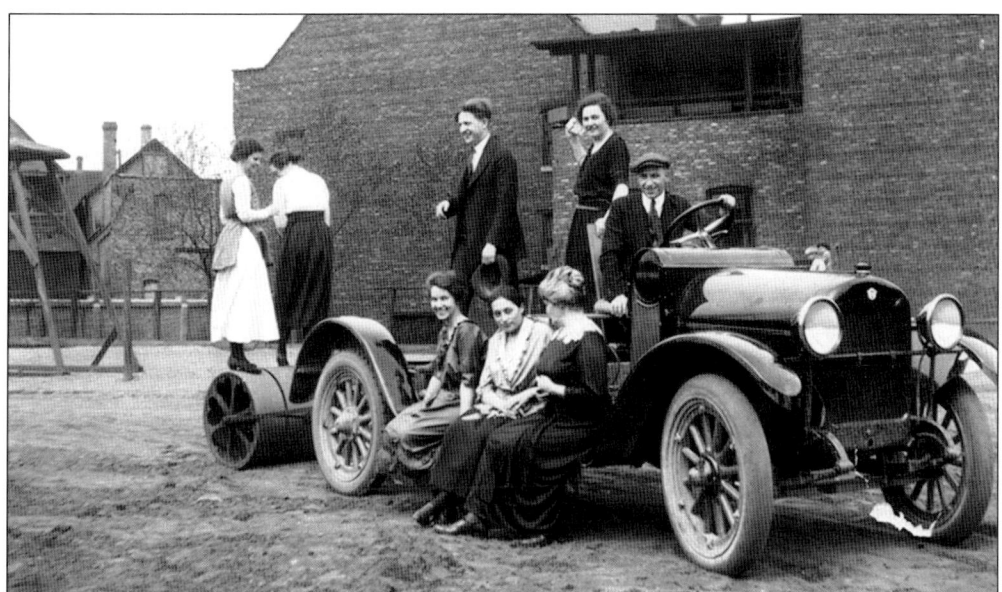

The Mary McDowell Settlement House was established by the University of Chicago in 1894 to help immigrants living on Chicago's west side. McDowell, known as the "Angel of the Stockyards," helped many immigrants by providing education, job training, and childcare. Above is the settlement's core staff, among them Ruzena Hudlicka ("Sister Hud"), whose Czech background must have helped the settlement in building trust among area Czechs. (Courtesy Chicago History Museum.)

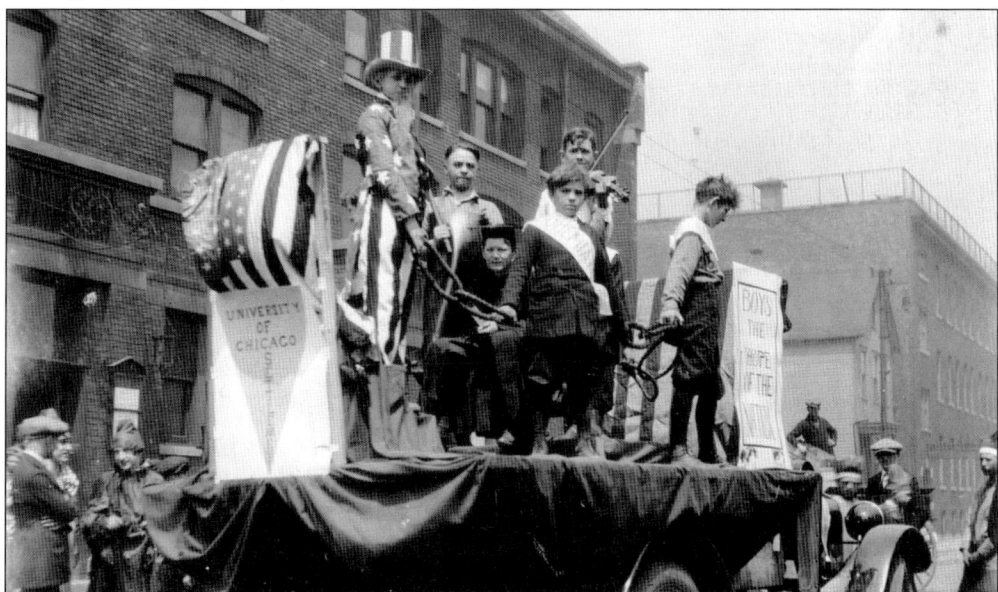

The McDowell House often participated in parades and other citywide events as a way to educate the larger public about the life of the ethnic poor amid them. Here a float represents the settlement house in a 1921 spring parade. The float shows boys from various ethnic groups, including Czechs (center, with *Bohemian* on sash), Poles, and other Slavic nationalities, symbolically "chained together" under the banner, "Uncle Sam welds the boys of all nations into one glorious manhood." (Courtesy Chicago History Museum.)

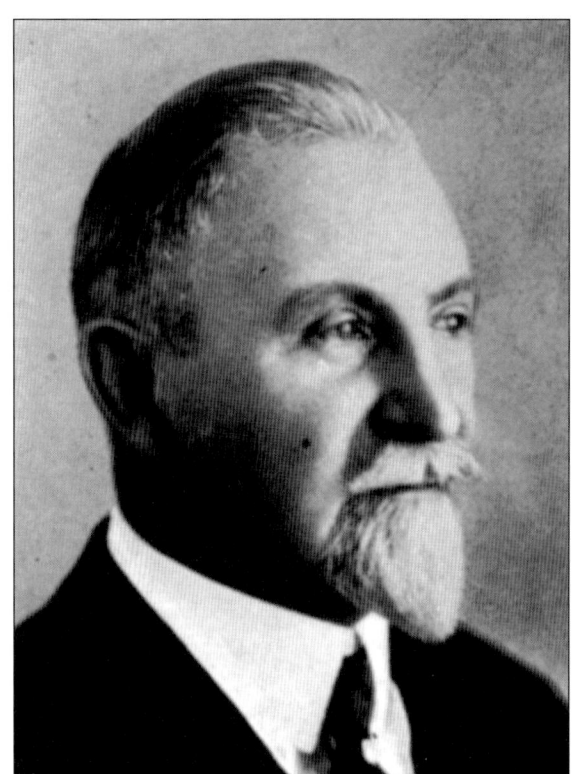

Rudolph Jaromír Pšenka was a true Czech American renaissance man. Invited to Chicago by the publisher August Geringer, Pšenka (born Pšenička) arrived in the city in 1901 and worked as an editor and author. In 1903, he married his bosses' daughter, Augusta Geringová and, having secured the trust of the at-times-taciturn Geringer, in 1909 he took over the position of editor in chief of the *Svornost*. (Author's collection.)

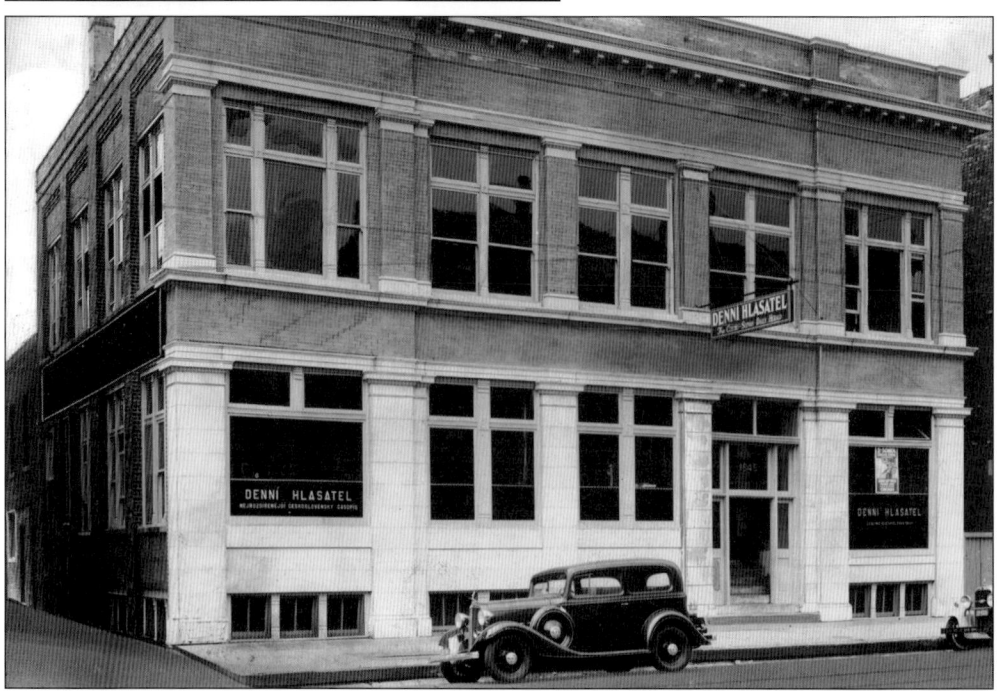

In 1891, the *Denní Hlasatel* (daily herald) newspaper, champion of workers' causes, came onto the scene. At their height, papers like the *Denní Hlasatel* and the *Svornost* could both claim a readership of over 50,000. (Courtesy CSA.)

This postcard from the beginning of the 20th century gives a strong impression of how profound the Czech flavor of Chicago was at that time and how deep was the sense among the Czech community of their belonging to Chicago. The postcard reads from the top, "These gals are our gals and this Chicago is our Chicago." The print below reading "Pozdrav z Chicaga" translates as "Greeting[s] from Chicago." (Courtesy CSA.)

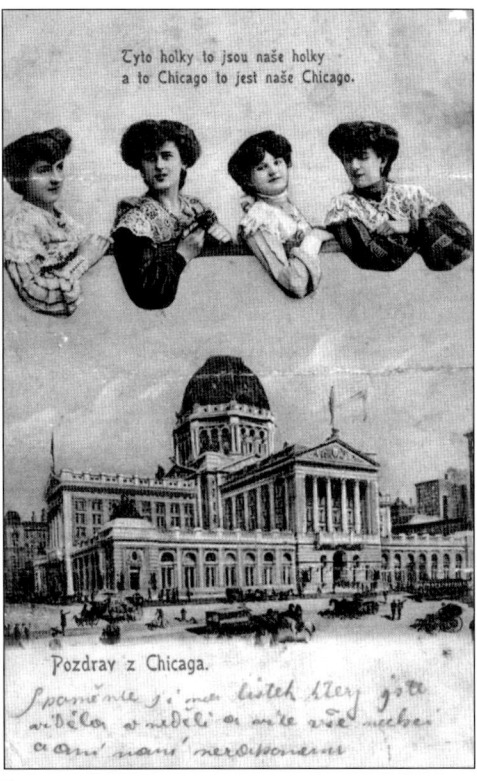

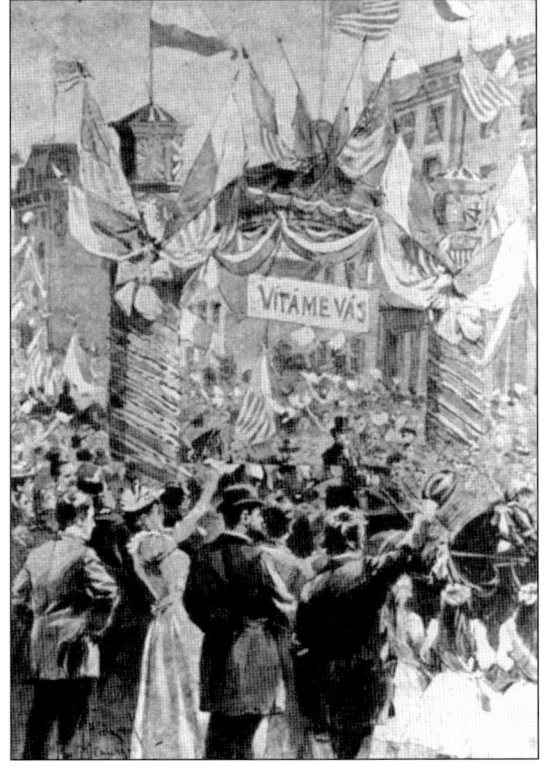

Czech American residents of Chicago welcome visitors to the 1893 World's Columbian Exposition. The banner reads, "[We] Welcome You" and is festooned with U.S. and, although the sketch is in black and white, the red and white flags of Bohemia proper. In a gesture that might be taken as politically symbolic of the Czech desire to gain independence, noticeably absent are flags of the Austro-Hungarian Empire, under which dominion the Czechs (Bohemians), Moravians, Silesians, and other groups lived at the time. (Author's collection.)

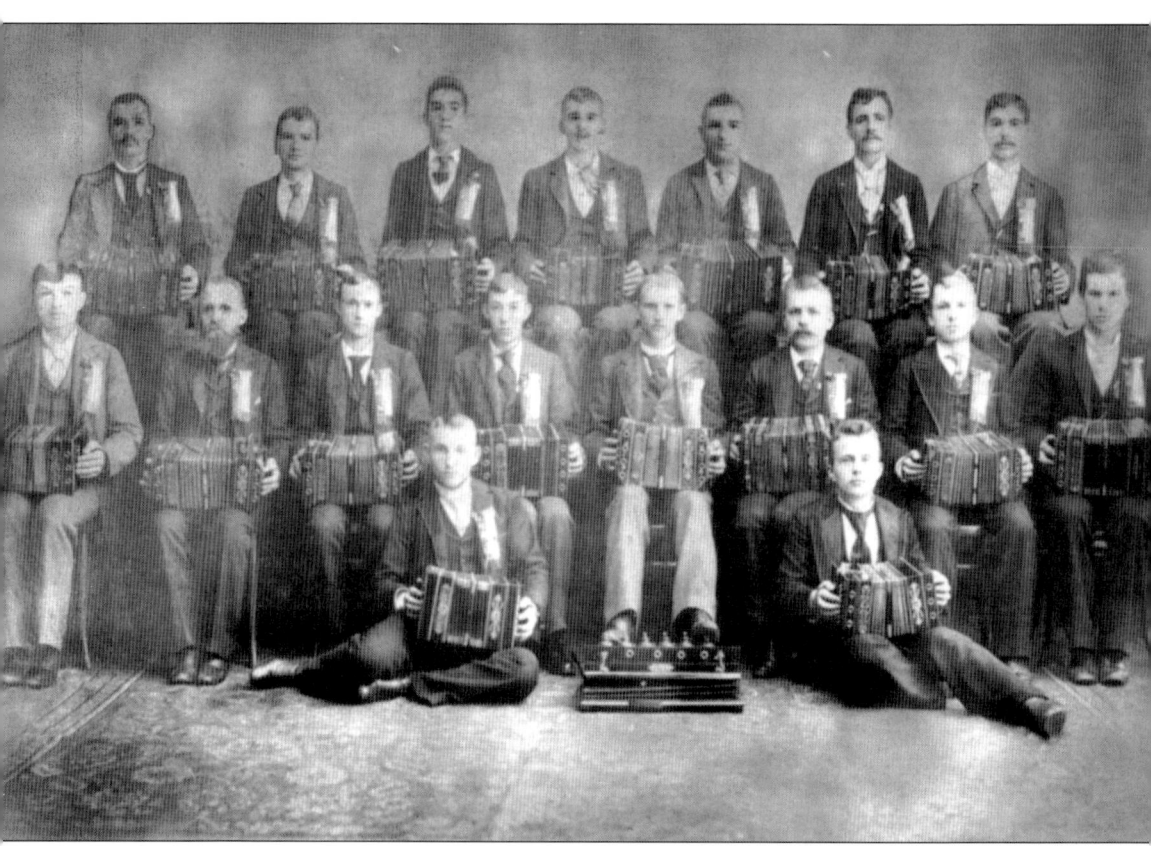

The První Česko-Americký Bando-Concertina Club (First Czech-American Bando-Concertina Club) was established in Chicago on February 6, 1893. Taken at the Schold photography studio on Halsted Street, this photograph features members, from left to right, (first row) František Slauf and Alois Kalčík; (second row) Josef Hora, Jan Konečný, Miroslav Korbel, Antonín Liška, Václav Fergl, Tomáš Košatka, František Košatka, and Jiří Kolnař; (third row) Antonín Mráz, Josef Kolář, Fratišek Suchý, Edvard Vopat, František Flusek, Josef Novotný, and J. Mauer. Václav Fergl is pictured here with his feet on concertina foot pumps. Fergl, along with Tom Košatka and Alois Kalčík, were cofounders of the club, and Košatka's family, who owned a music store in Pilsen, sponsored Fergl's naturalization as a U.S. citizen. Fergl settled on Eighteenth Street in Pilsen, just down the street from F. D. Němeček's popular photography studio. (Courtesy Evelyn Fergl [née Křenek].)

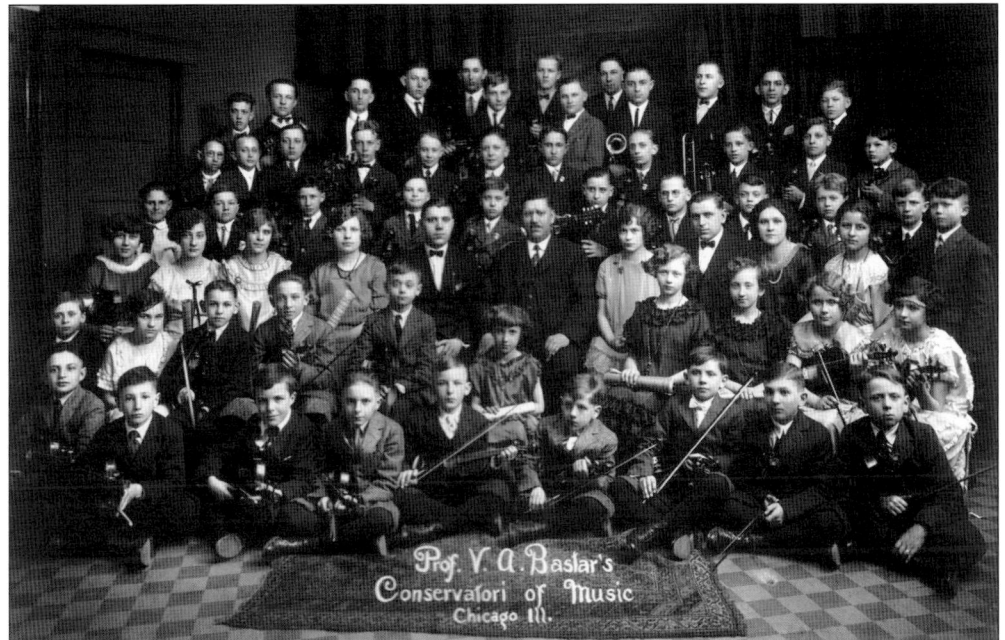

The Bastars, who operated a conservatory in Pilsen, were instrumental, no pun intended, in supporting the naturalization of Václav Fergl as a U.S. citizen. The help they gave to their compatriot was typical of the care the Czech community extended to those newly arrived in their midst. (Courtesy CSA.)

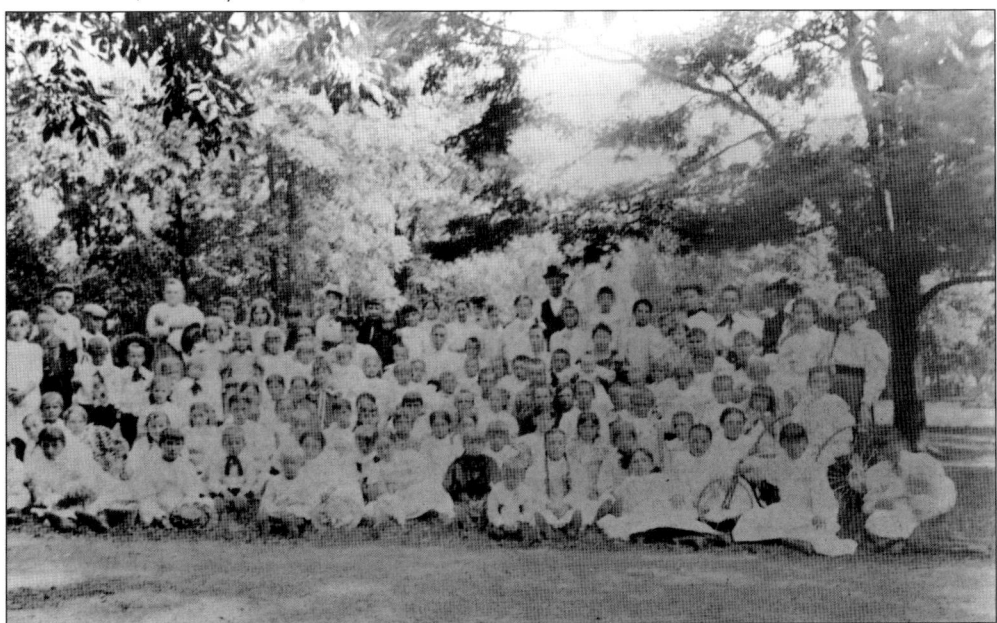

Above is depicted the congregation of Bohemian Methodist Episcopalian (located in Pilen at Nineteenth Place) on a church-sponsored outing to the Des Plaines campgrounds in 1896. A member of the church recalls that they would charter a train to take the families to the campground on the two-week retreat and that those with day jobs would commute back into the city every day. (Courtesy CSA.)

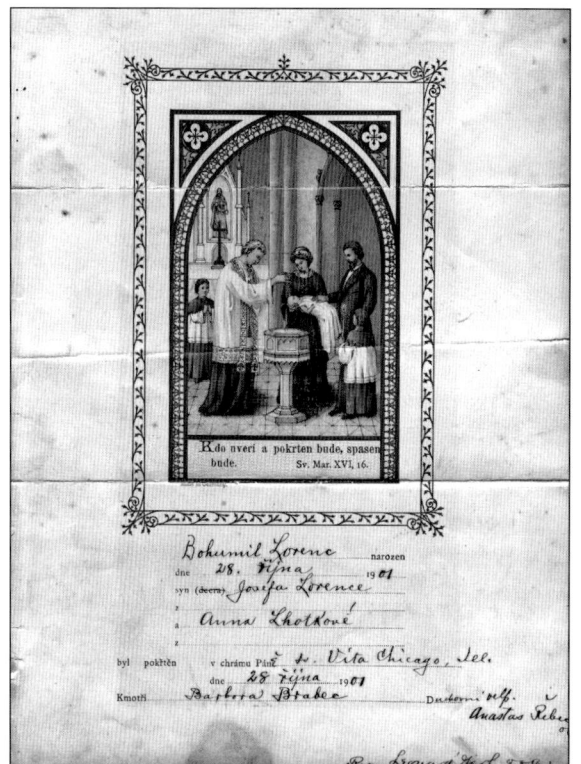

In 1888, the church and school of the largely Irish parish of St. Pius, which had relocated a few blocks southwest, was converted into a Czech Roman Catholic church, rectory, and school: the parish of St. Vitus. This certificate from 1901 commemorates the baptism of Victor Lorenc and is, notably, completely in Czech. The text to the illumination corresponds in the King James English to the line "He that believeth and is baptized shall be saved." (Courtesy CSA.)

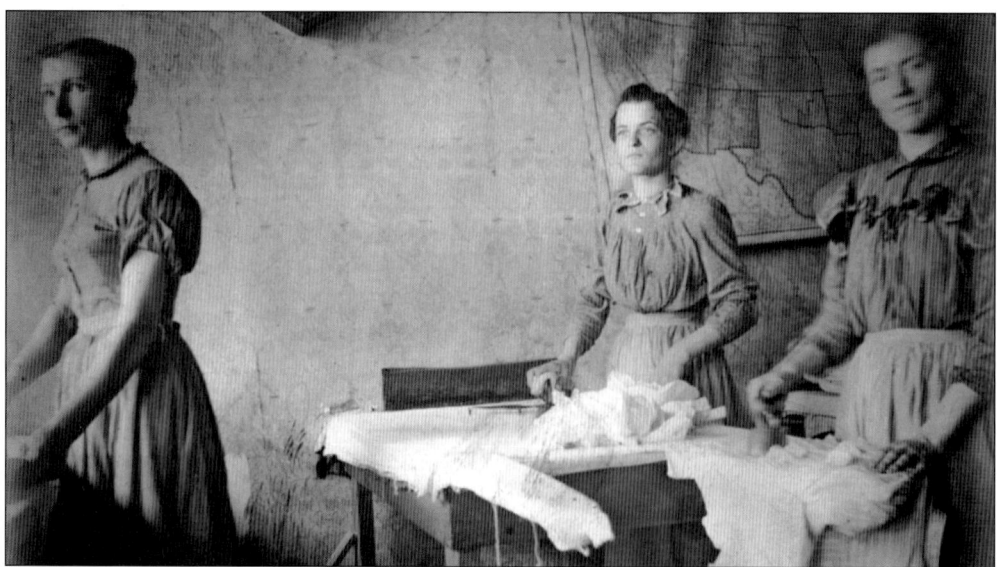

This photograph of workers of the Czech-owned Malina Laundry, at Twenty-fifth Street and Spaulding Avenue, was taken in 1896, proving how early the Czechs were working in the new community south of Pilsen. Lawndale was being touted to many Chicagoans as the neighborhood of opportunity, but the services that made such luxury possible were far less glamorous. Many Czech women made their living in the laundries and garment industries of the city and supported their families with their modest income. (Courtesy Chicago Public Library, Special Collections and Preservations Division.)

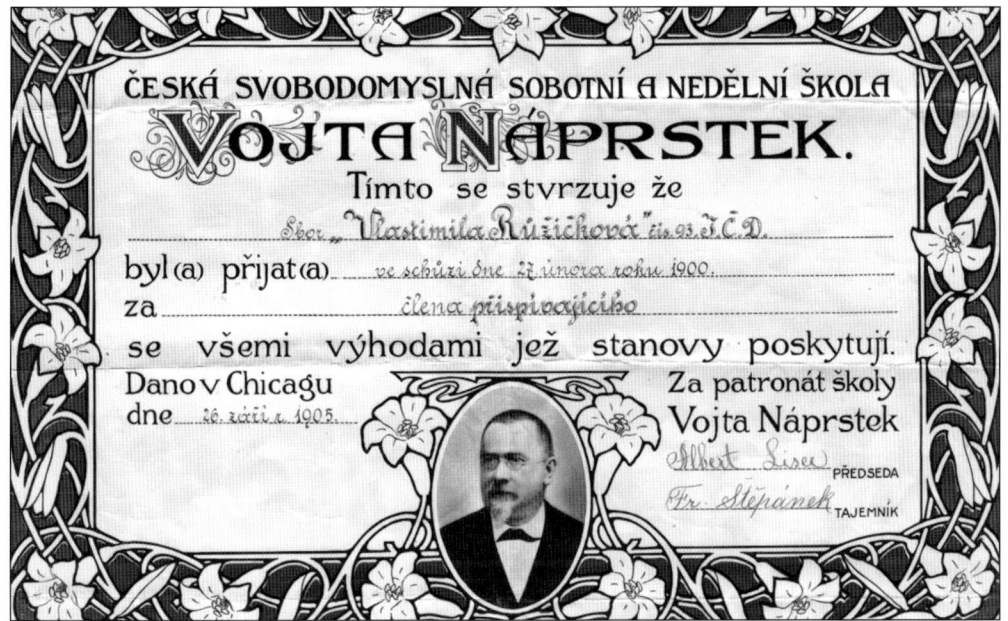

The Vojta Náprstek school was an important freethinking institution in Chicagoland, adamant as it was to retain and foster Czech language and customs in the New World. This certificate testifies that Vlastimila Růžičková, of the Union of Czech Ladies (Jednota Českých Dam), has completed the Vojta Náprstek Czech Freethinker Saturday and Sunday school. (Courtesy CSA.)

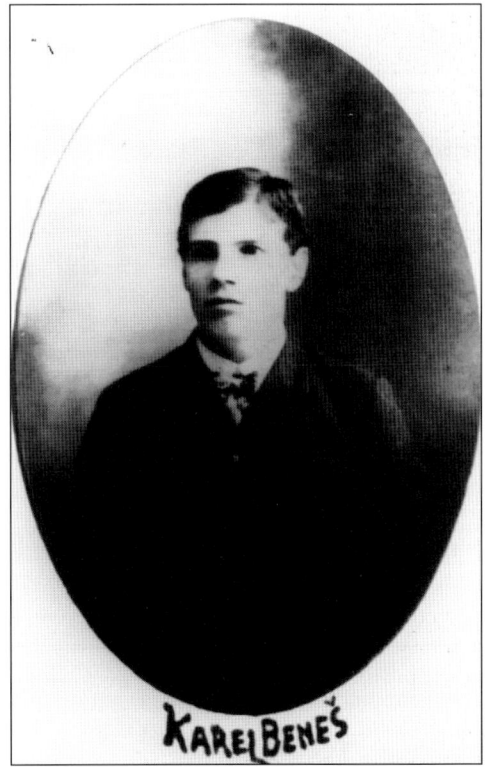

Karel Beneš, grandfather of Dorothy Beneš Duy, left his home in Bohemia and emigrated, along with his brothers Jan and František, to the United States between 1895 and 1900. They settled in Chicago's Pilsen neighborhood, and Karel opened a butcher's shop. He met Josefa Linhartová, who had come to Chicago from Bohemia via New York in 1899. By Dorothy's account, by 1900, September 30 to be precise, they were married at St. Procopius Church on Eighteenth Street. (Courtesy Dorothy Beneš Duy.)

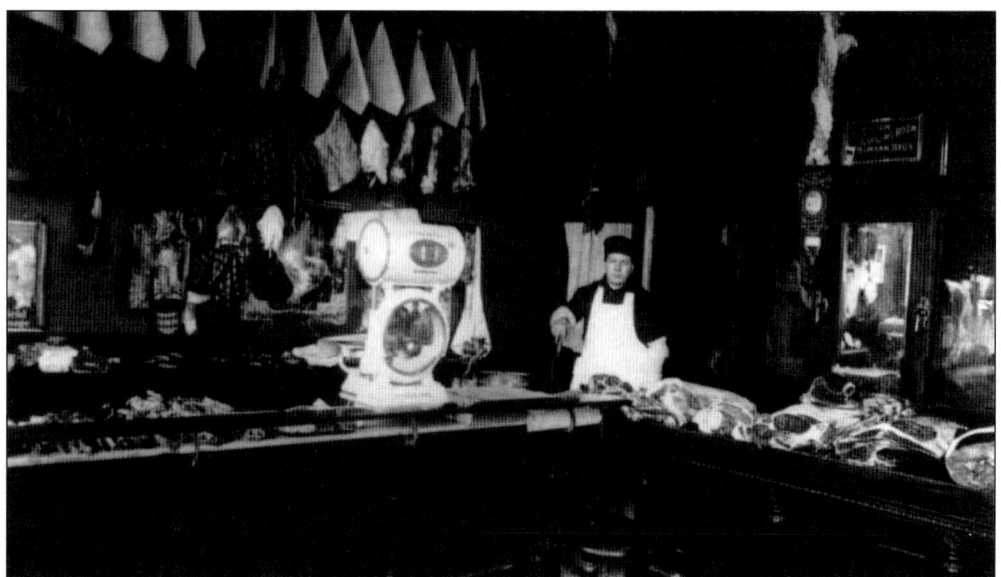

Karel Beneš stands in the center of his butcher shop in a photograph taken in 1907. The butcher's trade was a very popular one for Czech émigrés. Karel Beneš's business must have prospered as, by the second decade of the 20th century, as Dorothy recalls, the Beneš family was able to move—business and home—to the better-heeled neighborhood of Czech California. (Courtesy Dorothy Beneš Duy.)

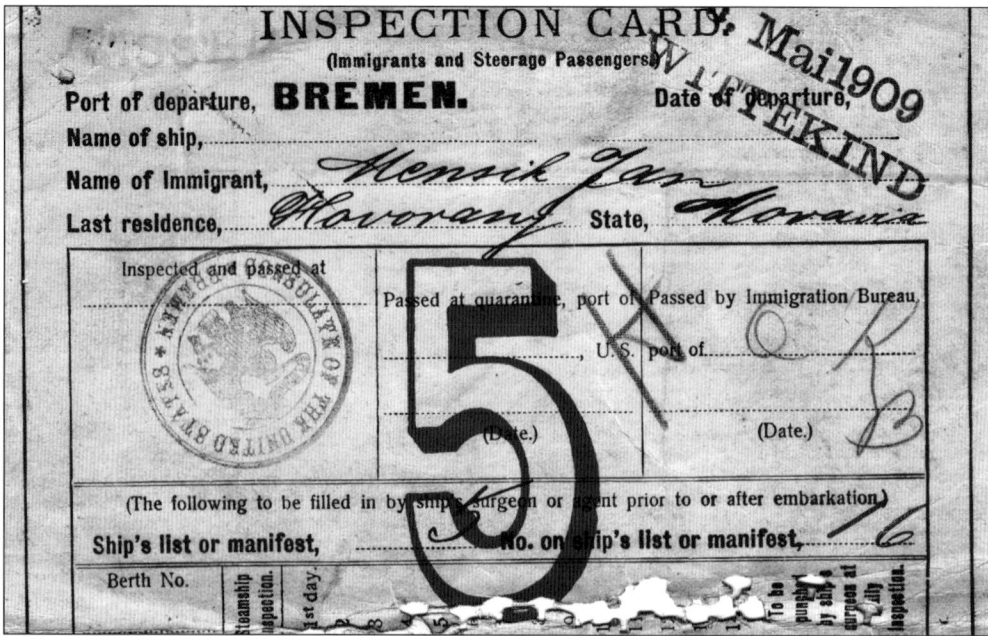

One of the ports of call of Jan Menšík's long journey to the United States was Bremen. This inspection card dated May 5, 1909, gives some sense of the kind of journey so many Czechs, still then subjects of the Austro-Hungarian Empire, endured to make it to the United States. The detail "immigrants or steerage passengers" underscores the frequently modest station of these émigrés and the amount of bureaucracy that faced them in their storied journey. (Courtesy Jean Mensik.)

The adventure of Růžena Čapová's (anglicized as Cap, and later to marry Jan Menšík) journey from the Hapsburg controlled Czech lands to Chicago is spelled out in this manifest. Čapová's journey from the port of Bremen, through the port of New York and then, eventually, her settlement in Cook County is drawn out in the administrative language of immigration, but as official as the document may be, the impression of the courage and strength of the young woman who made the journey is also inscribed. (Courtesy Jean Mensik.)

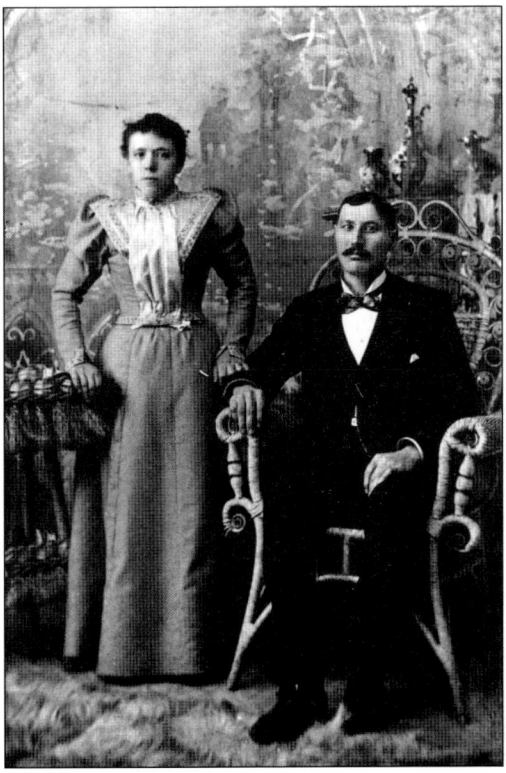

Emma Tomes and James (Václav) Palma were married on February 11, 1899. They had six children, one of whom, Rose, would be mother to Dorothy, who had the foresight to keep these memories for her descendants. James Palma worked for Western Electric, and his family was scheduled to be on the *Eastland* that fateful day in 1915, but as his granddaughter Dorothy recalls, "Someone in the family didn't feel well so they didn't go." (Courtesy Ray and Matthew Mulac.)

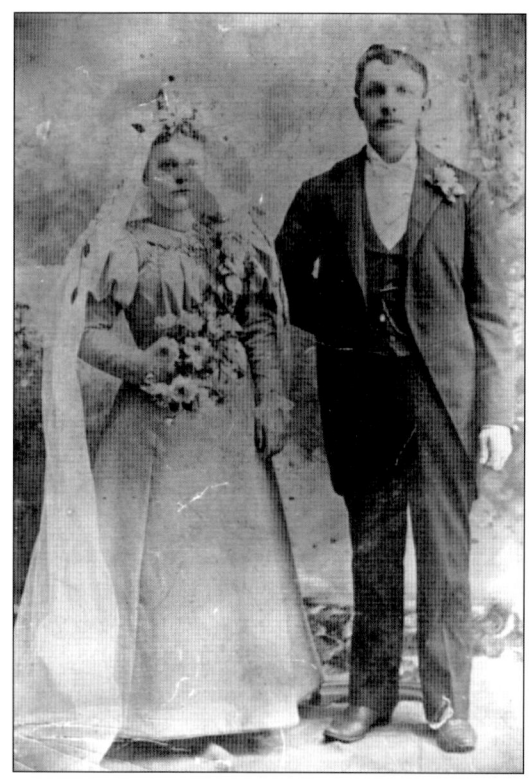

Josef Bezděk immigrated to the United States in 1892 at the age of 21, according to Dorothy (Bezděk) Mulac, Josef's granddaughter. He became a U.S. citizen in 1898 and one gets a sense of the lot of the new Czech émigré when Mulac reminisces about her paternal grandfather that it was only once he had a command of English that he was able to become economically independent. Only then was he able to "work in music stores" and then, "after much hard work, he was able to open a tavern." (Courtesy Ray and Matthew Mulac.)

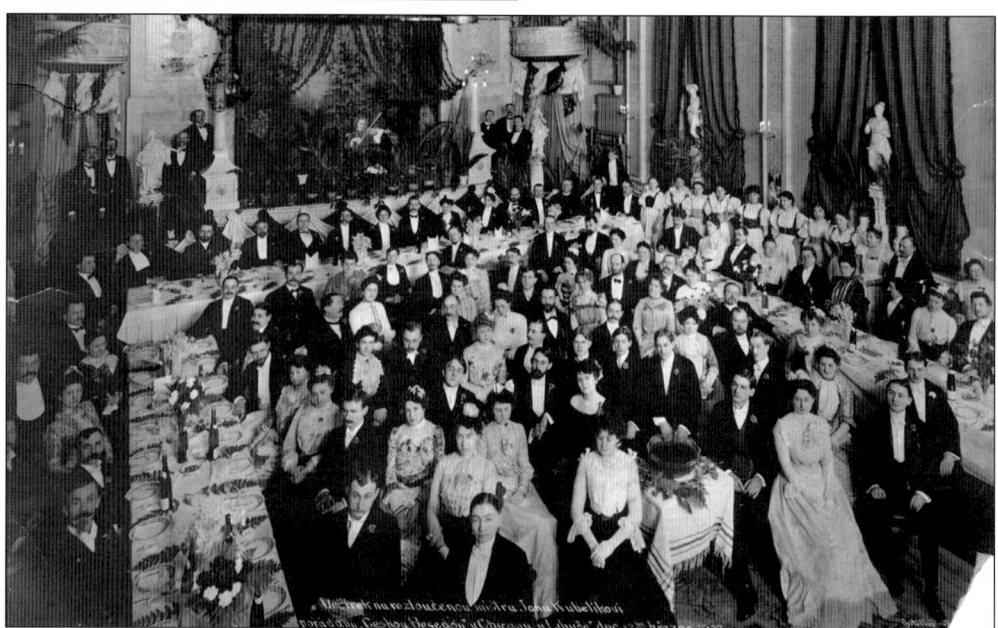

Violin prodigy Jan Kubelík made a tour of the United States in 1901–1902 at the age of 21. His appearances in Chicago were of great pride to its Czech population. In this 1902 photograph, prominent Czech Chicagoans fete Kubelík at a farewell dinner. Carl Sandburg even devoted a poem to Kubelík that begins, "Your bow swept over a string, and a long low note quivered to the air." (Courtesy CSA.)

Pilsen supported several photography studios—and the products of their work are included in this book—specializing in special occasion photographs. But preeminent among them was Francis D. Němeček's studio at 1439 West Eighteenth Street. It was also one of the most elegant buildings in Czech Pilsen. Designed by architect Frank Randak in 1907, it featured a beautiful slanted window roof that allowed natural light into the studio. The building today is home to the busy and popular Café Jumping Bean. (Courtesy Chicago History Museum.)

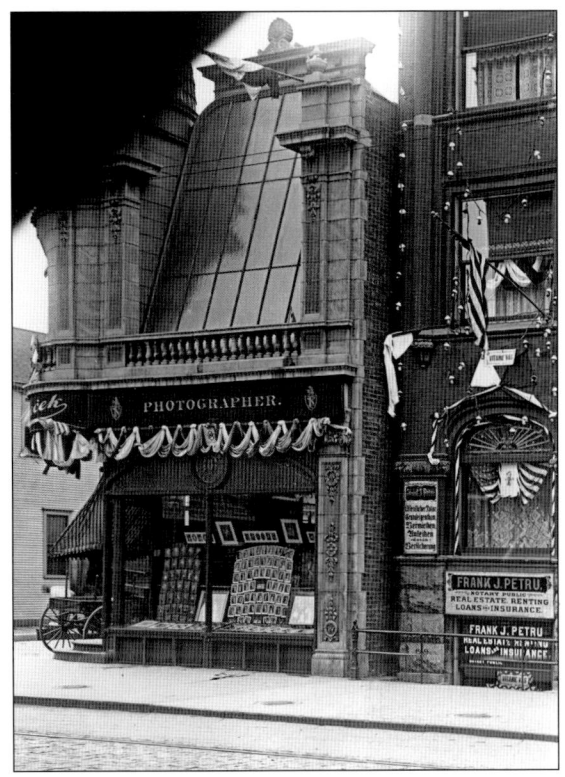

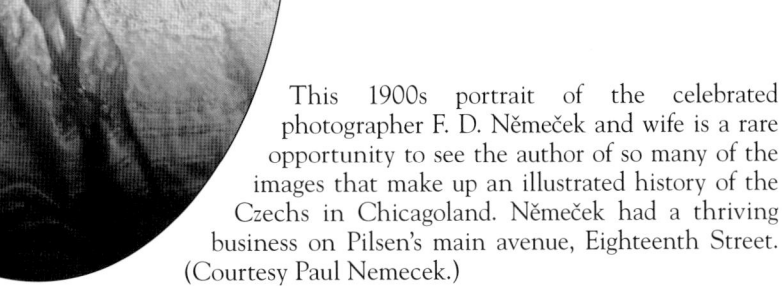

This 1900s portrait of the celebrated photographer F. D. Němeček and wife is a rare opportunity to see the author of so many of the images that make up an illustrated history of the Czechs in Chicagoland. Němeček had a thriving business on Pilsen's main avenue, Eighteenth Street. (Courtesy Paul Nemecek.)

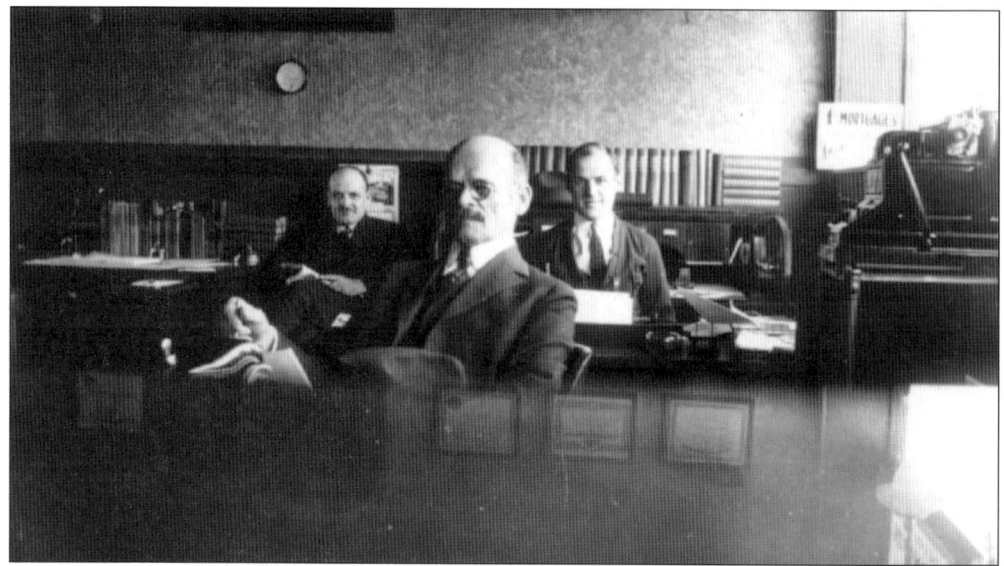

The offices of A. Furst realty company are seen in the second decade of the 20th century located at 4145 West Twenty-sixth Street in the growing community known as Lawndale or Czech California. In the foreground is the company's namesake. The real estate business was a lucrative one for Czechs in the second decade of the 20th century, and Czechs were more likely to patronize businesses owned by those they saw as compatriots when dealings were of such importance as the purchase of land or a home or the investment of money. (Courtesy Chicago Public Library, Special Collections and Preservation Division.)

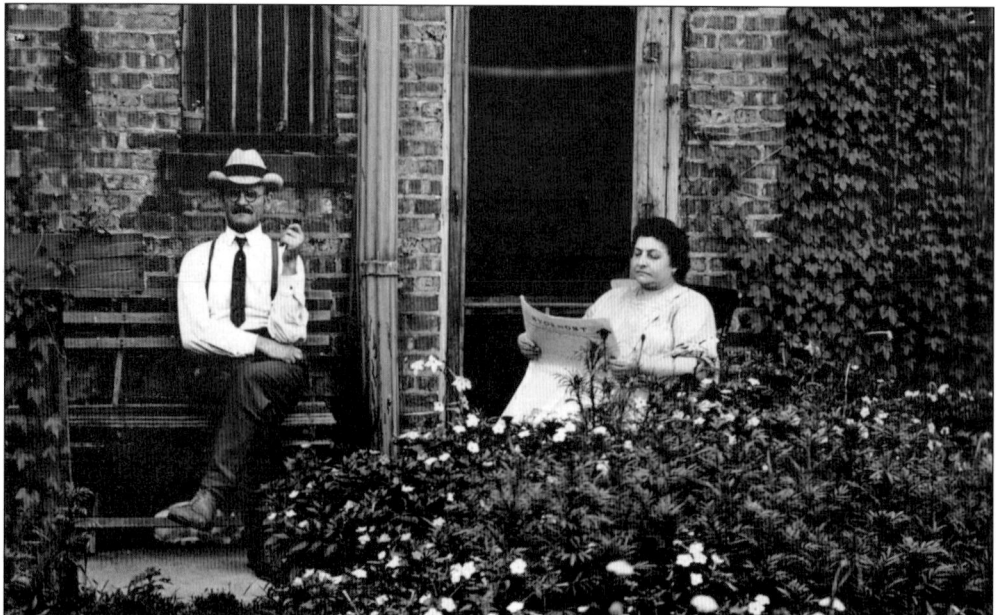

This informal photograph taken in 1921 of the Fursts, who owned a real estate business in Czech California, shows them in their backyard relaxing: Adolf Furst smoking a pipe while his wife reads the *Svornost* newspaper. That the paper is the *Svornost* tells that the Fursts were Czechs with freethinking political and ideological leanings. (Courtesy Chicago Public Library, Special Collections and Preservation Division, LCCC 1-247.)

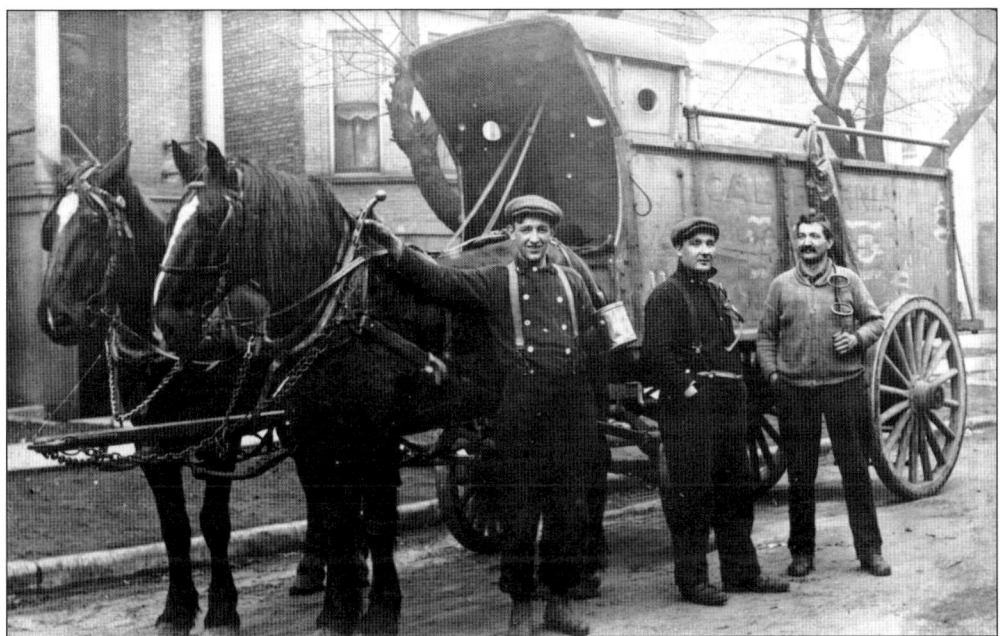

Josef Naxera came to Chicago from his native Bohemia and settled first in Chicago's Pilsen neighborhood; he, like many working-class Czechs in the city, was a carter and peddler of wares. Here he is shown with his ice wagon, around 1908, on his rounds through Pilsen. (Courtesy Frank Magallon.)

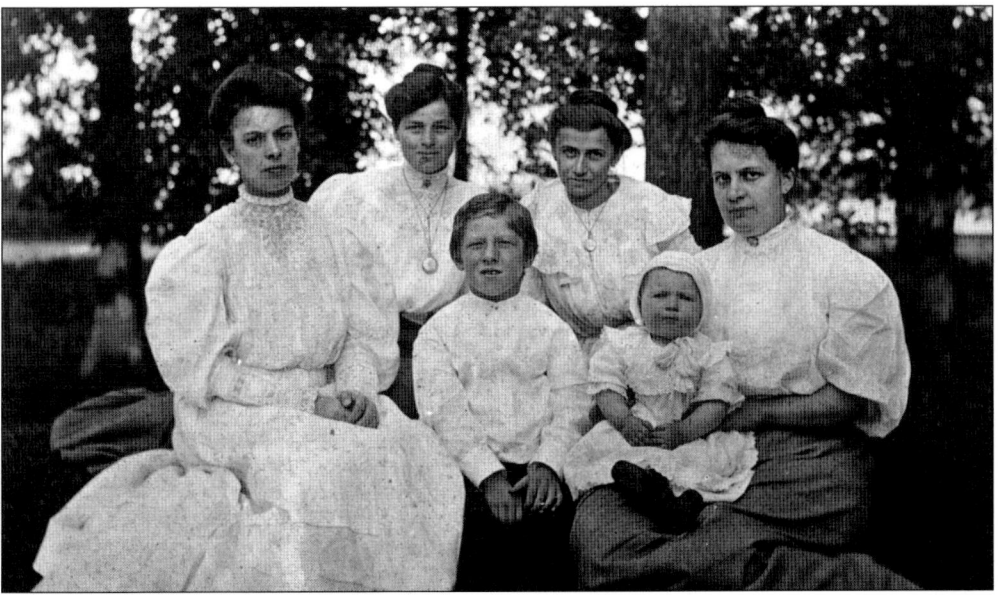

An intimate family portrait from 1906 shows the forebears of Marge Sladek Stueckemann. On the far left is Aunt Mary Knudson (née Pancer), Aunt Emma Závodský (née Pancer) sits to her upper right, Mary Sládek Hynek sits to her immediate right, and clockwise to her immediate right is the family's uniting matriarch, Marge's grandmother Anna Sládek (née Pancer). The two children sitting in the middle of the family circle are Clarence, Charles, Hynek (age eight), and the baby Blanche (age one). (Courtesy Marge Sladek Stueckemann.)

53

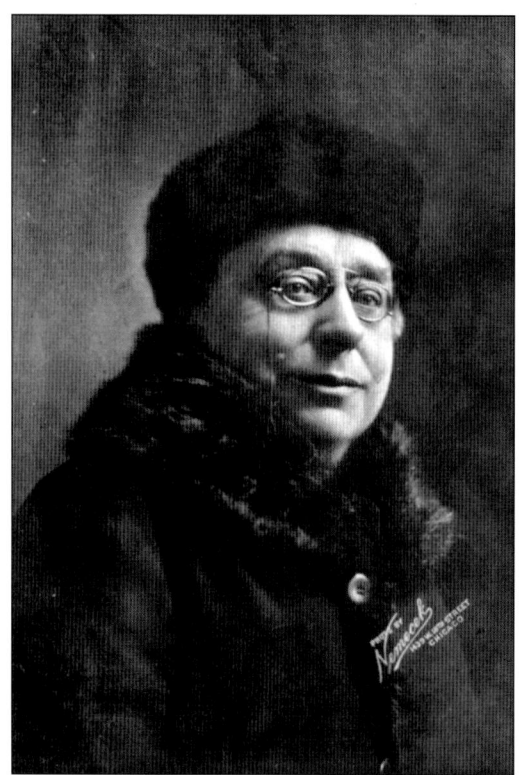

The professional acting troupe of the Ludvík Players, named for the patriarch of the troupe, František Ludvík, came to Chicago as part of a tour of the United States. Their success in Chicago was so extraordinary and the welcome so warm that they decided to settle in Chicago, making Thalia Hall their home stage for over 30 years. František's wife, Bohumila Ludvíková, and their children František Jr. and Marie were also perennially popular stage stars. (Courtesy CSA.)

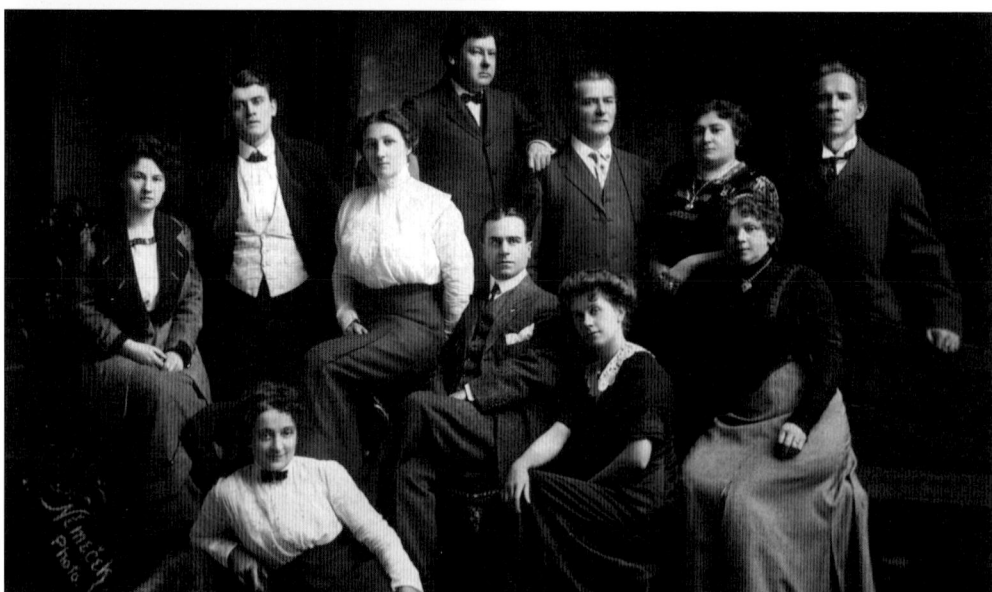

The Ludvikovci encouraged theatrical activities around Chicagoland, and in their several decades in the city, with their home stage at Thalia Hall, they fostered talent among young men and women with aspirations to careers on the stage and, increasingly, in film. Above are the *dorostov*, or young generation, of the Ludvík players in a 1913 portrait, taken on the occasion of the 20th anniversary of the Ludvik troupe's stay in Chicago. (Courtesy University of Chicago, Archive of Czechs and Slovaks Abroad.)

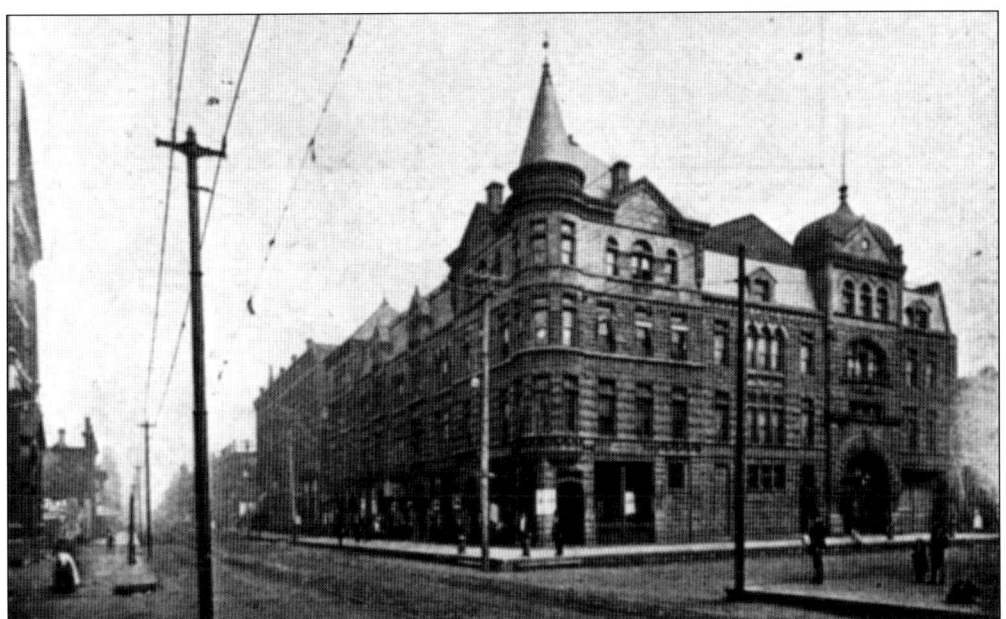

Thalia Hall on Eighteenth and Allport Streets opened in 1882 to great accolades, and the Czechs finally had a stunning artistic hall of their own. Here Czech plays were staged, meetings were held, and schemes for Czechoslovak sovereignty were concocted. Architects Faber and Pagels took their inspiration from the Romanesque buildings of Europe and designed Thalia's interior to be plush and spacious. (Courtesy CSA.)

Of the actors and singers on the Czech Chicago stage, Josef Krejčí and Marie Havelková were two of the most popular. Here they are shown in a postcard scene captured from the play *Polská Krev* (Polish blood) in which they starred as Bolo (Krejčí) and Helena (Havelková). Krejčí was a very celebrated baritone who had come from Prague's music conservatory to grace the stages of Chicago. (Courtesy University of Chicago, Archive of Czechs and Slovaks Abroad; photograph by Pleschner Studio.)

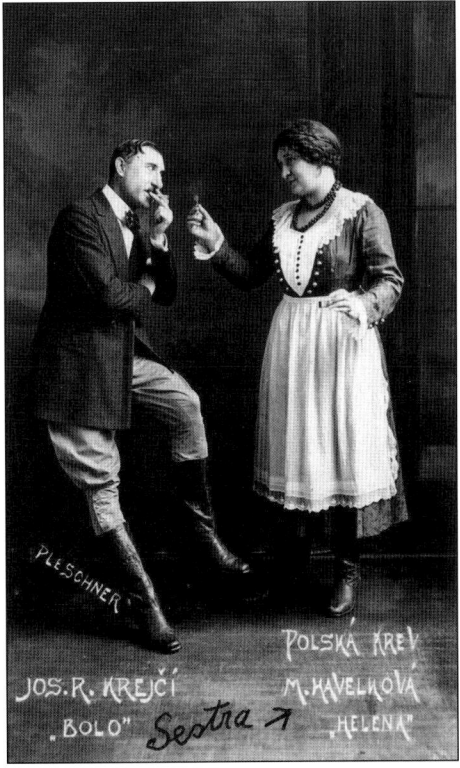

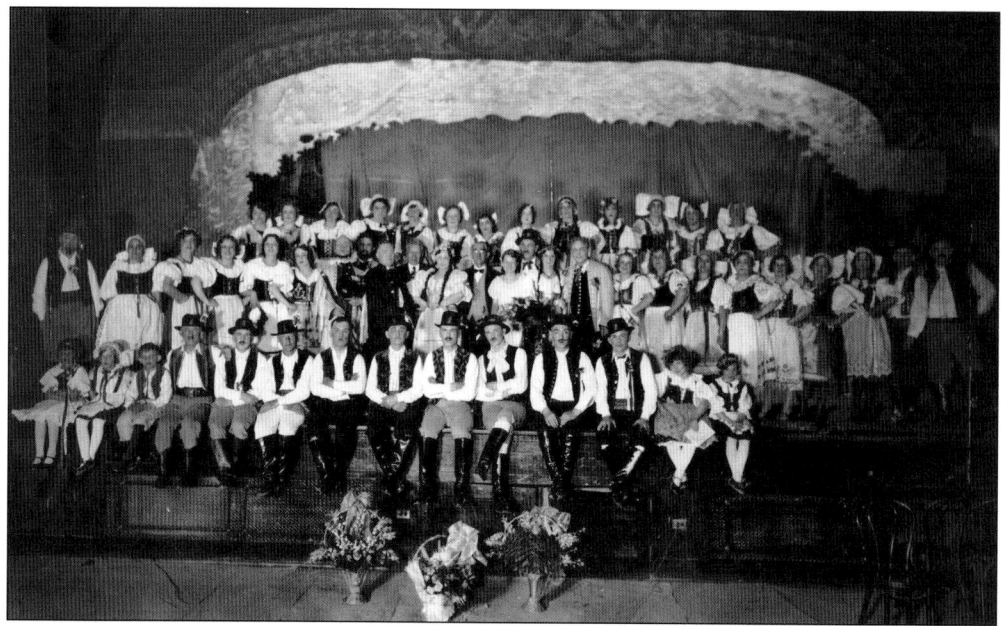

A production of the play *Zmařená Svatba* (the stymied wedding), subtitled "a national opera in three acts," attests to the strong national spirit Czechs in Chicago maintained. Here the large cast collects for a group photograph, and from the picture it is clear that amateur theatricals were not only a means by which to instill and cultivate national feeling but also a way for Czechs of all ages to become involved in the life of the community. (Courtesy CSA.)

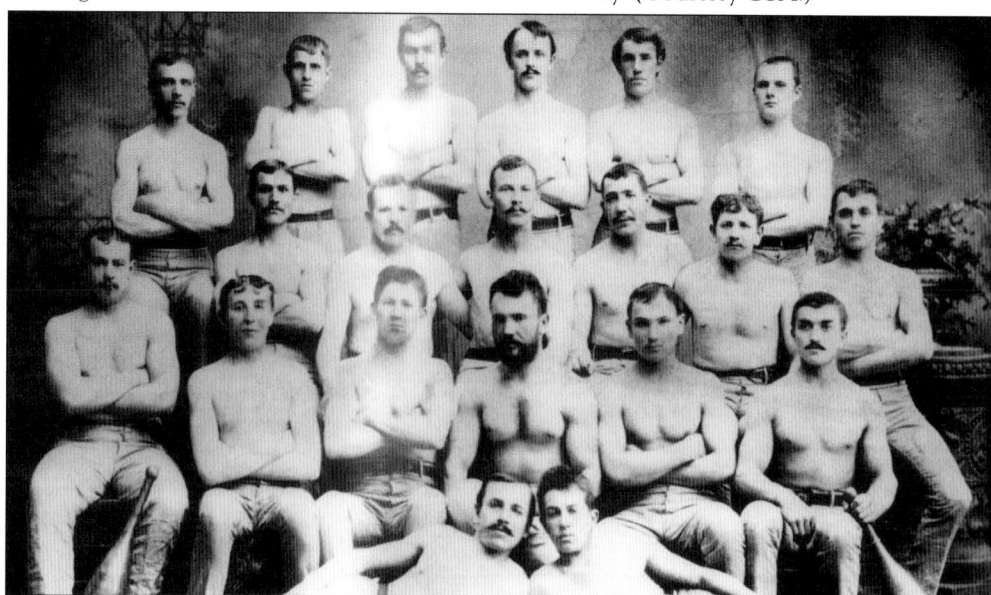

In 1886, the Cvičicí Členové Tělocvičné Jednoty Sokol Čechie (practicing members of the Gymnastic Union of Bohemian Sokol) was still nascent but sturdy. Prominent among those here is Karel Štulík. Among other members are F. B. Křenek (top row, left) and Tom Křenek (second row, right). Tom Křenek is grandfather to Evelyn Křenek Fergl, who grew up in Czech Berwyn and attended the heavily Czech-inflected Morton West High School. Evelyn now lives in Detroit, but her Czech Chicago roots are strong. (Courtesy Evelyn Fergl.)

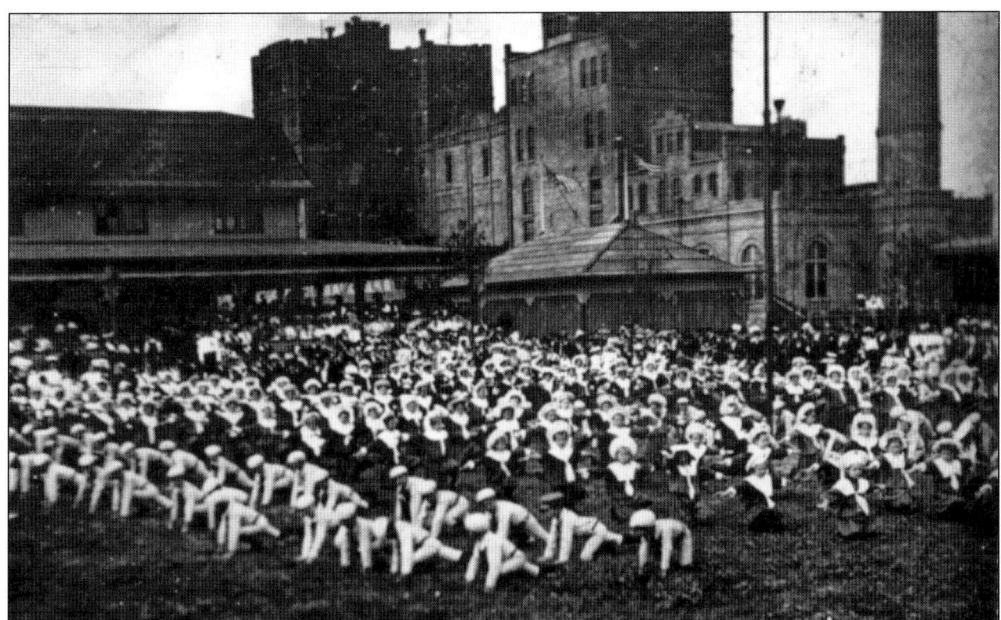

Sokol field competitions drew together competing lodges with their elite gymnasts and, as seen here in a photograph from around 1900, meticulously rehearsed and choreographed calisthenics routines. Sokol competitions kept alive the notion of a "fit mind in a fit body" and cultivated a connection between Czechs in the New World and their brothers and sisters in the Czech lands. (Courtesy Chicago Public Library, Special Collections and Preservation Division.)

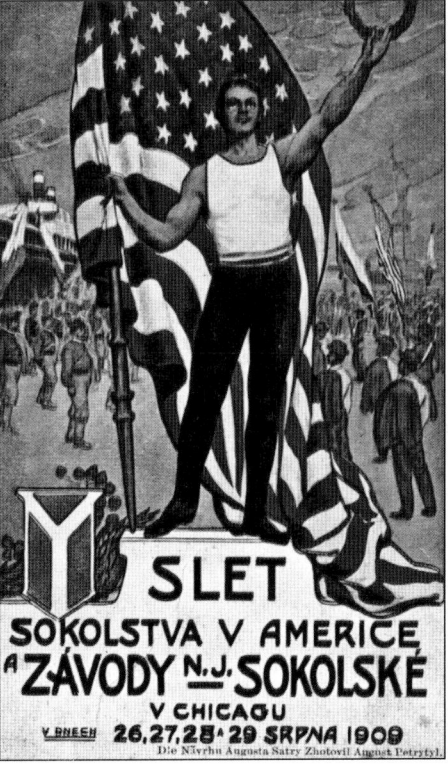

The poster announces the 1909 *slet* (literally flocking, or meet) of the Sokol organization in America. The pride of the Slet's host city is clear in the Y in the lower left, a symbol that represents the Chicago River's outline (south and north branches) and its importance in the city. (Courtesy University of Chicago, Archive of Czechs and Slovaks Abroad.)

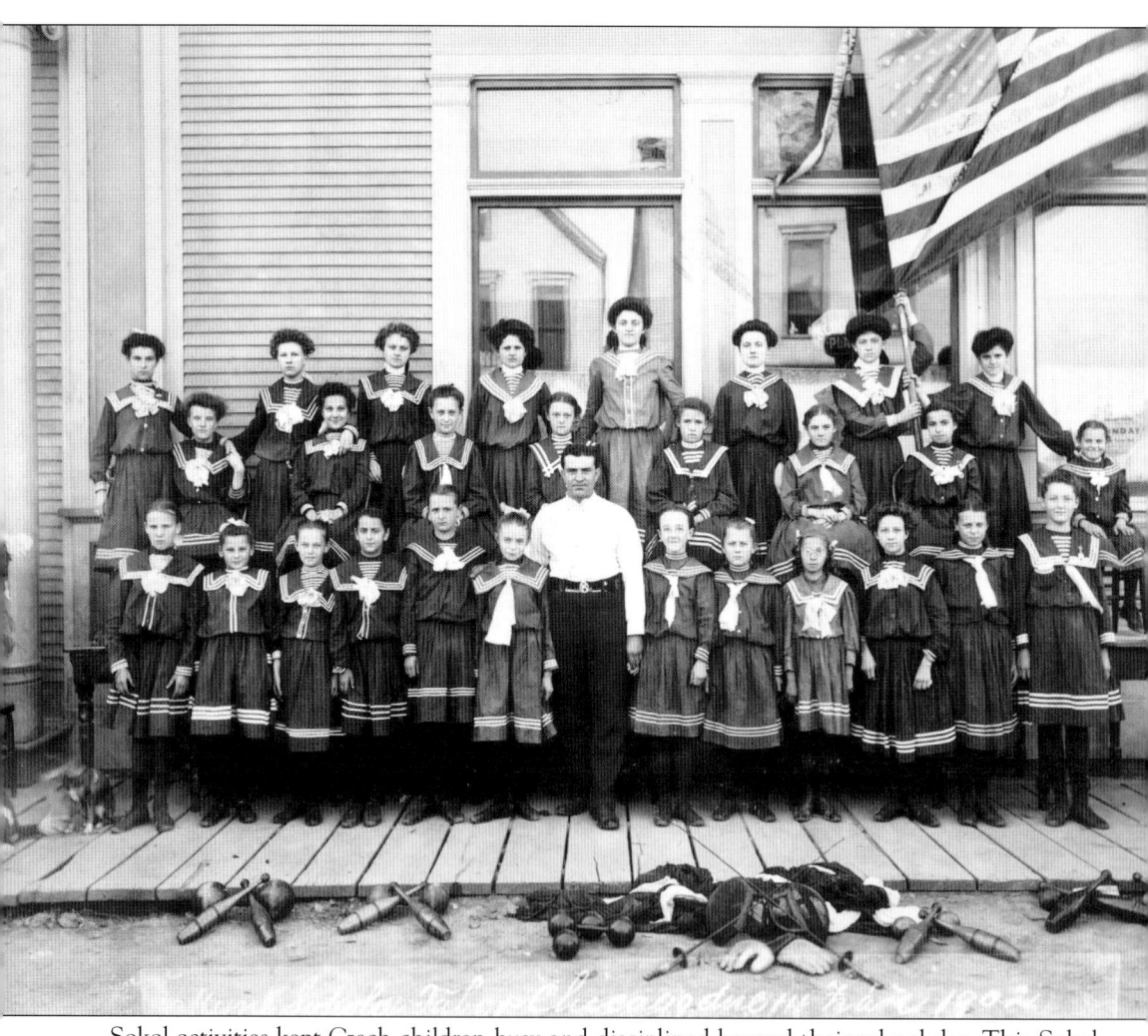

Sokol activities kept Czech children busy and disciplined beyond their school day. This Sokol gymnastic union poses for a formal group picture in 1902. Note the new plank board sidewalks, a reminder that in the 1860s Pilsen's street level was "lifted" between 4 and 14 feet to meet new city grade laws. Some homeowners decided to load their house frames onto wheels and roll them to new plots; most, though, turned their second floors into ground floors with bridges leading to the new front door. The vaulting of sidewalks in Pilsen led to gaping views under the sidewalk—*nad sidewalce*—that were the stuff of nightmares for many a Bohemian child. The "raising of Chicago" was ordered as early as 1855, but it took several decades for the city to attend to some of its less affluent neighborhoods. The raising of the street level also made for interesting below-street-level gardens in Pilsen and other neighborhoods, earning Pilsen the nickname "Garden City." (Courtesy Chicago Public Library, Special Collections and Preservation Division, LCCC 1-446.)

Josef Novák, one-time chief editor of the newspaper *Spravedlnost*, is depicted in this portrait. The *Spravedlnost* (justice) was founded in 1905 as a socialist-anarchic weekly, and it was the organ of the Czech contingent of the U.S. social-democratic party. Novák distinguished himself as one of the very first volunteers to join the Czechoslovak Legion, a military company formed during World War I with the mission of securing an independent Czechoslovakia. (Courtesy University of Chicago, Archive of Czechs and Slovaks Abroad.)

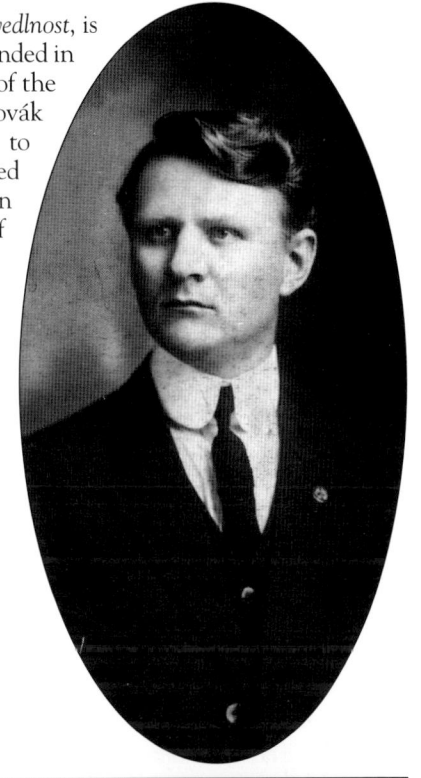

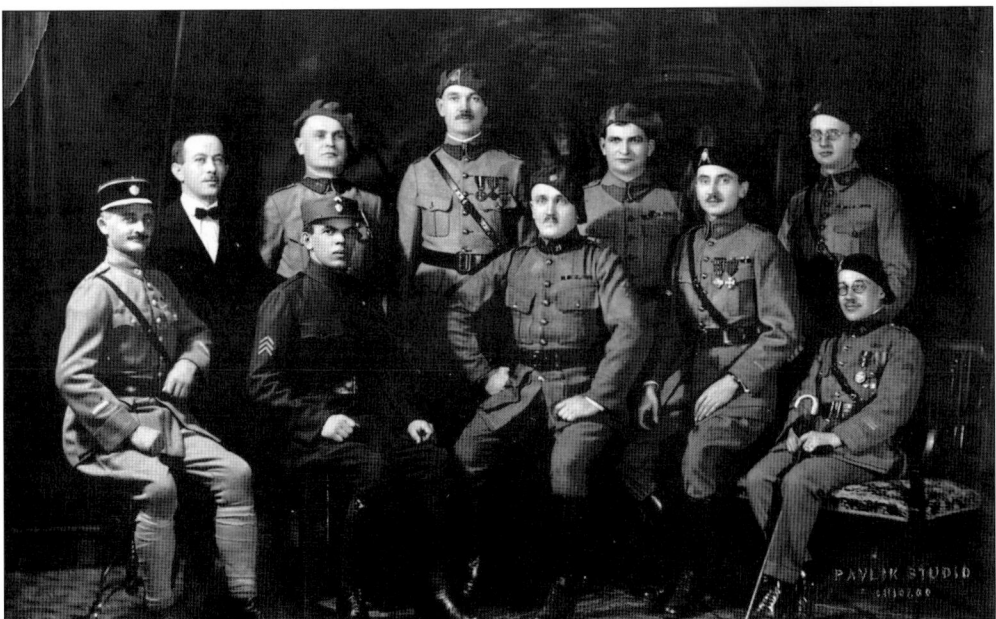

This group portrait shows the Chicago faction of the Czechoslovak Legionnaires. Without the support of Czech Chicagoans in World War I, both as servicemen and as agitators for a free Czech state, the beginnings of Czechoslovakia may not have been so assured. The magnitude of Chicago's contribution to the founding of a free Czechoslovakia is yet to be fully appreciated. (Courtesy CSA; photograph by Pavlík Studios.)

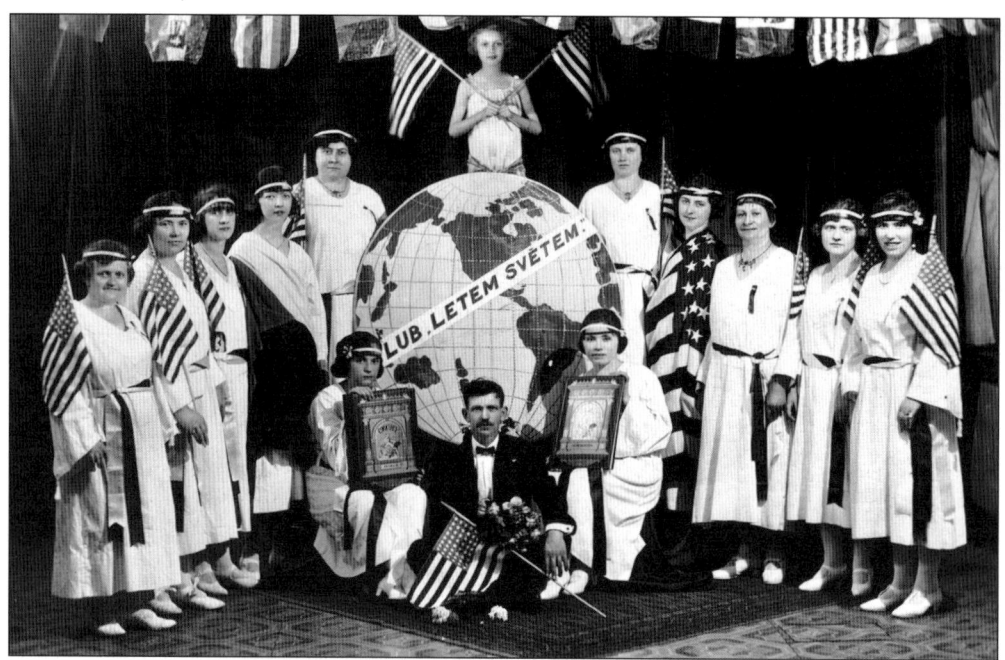

Other clubs outside of Sokol flourished also, especially those with a strong arts, music, and theatrical component. This image of the Club Letem Světem (round the world) testifies to the patriotic fervor the Czechs felt toward their new home. The books the two girls flanking the man in the foreground are presenting, however, make the deeply Czech character of this club clear. (Courtesy University of Chicago, Archive of Czechs and Slovaks Abroad; photograph by Pavlík Studio.)

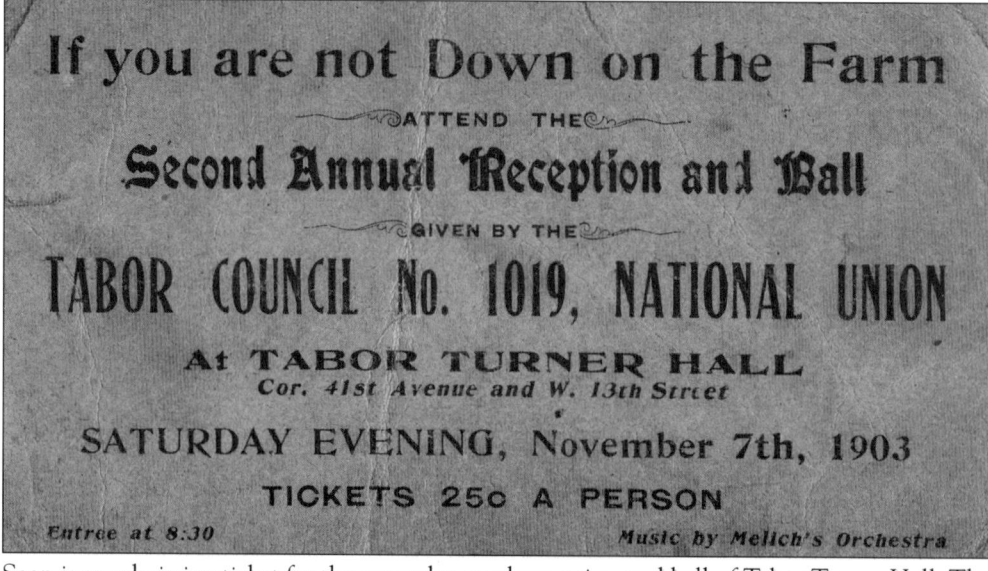

Seen is an admission ticket for the second annual reception and ball of Tabor Turner Hall. The hall at the corner of Forty-first Avenue and West Thirteenth Street was in the heart of Merigold, or Nový Tábor, as the Czechs dubbed it. The fact that the ticket is entirely in English and uses the colloquial phrase, "If you are not Down on the Farm," is signal for this author of deepening assimilation of the Czechs to their Chicago environment. (Courtesy CSA.)

Jaroslav Zmrhal was one of the city's brightest luminaries. He received his doctorate from the University of Chicago—the picture here occasions his graduation—and soon after, in 1921, was appointed district superintendent of the Chicago Public Schools. Throughout his life, Zmrhal campaigned for the teaching of so-called "immigrant" languages, wrote primers and readers, and expanded the language curriculum to the extent that his reforms are still felt today. (Courtesy CSA.)

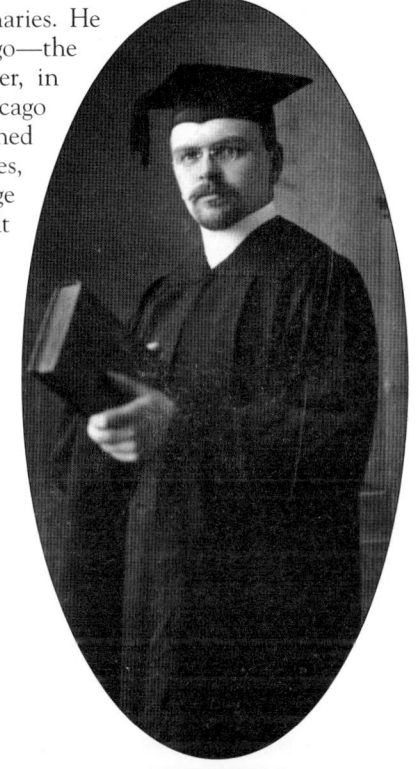

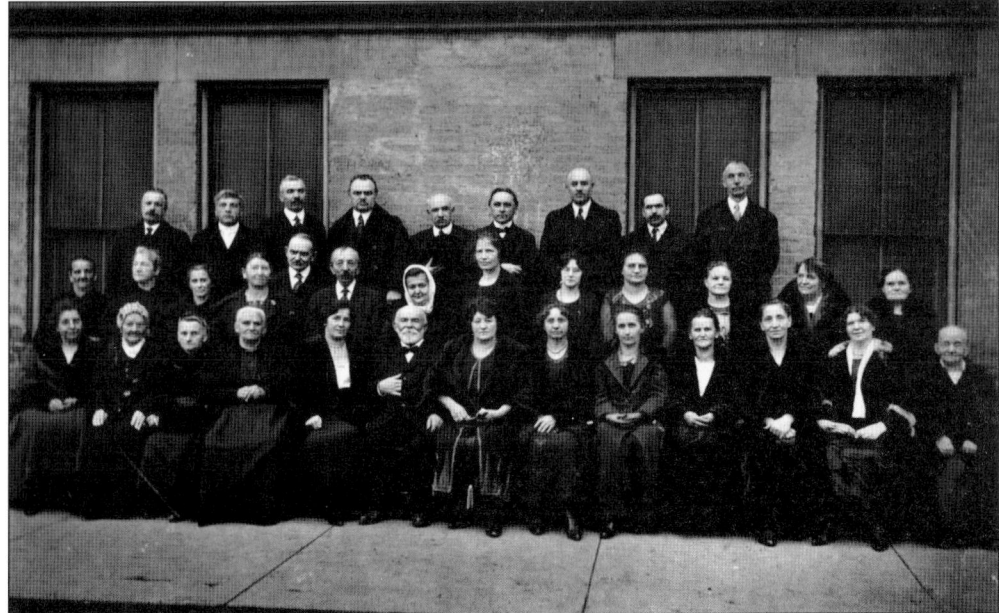

The year 1914 marked the 20th anniversary of the Bohemian Baptist Church. This photograph shows not only the numbers of the group but also the early signal settlement of the western suburbs by Protestant congregations. Jaroslav Zmrhal and his wife, Agnes Zmrhal (née Palma), were also active in the Baptist church and are pictured here among other congregants. (Courtesy University of Chicago, Archive of Czechs and Slovaks Abroad.)

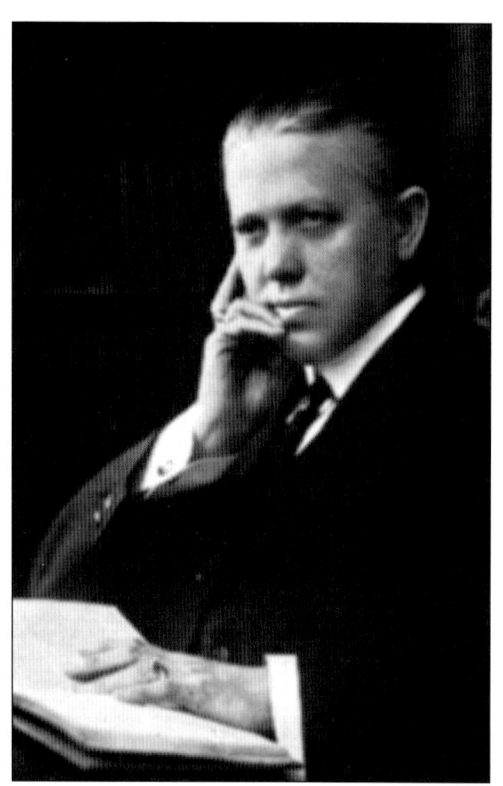

Born in Prague in 1872, Jaroslav Vojan received his law degree from Charles University in Prague in 1898. He made the trip to the United States in 1904, and in 1909, he was appointed to Chicago's Czech-American Press Bureau. Vojan was the founder in 1912, and first president, of the Bohemian Arts Club; throughout his life he was a leading freethinker and community activist. (Author's collection.)

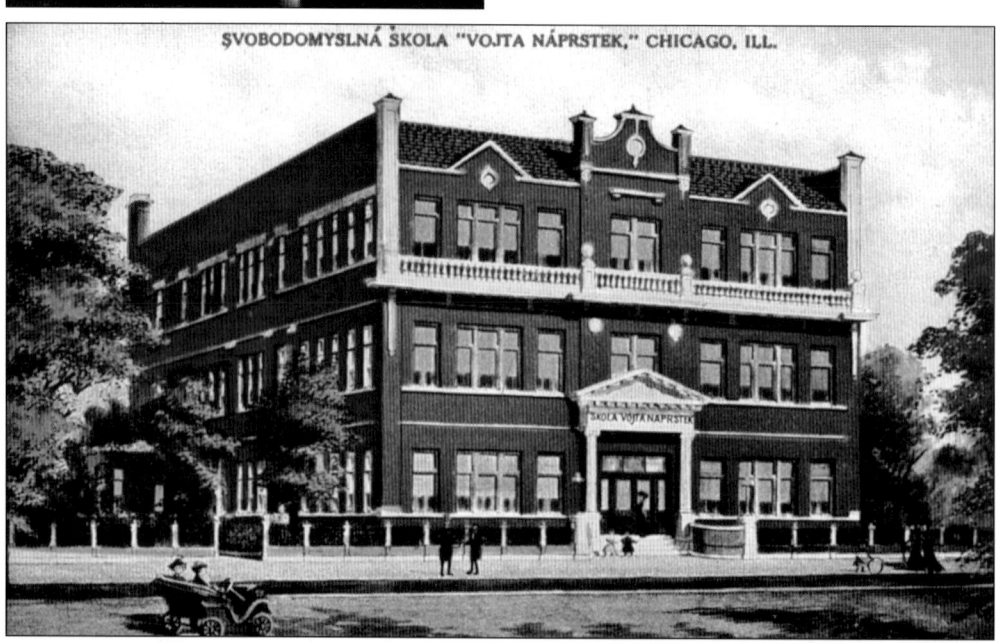

By 1936, the Náprstek School was one of three full-time freethinking schools in Chicago. Svobodná Obec (free commune) was the "oldest Czech rationalistic body" in the United States in 1870. According to Jaroslav Vojan, the freethinker philosophy is based on "a junction of rationalism and positivism. It strives for progress in all branches of human life, for progress of thought as well as for economic and social progress." (Courtesy CSA.)

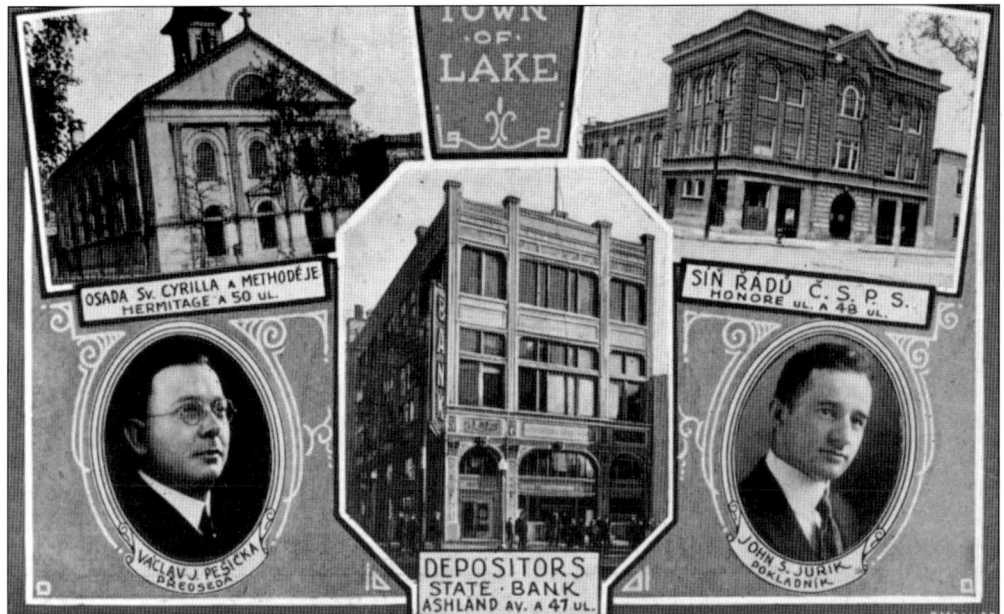

Macha's booklet of postcards is witness to how rich the Czech Chicago experience was. This view of Town of Lake converges on the Depositor's State Bank, with its president Václav Pesička and treasurer John Jurík. Town of Lake had its Czech Catholic center at the church of SS. Cyrill and Methodius, and, at the corner of Honore and Forty-eighth Streets, was the lodge of the ČSPS. (Courtesy CSA.)

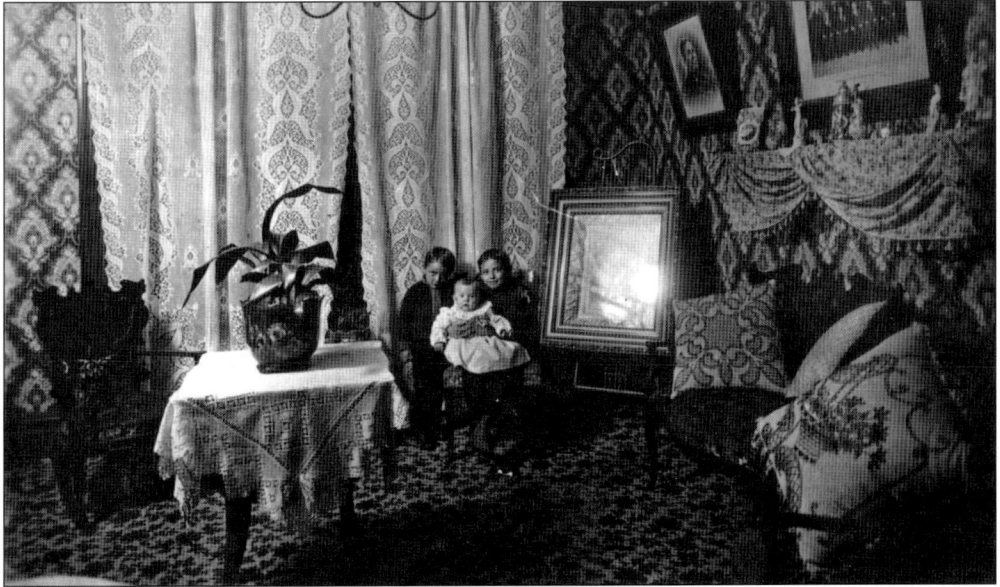

František Slauf, also pictured among the Bando-Concertina Club members, and his wife, Marie, thrived in Chicagoland and, like the Vlčeks, were able to settle in the new Lawndale neighborhood in rather elegant surroundings. This image of their children sitting in what is the well-appointed salon of their home on Karlov Street, is perhaps emblematic of the increasing wealth and affluence of the community. (Courtesy Chicago Public Library, Special Collections and Preservation Division, LCCC 1-361.)

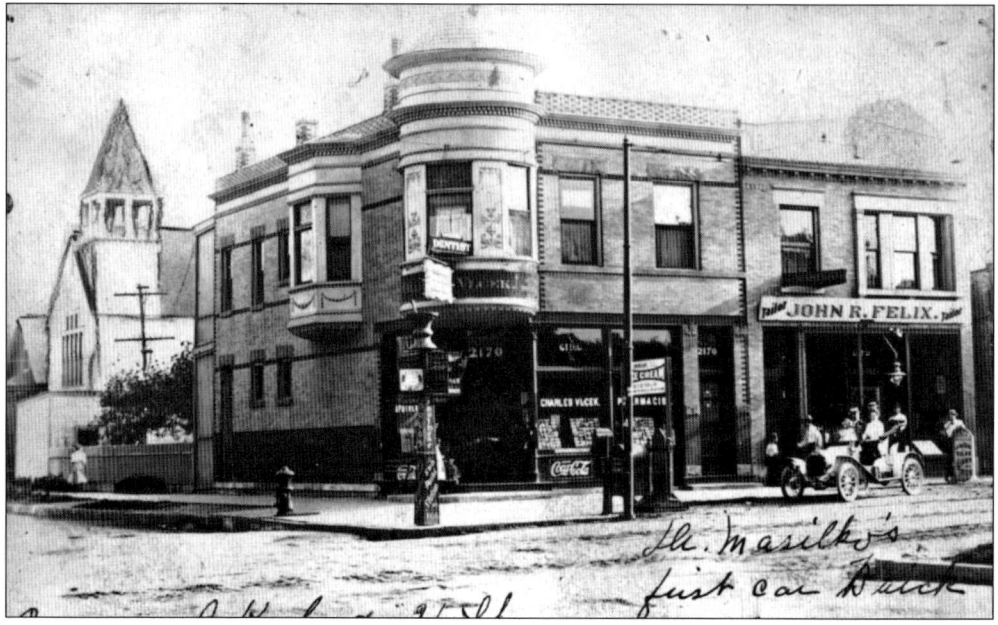

This image from 1908 of Charles Vlček Pharmacy on Twenty-sixth Street makes it clear that even as early as the beginning of the 20th century the area west of Pilsen was being colonized by Czech folk. It also indicates that Czechs as a group were upwardly mobile, with the possibility of intracity migration to areas considered by their developers in this way. Increasingly, Czech families were settling directly in "Ceské Kalifornie." (Courtesy Chicago Public Library, Special Collections and Preservation Division.)

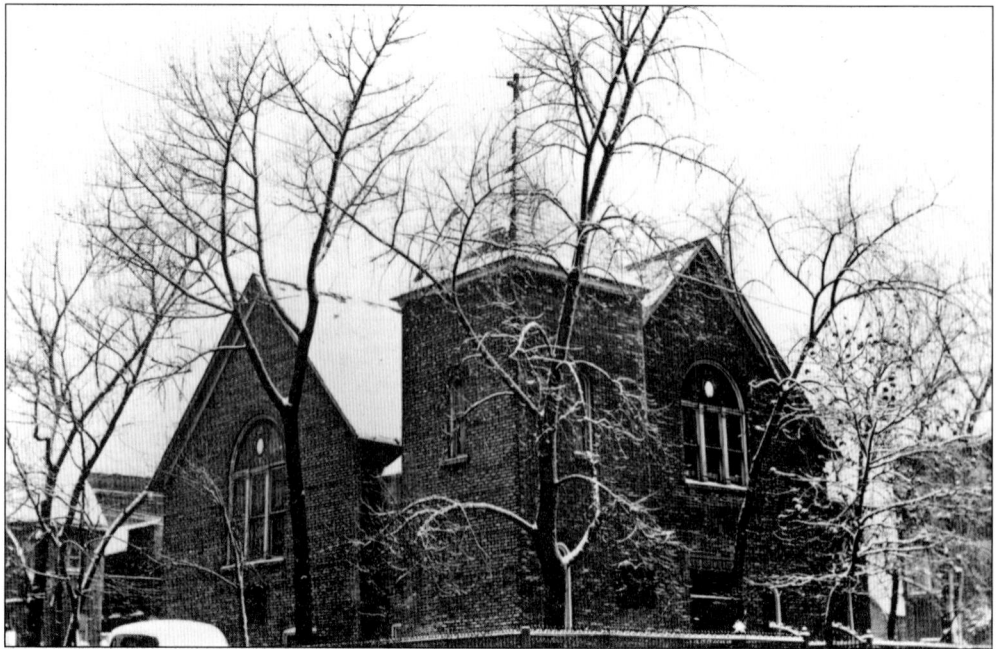

Of the Czech Protestants in Chicago, the Bohemian Methodist Episcopalians arguably had the strongest political voice. They established themselves early on around the Jan Hus Church on Sawyer Avenue and Twenty-third Street in Czech California, today's Little Village. (Courtesy CSA.)

Three

CALIFORNIA DREAMING AND WINTER'S DAYS

By 1910, there were more than 100,000 Czechs in Chicago. The community expanded westward into the area known as Lawndale-Crawford. With arteries on Twenty-second and Twenty-sixth Streets, the neighborhood was so dominated by Czechs that it became known as Česká Kalifornie (Czech California), after one of the settlement's thoroughfares.

With each year the Czech community was proving to "established" Americans that they were a model ethnic group, one contributing to the wealth and moral fiber of its adopted homeland. With the advantage of larger plots and the new bungalow architectural style, Czech California was now the Czechs' community of choice. Here banks proliferated so that by 1920 the total savings in Czech-owned and Czech-patronized banks was calculable at $12 to 15 million.

Pains were taken by the Czech community to preserve its language and cultural identity while also "learning" to be ideal U.S. citizens. This was no small task for a people who until 1918 did not have a sovereign nation to which to refer. But with the specter of war looming in central Europe, the Czechs of Chicago saw an opportunity for their native land to gain autonomy, and they were instrumental in its establishment.

In the early 1900s, the Western Electric Hawthorne Works on the city's edge, between Czech California and the town of Cicero, offered gainful employ to thousands of Czech workers. Such success for the Czech community would be tragically dimmed by the events of July 1915. The *Eastland* disaster counts as one of the saddest chapters of Chicago history. It was especially heartbreaking for the Czech community: of the over 800 victims of the *Eastland*, more than a third were of Czech ancestry.

But the Czech community bounced back, showing its resilience in its many high-ranking civil servants. Most famous among them was Antonín Čermák. His celebrated mayoral term and his heartrending assassination were watersheds in the life of the Czech community and the city as a whole. The Czech penchant for organization and zeal for liberty came together perfectly in the 20th century to make for the profile of Czech Americans in Chicagoland's political life.

The years 1914 to 1938 for the Czech Chicago community were filled with triumphs, often followed by tragedies; but as horrific as the losses of 1915 and 1933 were, nothing could prepare the Czechs in Chicago, or the world at large, for the events of 1939.

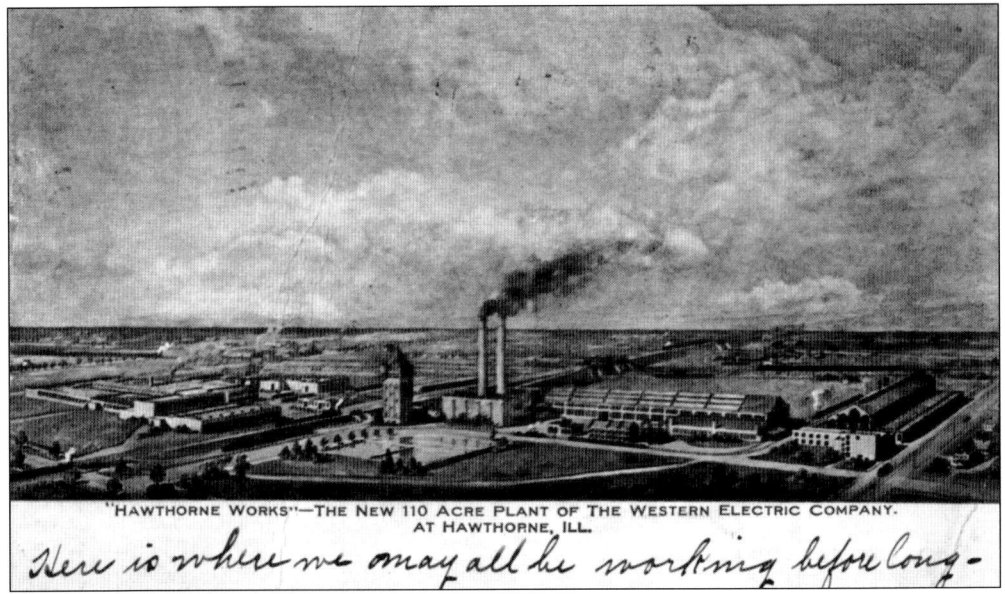

"Here is where we may all be working before long" is both prophetic and poignant. The author could not have been more correct: at its height, over 20,000 people worked for Western Electric's Hawthorne Works, one of the major employment opportunities for the large Czech working and middle class from 1904 through 1983. In Western Electric's Cicero operations, the city had a veritable behemoth of an industry, and Czechs were lured by the thousands and began moving westward, again, to where the jobs were. (Courtesy Frank Magallon.)

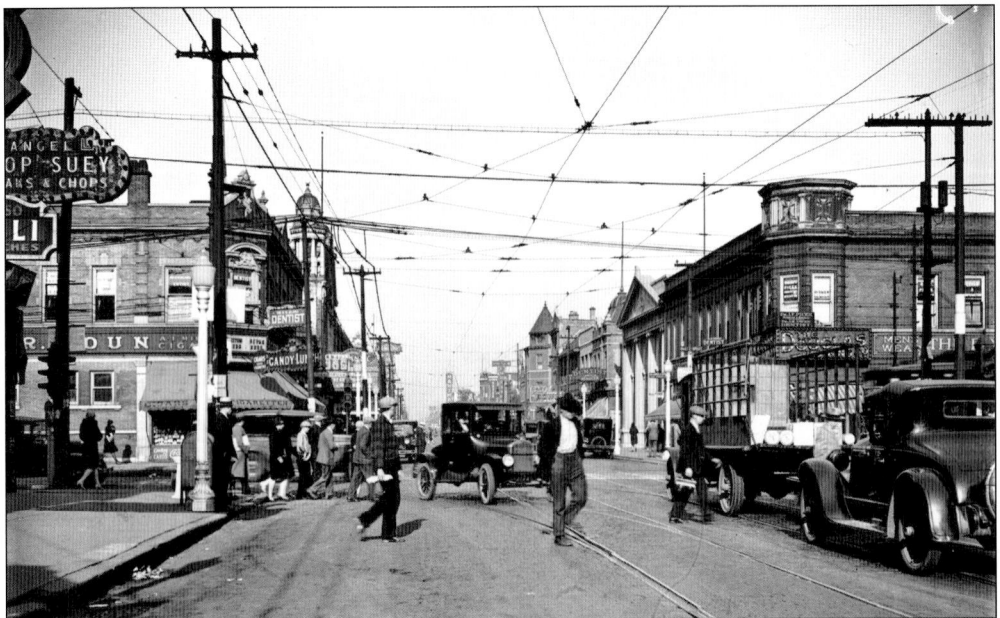

The main business arteries of Czech California, as the Czechs called the Lawndale settlement to the west of Pilsen, were Twenty-sixth Street and Crawford (today's Pulaski) Avenue. The picture above shows the dynamism of life—note the Chinese restaurant in the predominantly Czech enclave and the web of tramlines—and the growing wealth—note the car, from older models to the latest style—in the new neighborhood. (Courtesy Chicago History Museum.)

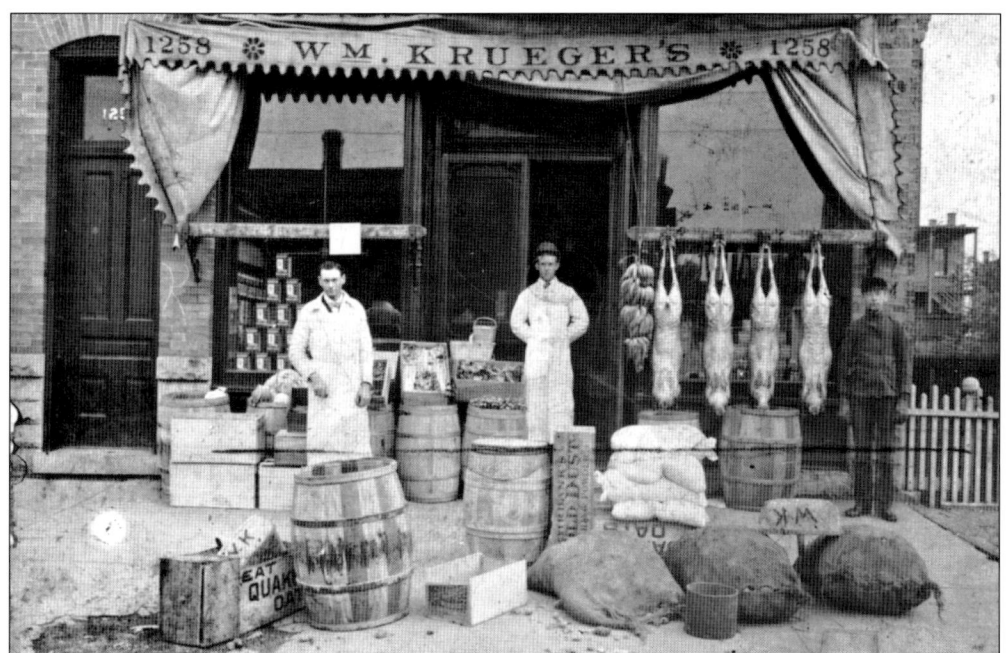

Krueger's grocer is seen at Twenty-sixth Street and Lawndale Avenue in the early 1900s. The foods offered, the conditions of the buildings, and the dignity written on the face of the merchants serving their community speaks volumes about the Czech immigrant experience. (Courtesy Chicago Public Library, Special Collections and Preservation Division, LCCC 2-1.)

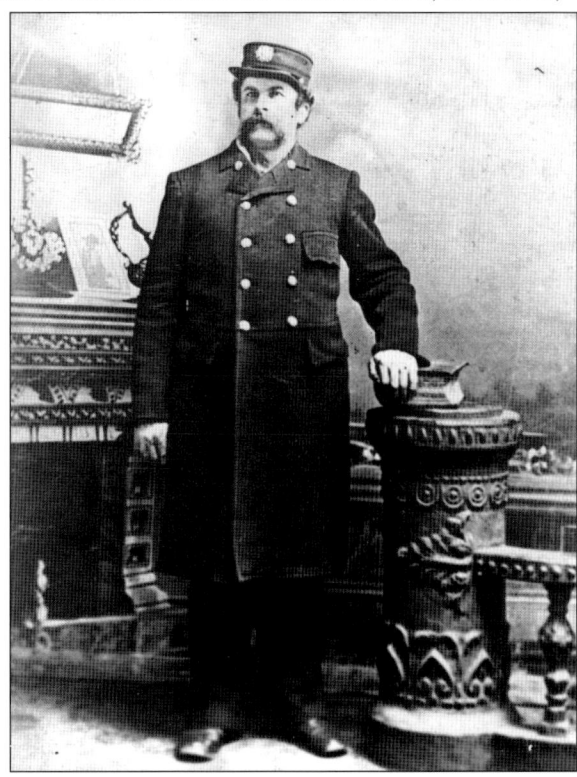

John Belský, organizer of the Lawndale Fire Department, poses here for what was likely a portrait celebrating his installment as chief. The position was prestigious, and Belský's ability to reach it before Lawndale was completely Czech dominated confirms the success of Czechs to capture high municipal offices and to prove themselves models of responsible American citizenry. (Courtesy Chicago Public Library, Special Collections and Preservation Division.)

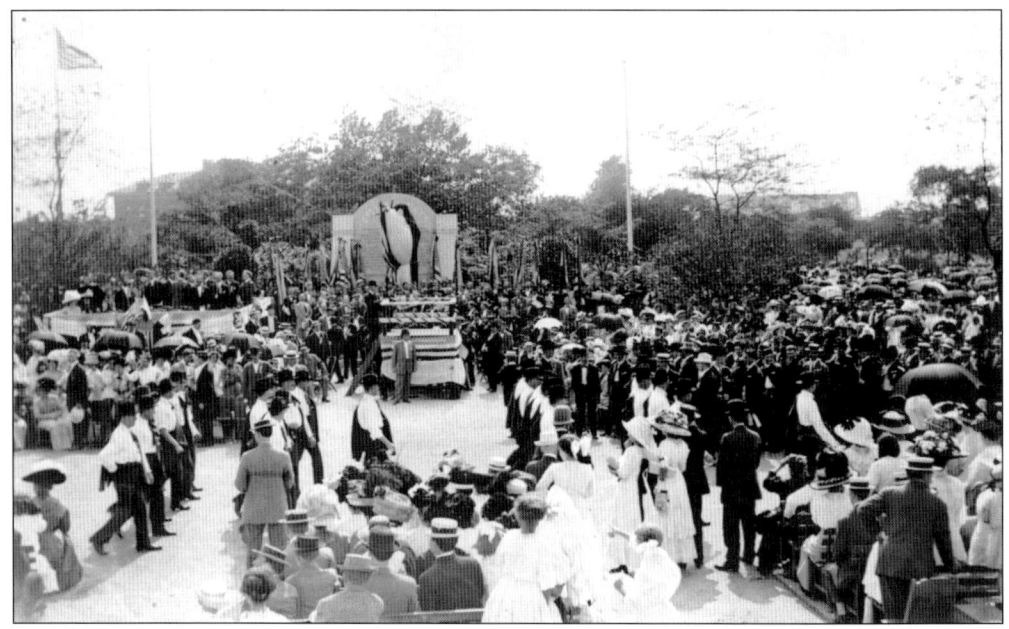

Czech California's central green space was Douglas Park. So wedded was Douglas Park to the Czech community that in 1911 it was chosen as the site for a monument to the Czech national hero, the writer Karel Havlíček Borovský. When the Czech community picked up roots and moved to the western suburbs, the Havlíček memorial was moved to the city's lakefront. (Courtesy Chicago Public Library, Special Collections and Preservation Division.)

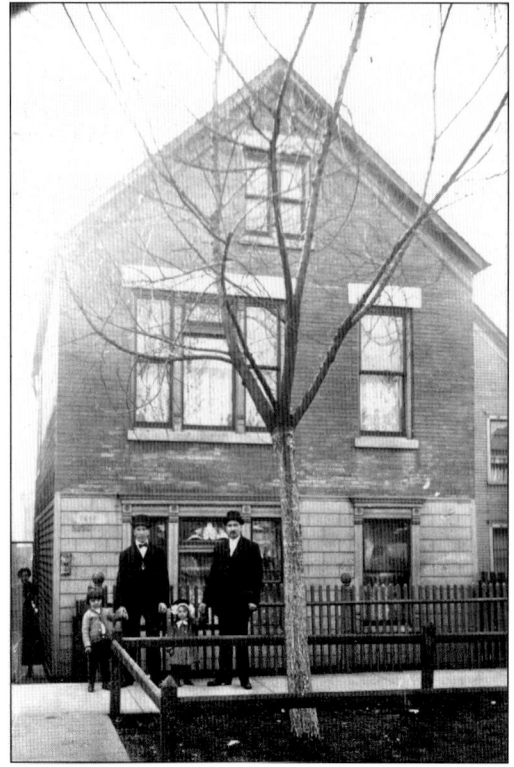

The move to Lawndale for a Czech family was in many ways tantamount to the attainment of the American dream. Standing before a new home on Homan Avenue are, among others, L. Bohumil Havranek and Stanley J. Ryba. (Courtesy Frank Magallon.)

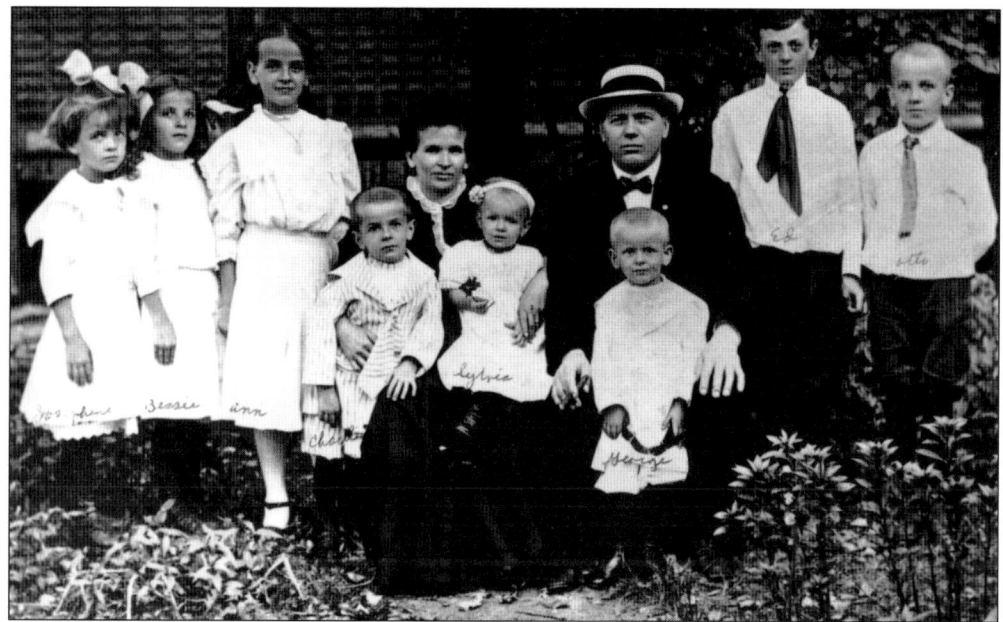

Karel and Josefa Beneš had 11 children, of whom 8 are pictured in this 1913 photograph taken at their home in Czech California in the second decade of the 20th century. Not yet born were three others, one of whom was Dorothy Beneš Duy's father, Václav, or James. After the death Josefa, the Beneš family moved again, like many of their Czech neighbors, to the near western suburbs. (Courtesy Dorothy Beneš Duy.)

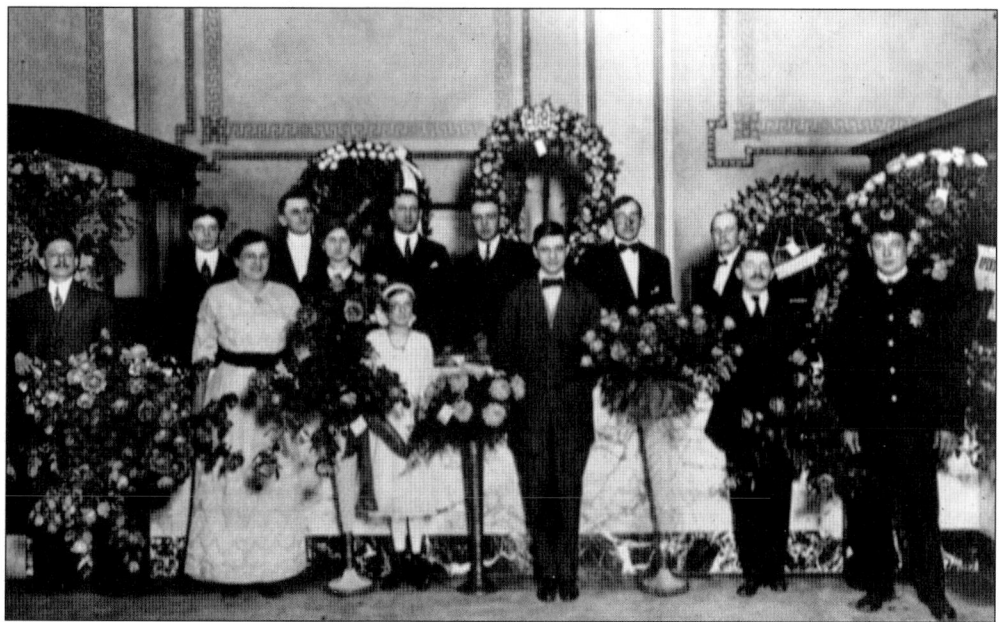

Employees pose proudly at the opening of the Lawndale Bank in 1912. Both the Lawndale State Bank, on Twenty-sixth Street in the new Czech California neighborhood, and its older sibling, the Lawndale National Bank, were joint ventures of founders Charles Hajíček, Josef Salat, Josef Polak, and Josef Kopecký. The success of financial ventures in the newly colonized neighborhood attests to the thrift and industriousness of the Czech community. (Courtesy CSA.)

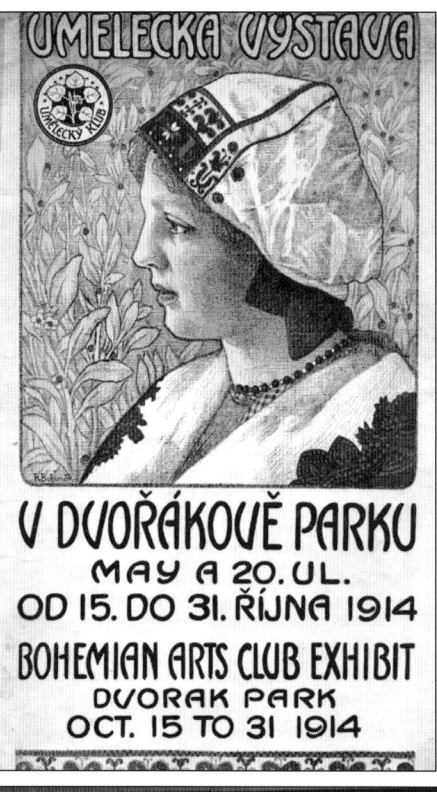

The Bohemian Arts Club (Umělecký Klub), to which many Czech community leaders belonged, was founded by Jaroslav E. S. Vojan in 1912. It regularly sponsored artistic performances and events that put emphasis on Czech painters, musicians, and actors. One of its most successful events was an art exhibit held in Dvořák Park from October 15 to 31, 1914. (Courtesy CSA.)

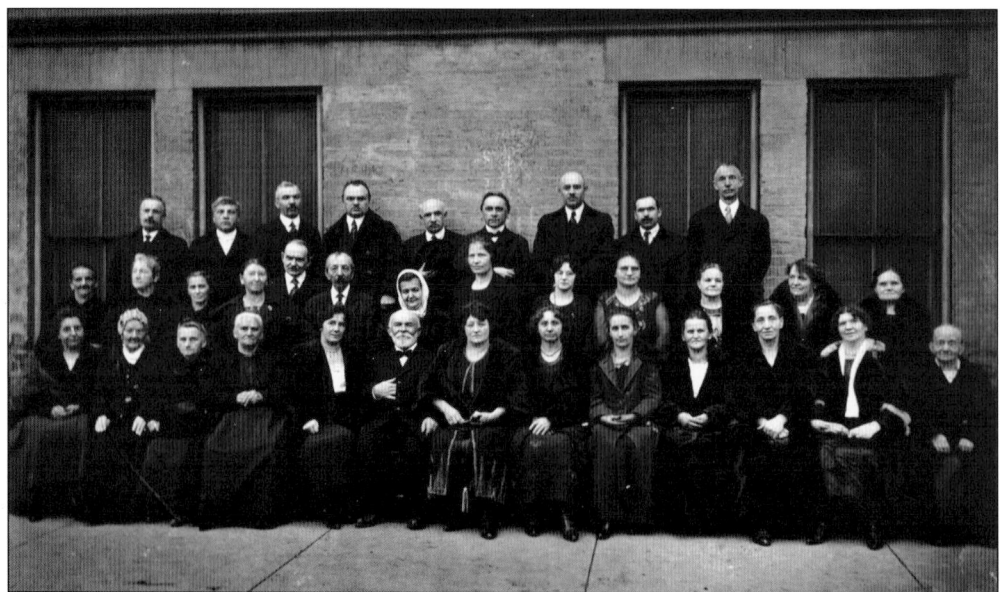

Members of the congregation of the First Bohemian Baptist Church on Millard Avenue in Czech California pose here in 1914 to commemorate the 20th anniversary of their founding. Protestants constituted a small minority among Czechs in Chicagoland, with meaningful differences among Baptists, Methodists, Presbyterians, and the Czech Brethren. Other Baptist congregations could be found at South Trumbull Avenue, also in Czech California, and in Berwyn, Cicero, and Brookfield. (Courtesy CSA.)

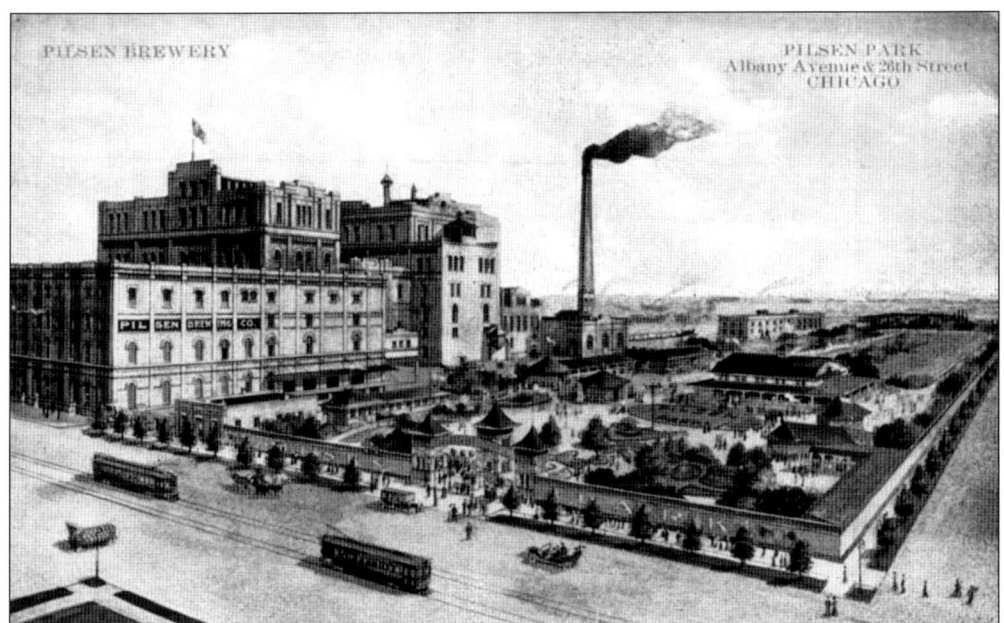

Pilsen Park, at Twenty-sixth Street and Albany Avenue, was the most important hub of Czech social and political life in the 20th century. In 1907–1908, shareholders of the Pilsen Brewing Company built up their adjacent lot and opened Pilsen Park. It featured gardens, a restaurant and tavern, assembly and dance hall, and a gazebo, site of many a marriage proposal. The park (and brewery) closed its gates in 1967. (Courtesy CSA.)

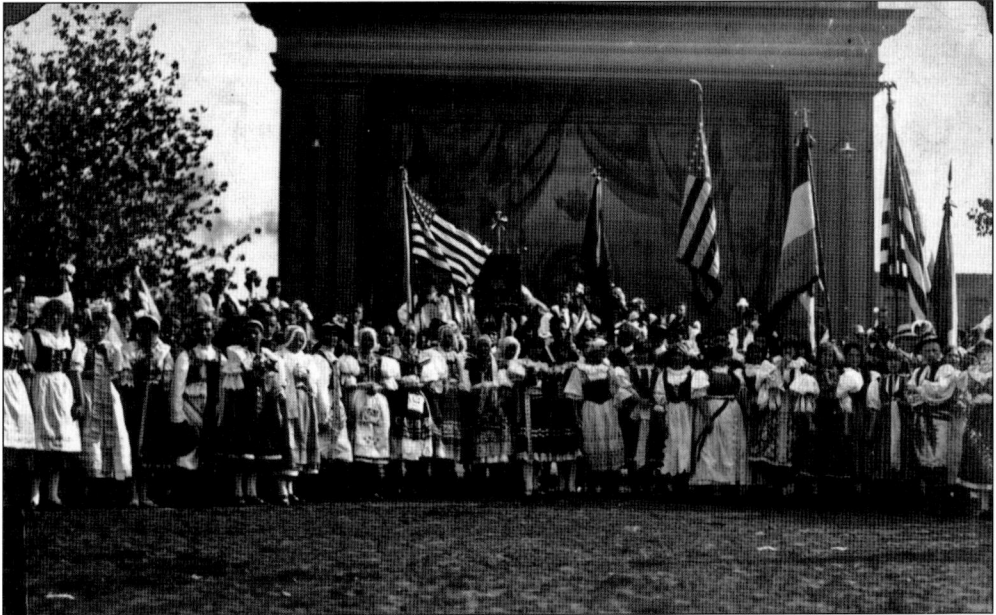

On July 28, the same day Austro-Hungary declared war on Serbia, Chicago's Czech leaders along with their counterparts from the greater Slavic community, came together at Pilsen Park. James Štěpina, of the Czech National Alliance, urged the crowd to write to friends and family in Austrian-controlled Czech lands to resist conscription, and if resistance was not possible, to turn sides and fight with their Serbian brothers. (Courtesy CSA.)

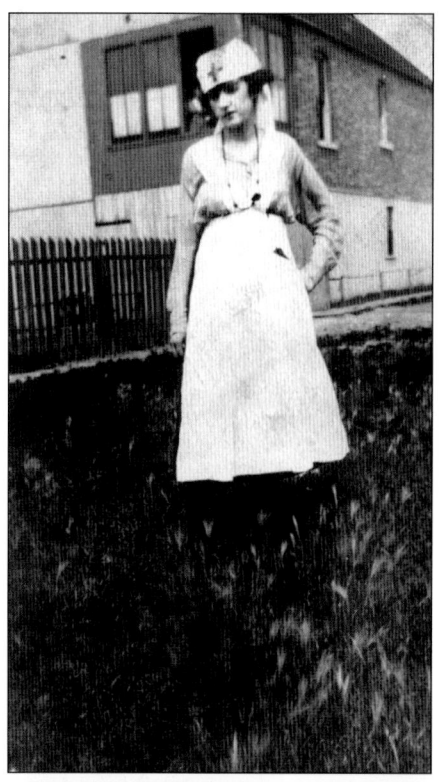

Lillian Naxera Peca is seen in her World War I volunteer uniform at the lot adjoining her family home at South Kenneth in Czech California. Through hard work and thrift, like so many other Czech émigré families, they could afford a nice home in the up-and-coming neighborhood and to purchase the adjoining plot for a growing family. (Courtesy Frank Magallon.)

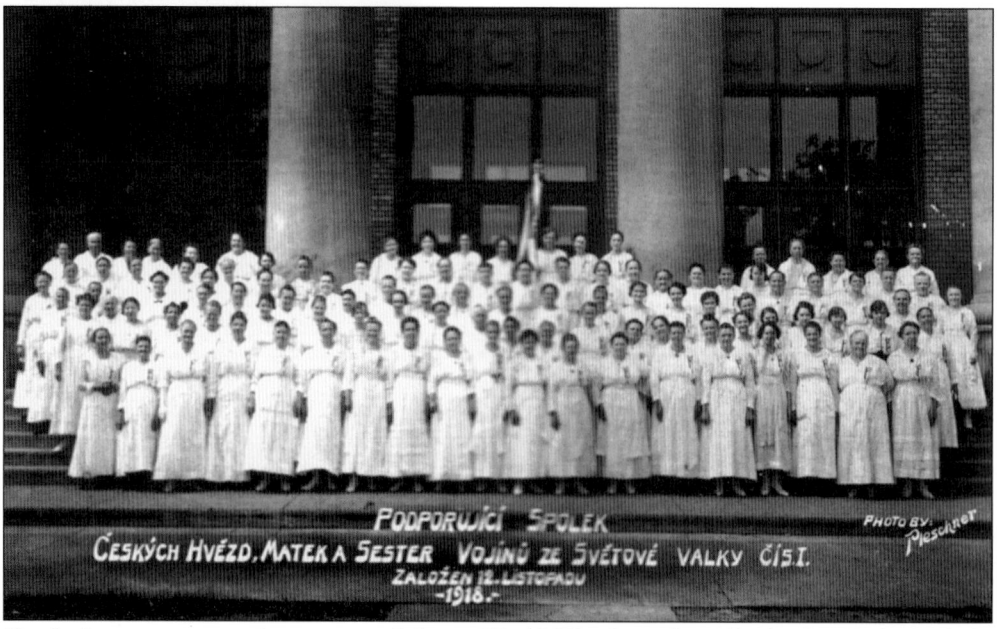

Czech Americans sent their sons to fight in World War I on the Allied side. With the help of charismatic leaders, Czechs under Austrian rule were able to turn sides, oppose Austria and Germany, and win national sovereignty. This 1916 image is of the "supportive union of Czech stars," mothers and daughters who had lost their loved ones in battle. (Courtesy CSA; photograph by Pleschner Studio.)

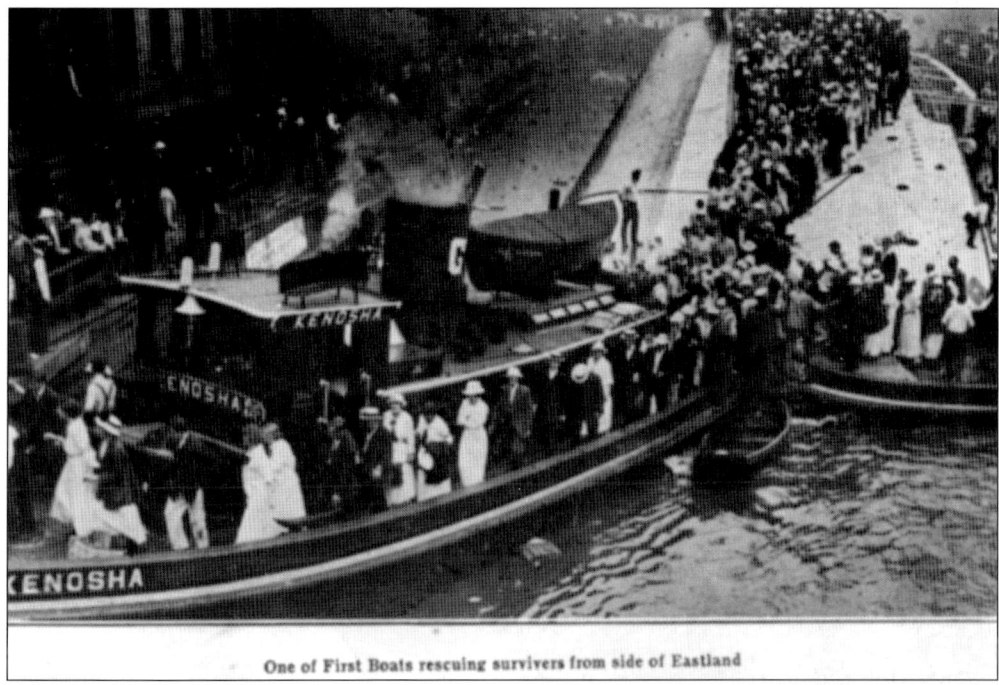

One of First Boats rescuing survivers from side of Eastland

On the morning of July 24, 1915, employees of Western Electric boarded steamboats bound for the company picnic in Michigan City, Indiana. Employees were encouraged to bring the entire family to enjoy a day of leisure. Of the steamboats hired for the trip, the *Eastland*, certified to hold 2,500, was overloaded with 2,572. As the *Eastland* cast off from near Clark Street Bridge, she listed and turned into the putrid waters of the Chicago River. A total of 844 passengers perished in the disaster, many drowned by being trapped under the boat's weight. Of these 844, over a third were of Czech extraction. In some cases, entire families—like the Sindelars—were lost. Stella Sladek too, pictured on the right, drowned that day, but her youth and beauty are captured for eternity in a portrait by Marchand Studios. (Courtesy Frank Magallon.)

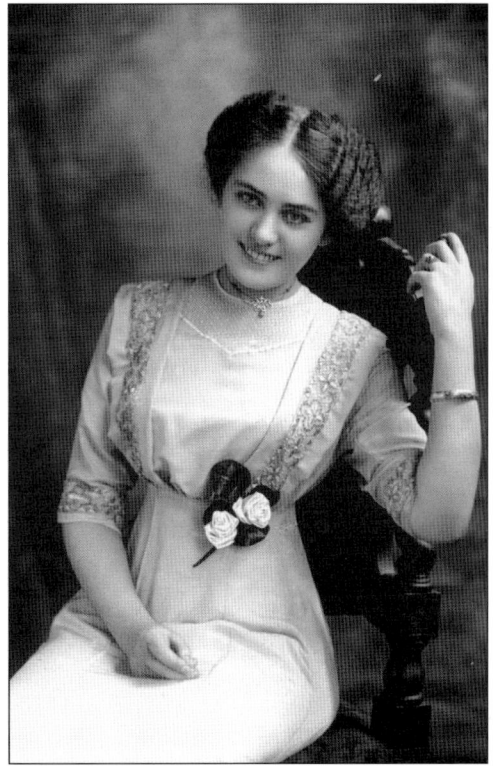

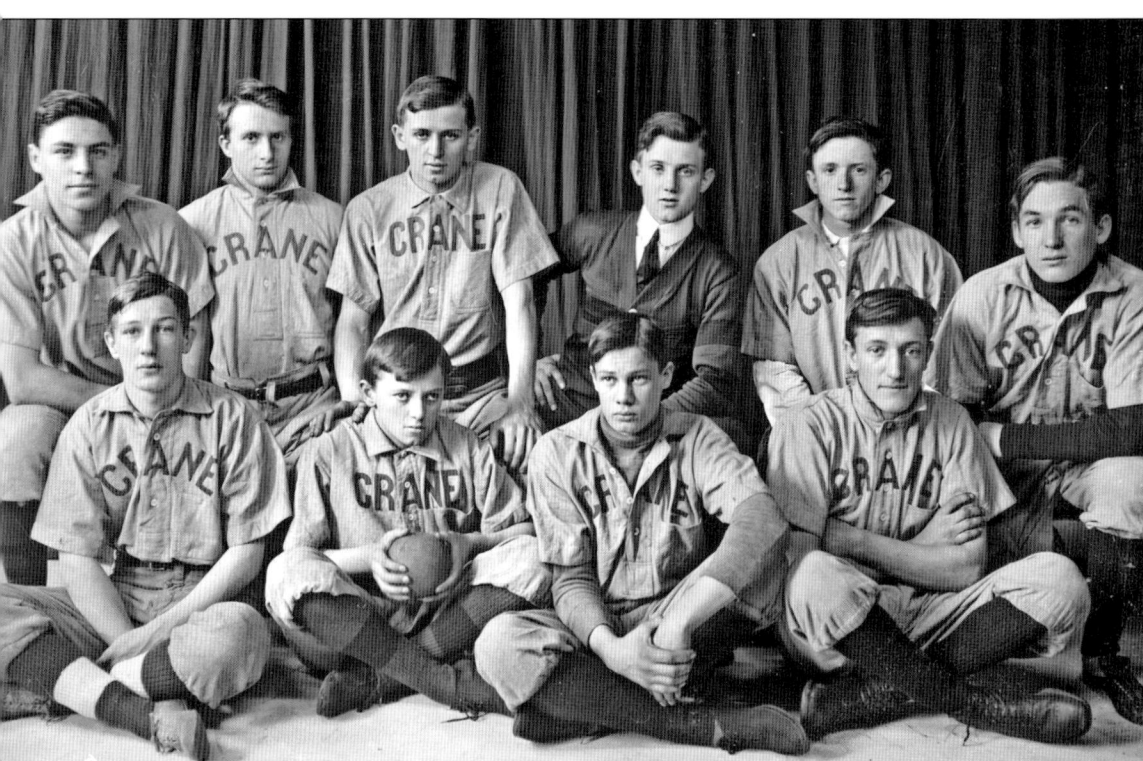

An indoor baseball league had formed in Chicago among the schools of Cook County at the end of 1895. For the next decade, Crane (formerly called English), along with a few other west side schools, with their ample Czech student body, dominated the sport. At the height of indoor baseball's popularity the Czech Halas brothers, Walter (a pitcher), Frank, and George, were among the best players in the country. Pictured here is Crane's 1910 line-up: F. Fessenden, G. Halas, D. Cochran, and P. Cohen, F. Albaugh, J. Klecka, E. Lemke, F. Dyer, and W. Halas. George Halas, born in Chicago in 1895, also played for the Western Electric baseball team and was expected to board the SS *Eastland* on the morning of July 24, 1915, for the company's picnic. The story has it that he overslept and missed the boat; he would of course go on to coach and own the Chicago Bears football team. (Chicago History Museum, SDN-008471; photograph by Chicago Daily News.)

The *Western Electric News* August 1915 issue, the first issue after the *Eastland* disaster, depicts in somber tones a memorial to the 841 passengers and 4 crew members who drowned that day. The issue contains lists of the dead. Over a third of the names within belong to employees of Czech heritage. (Courtesy CSA.)

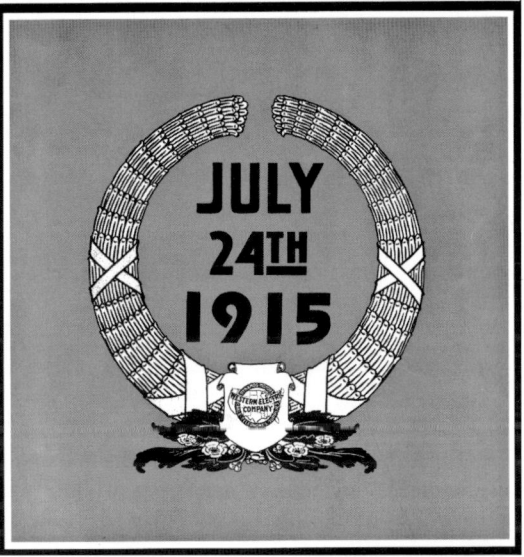

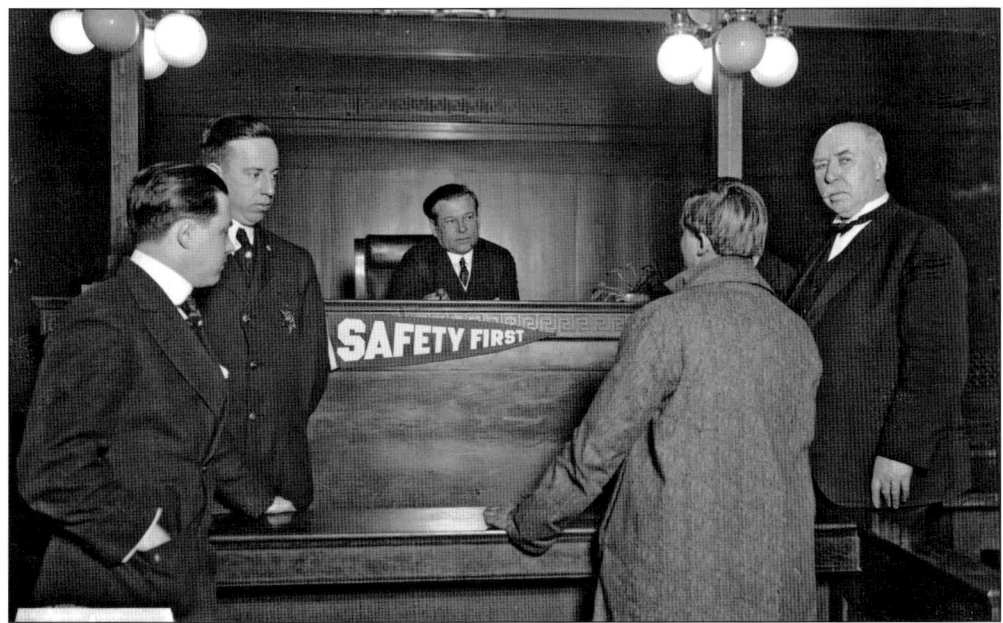

Judge Adolph Sabath, who emigrated from Bohemia in 1881, is pictured here in his courtroom in 1918. By 1928, Sabath was chief justice of the Superior Court of Chicago, but he never forgot his native town of Záboří, where he established a home for the poor. He was also instrumental in convincing the U.S. government to recognize the Czech government in exile during World War I. (Chicago History Museum, DN-0065743.)

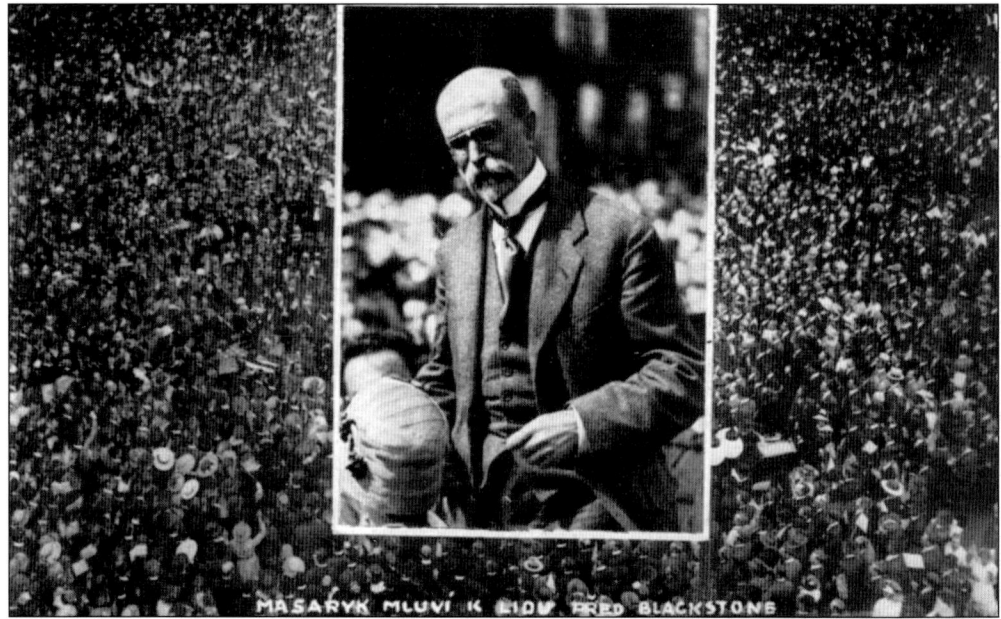

On May 5, 1918, Tomáš Garrigue Masaryk (1850–1937) made a triumphant visit to Chicago, where he stirred up fervor for an independent Czechoslovakia, free of imperial rule. He had designed a tour of the United States with Chicago as one of his first and most important stops. It was here that the Czech population was most active and here that he had a powerful ally in Chicago industrialist Charles R. Crane. (Courtesy CSA.)

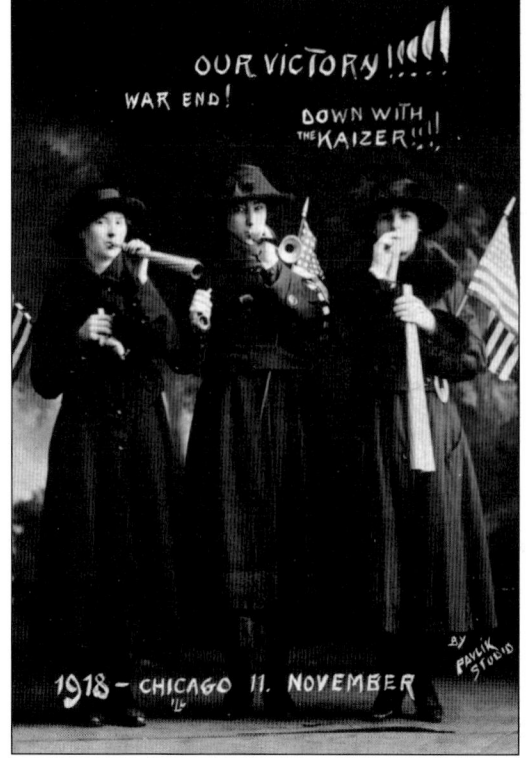

This postcard from 1918 celebrates the Allies' World War I victory over Germany. The young women depicted tooting on horns and holding U.S. flags are all Czech Americans, for whom the victory was twofold: for their U.S. homeland and their fatherland, whose independence was secured because of the Allied forces' victory. (Courtesy CSA.)

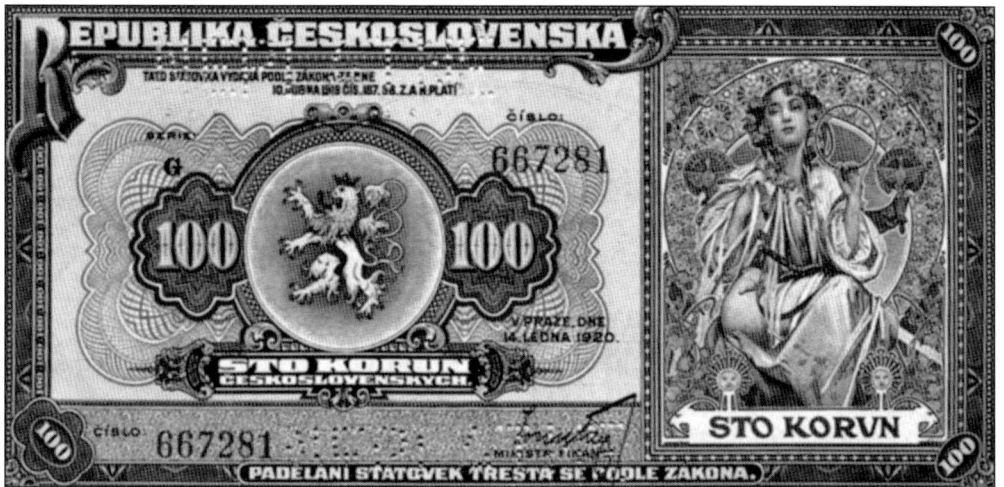

When Charles R. Crane, Chicago millionaire, invited art nouveau sensation Alfons Mucha to Chicago, one of Crane's daughters, Josephine, became the artist's muse. It is Josephine's aspect that is the inspiration for the Slavonic goddess depicted above in the 100 crown (Sto korun) note of the Republic of Czechoslovakia. (Author's collection.)

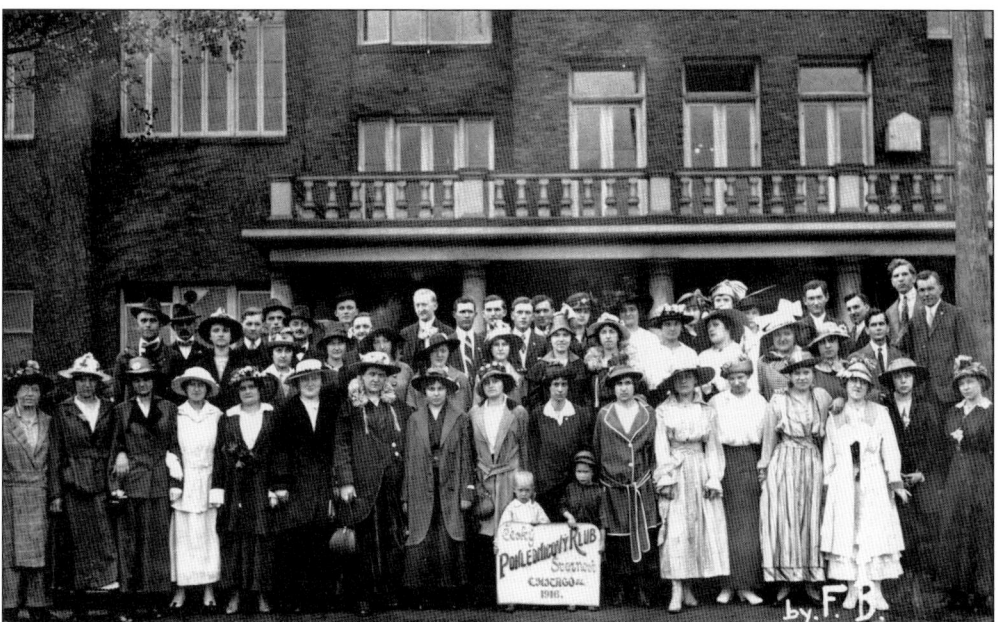

In addition to being members of Sokol lodges and other societies, such as the Odd Fellows and Rebekah lodges, the Masons, and amateur singing and dramatic groups, the picture above shows how far the spirit for fraternity and sorority go among Czech Americans. The young child in the front helps to hold up a placard that reads "The Czech Postcard Club. Svornost. Chicago, 1916." (Courtesy University of Chicago, Archive of Czechs and Slovaks Abroad; photograph by F. B. [likely Frank Boudnek].)

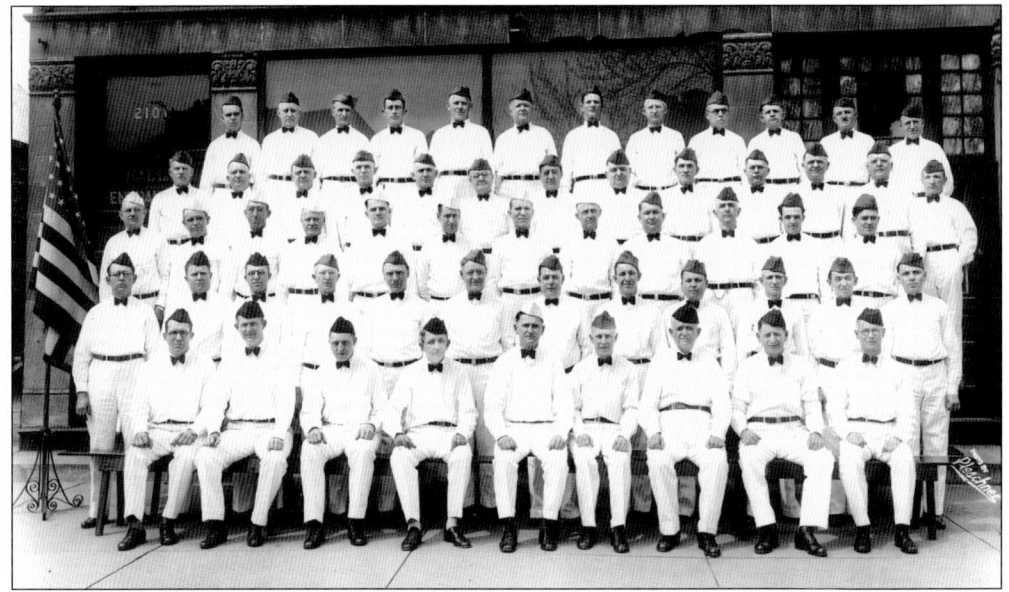

While most Czechs are association- and community-minded, some chose to join charitable societies with not exclusively Czech ties, like the Independent Organization of Odd Fellows (IOOF). The IOOF is a storied old institution; it can trace its roots back to 17th-century England, and, like the Masons, has complex initiation rites and symbologies. This photograph shows the Czech IOOF lodge named for Moravian-born national revivalist František Palacký. (Courtesy CSA.)

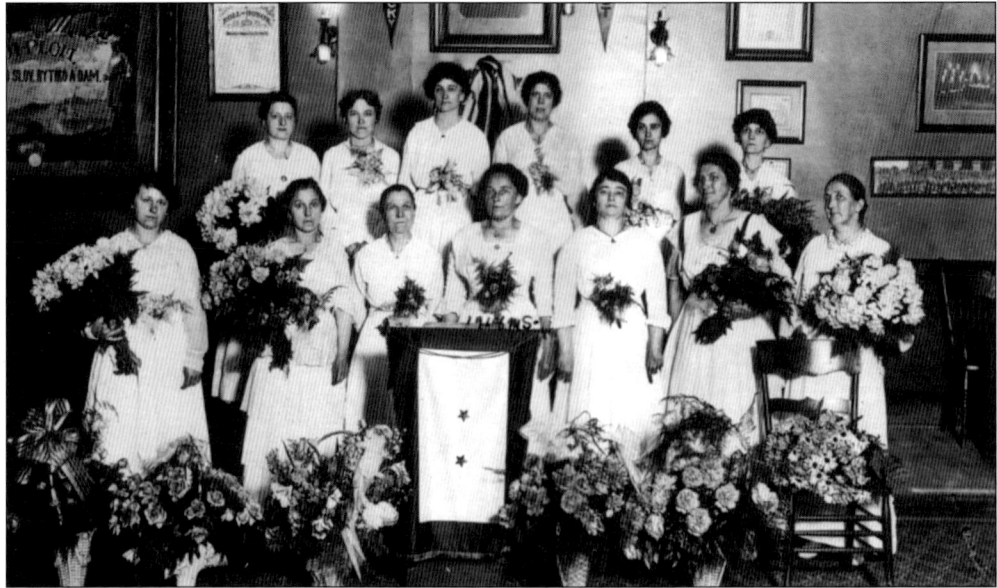

Although in more recent times the IOOF has admitted women, in 1918, when this photograph was taken, the IOOF had a separate sister organization named Rebekah. Rebekah's benevolent work has made an enormous impact on communities around the world. This image shows Rebekah sisters beneath the Odd Fellows's insignia—the three interlocking chain links—that symbolizes its tripartite credo of truth, love, and friendship. (Courtesy Czechoslovak Society of America, Museum and Library; photograph by J. F. Malý.)

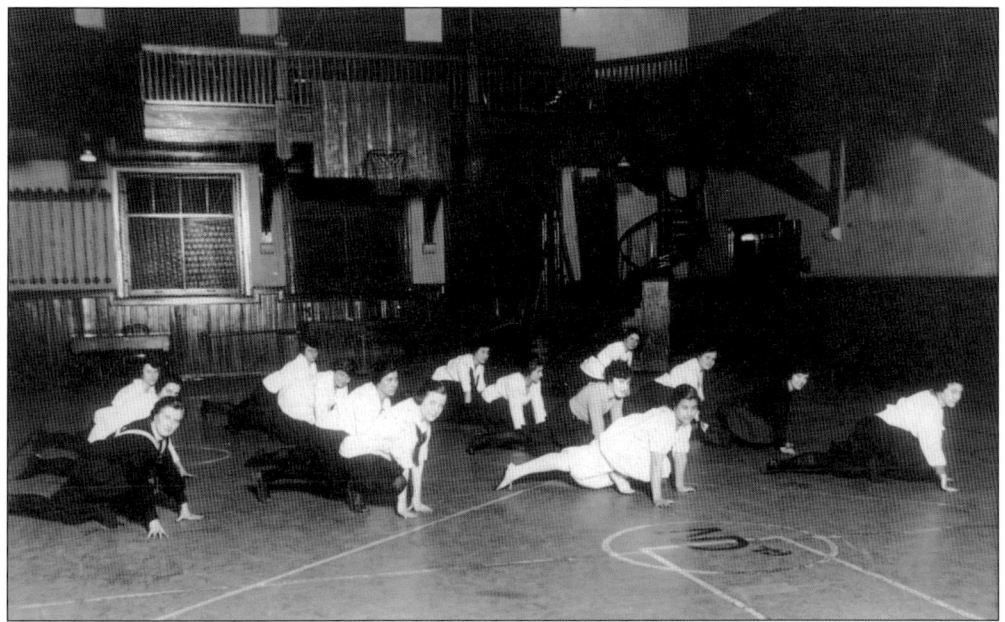

Female Sokol members practice in a gymnasium around 1919. The large-scale involvement of women, men, and children of all ages in the Sokol movement was key in keeping the Czech community in Chicago tied to its heritage, while also educating them in a broader sense of national belonging in their newly adopted homeland. (Courtesy Chicago Pubic Library, Special Collections and Preservation Division, LCCC 1-157.)

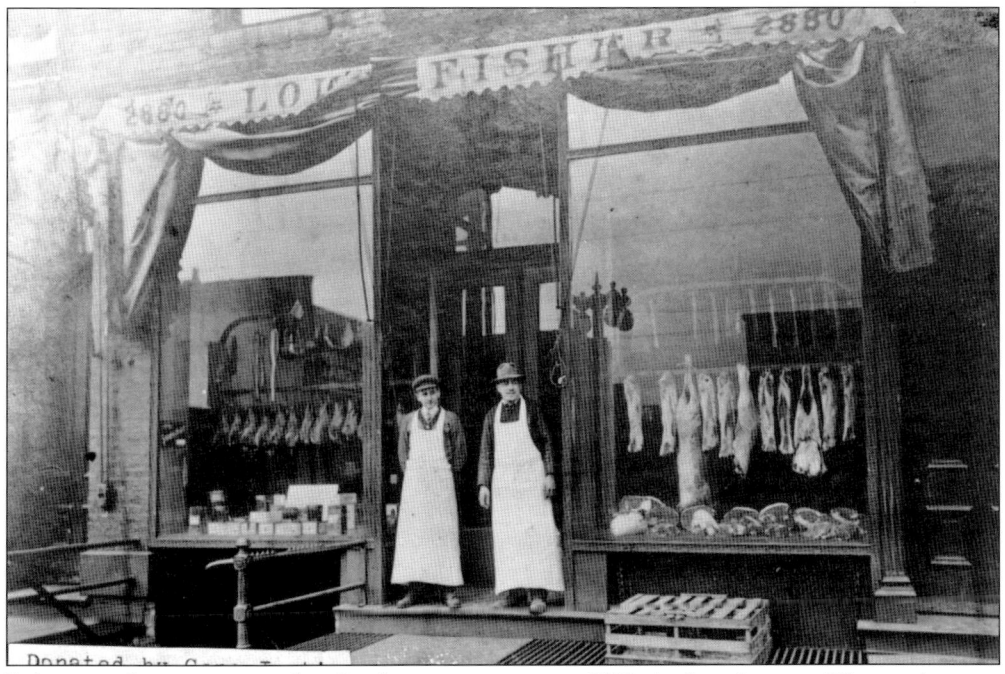

Fishers market was a popular Czech grocery store at 2880 Archer Avenue. The market was opened in the early 1900s. (Courtesy CSA.)

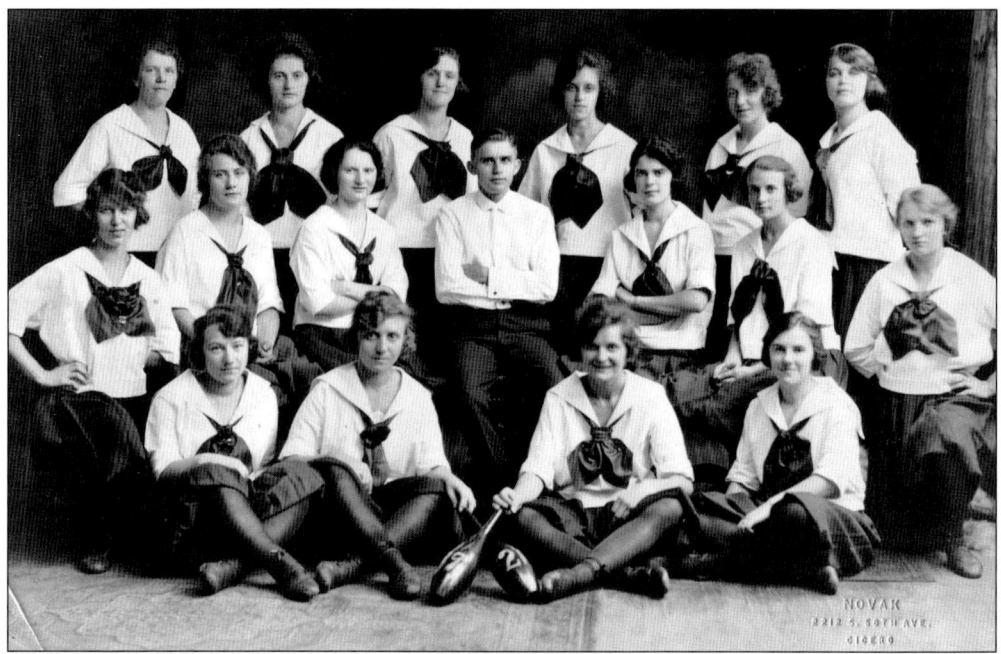

The female members of Sokol groups, known in Czech as Sokolice, were just as active as their male counterparts. Sokol athletes often distinguished themselves as gymnasts and track-and-field stars and many have gone on to represent the United States in Olympic competition. Here young Sokolice of the lodge Havlíček-Tyrš, located in the Czech California neighborhood, pose around 1921 with their male trainer at center. (Courtesy University of Chicago, Archive of Czechs and Slovaks Abroad; photograph by Novak Studio.)

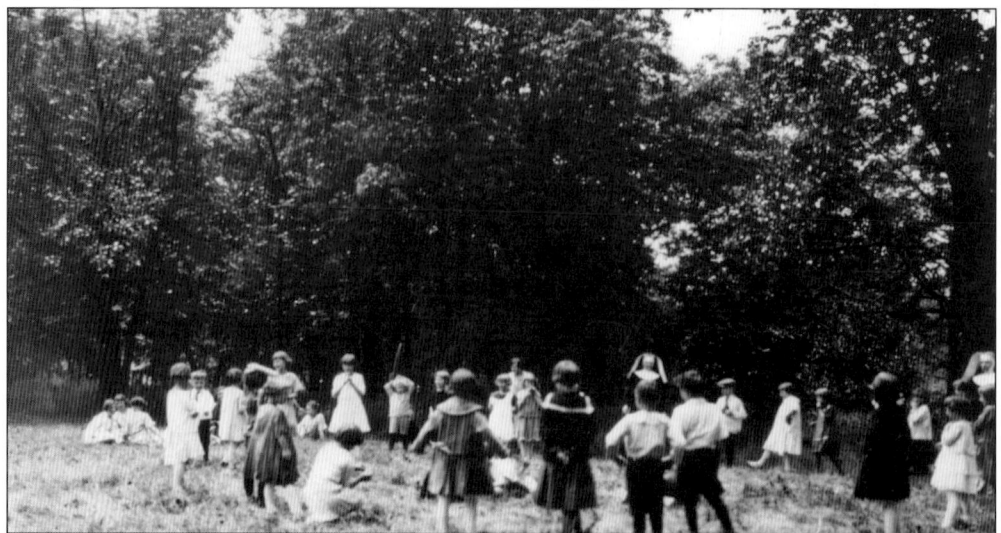

Pictured above are the children of Blessed Agnes School on an excursion to park grounds at Twenty-second and Des Plaines Streets in 1924. They are shown picnicking, a favorite pastime of Czechs carried over into their life in America. Blessed Agnes was one of the most populous of the Czech Roman Catholic Schools in the city at the time, and the church and school were important centers of Czech Catholic life in the metropolis. (Courtesy Chicago Public Library, Special Collections and Preservation Department, LCCC 1-449.)

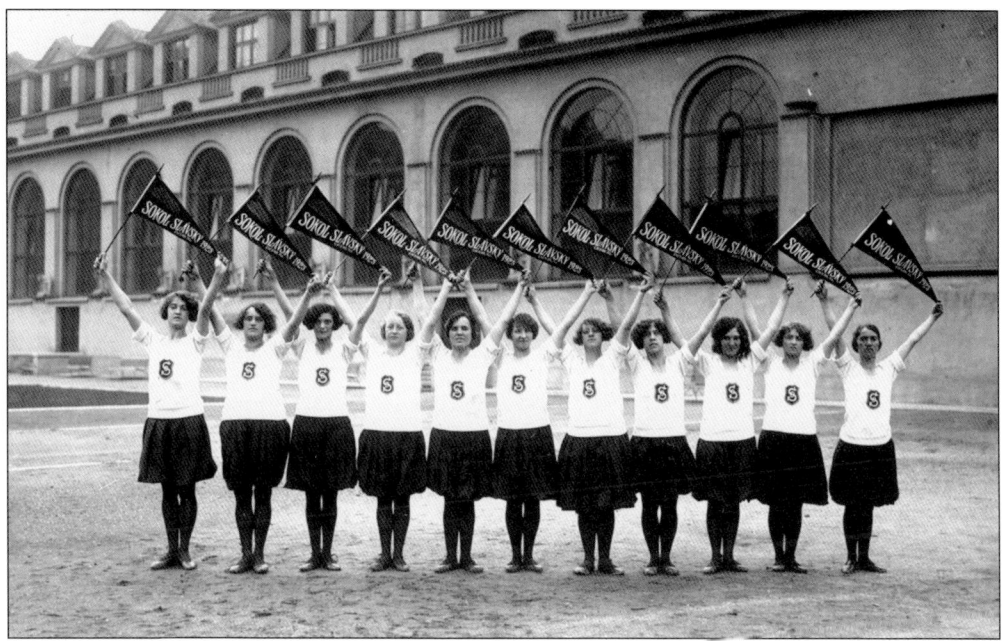

In 1925, Sokol Slávský, one of the oldest Sokol lodges in Chicago, sent its Sokolice, female Sokol members, to Prague to participate in the Sokol slet organized there. In this publicity still, one of several that shows the young women in various poses, they hold their Chicago pennants up high with due pride. (Courtesy University of Chicago, Archive of Czechs and Slovaks Abroad.)

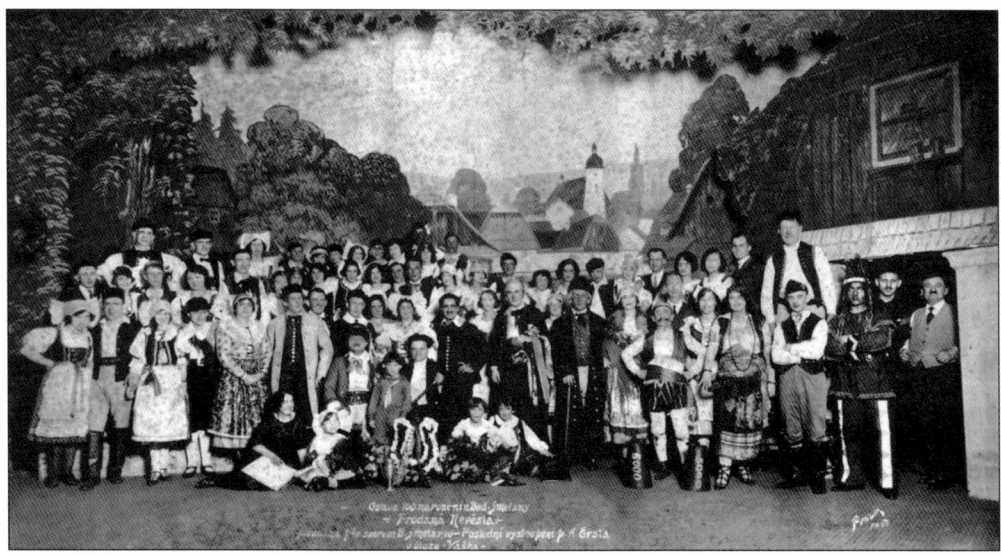

On May 4, 1924, Bedřich Smetana's opera *The Bartered Bride* (Prodaná Nevěsta) was performed by the group Pěvecký sbor B. Smetana to celebrate what would have been Smetana's 100th birthday. The caption tells that this was the final performance of tenor A. Erst, in the role of Vašek. The Czech will to retain ethnic identity and uniqueness is often bound up with theater and performance. (Courtesy Czechoslovak Society of America, Museum and Library; photograph by Pavlík Studio.)

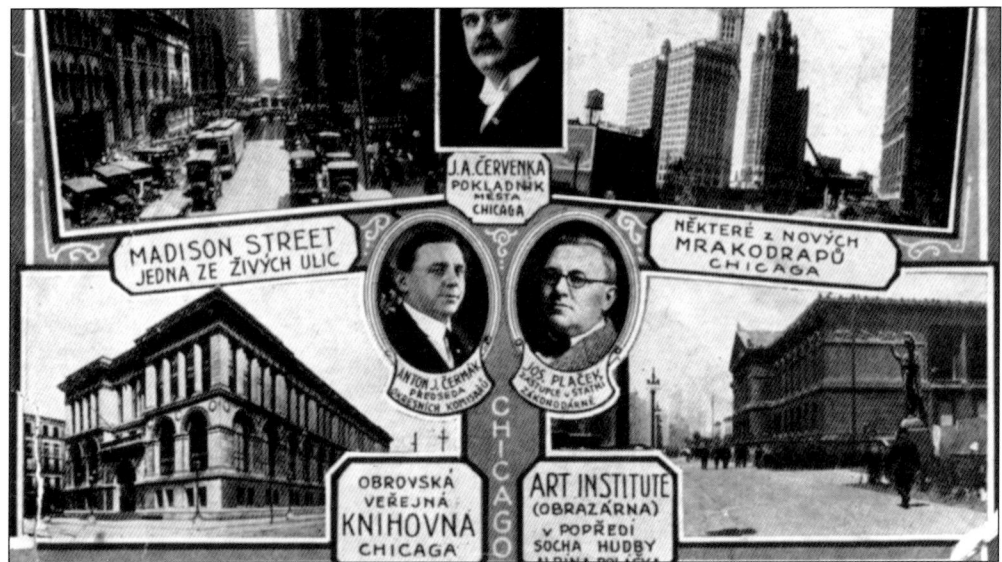

Ernst F. Macha's 1925 series of postcards shows how vibrant Czech Chicago was in the early years of the 20th century. In this postcard, the highest-ranking Chicago municipal leaders of Czech ancestry, John Červenka, Chicago city treasurer; Antonín Čermák, president of the city commissioners; and Josef Plaček, representative to the state legislature, are featured against the backdrop of the Chicago skyline, making a symbolic link between the grandeur of the city and its brightest Czech sons. (Courtesy Czechoslovak Society of America, Museum and Library; photograph by E. F. Macha.)

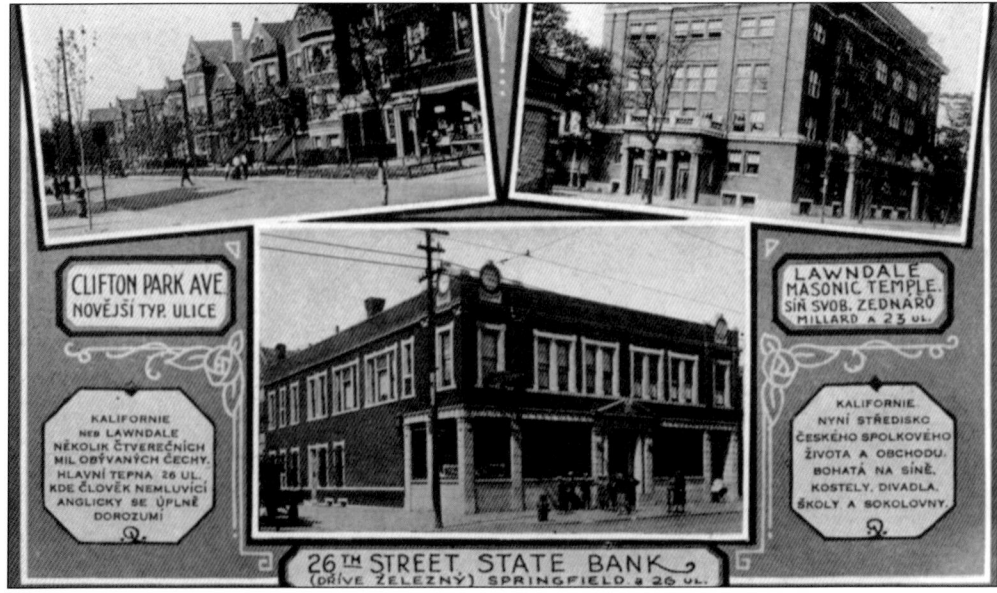

Macha's postcards of Czech California highlight the neighborhood's newness and largesse. The inset on the left side announces with pride that in "Kalifornie or Lawndale" are "several square miles tenanted by Czechs." The "main artery is 26th Street, where a person not speaking English can be fully understood" and "Kalifornie is now the center of Czech communal life and business. It is rich in halls, theatres, schools, churches and Sokols." (Courtesy Czechoslovak Society of America, Museum and Library; photograph by E. F. Macha.)

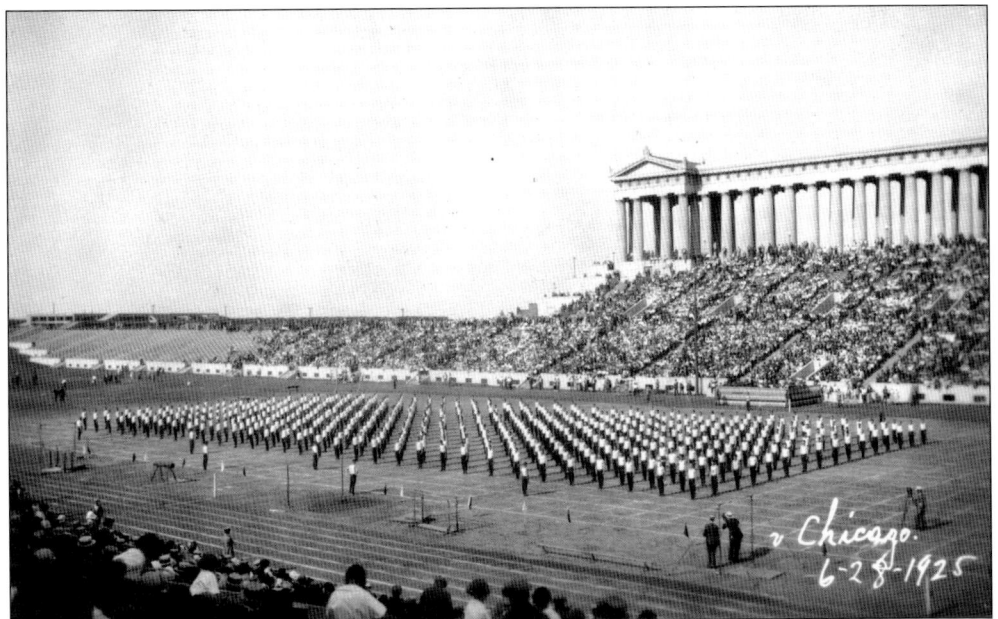

The first All-American Sokol slet (gathering or flocking) was held in the summer of 1925 in Chicago's Soldier Field; it drew Sokol lodges and members from all of the country, attesting to Chicago's central place as a Czech American city. This beautiful panoramic view gives an excellent sense to those uninitiated in Sokol traditions of the kind of mass athletic choreography for which the "falcons" are famous. (Author's collection.)

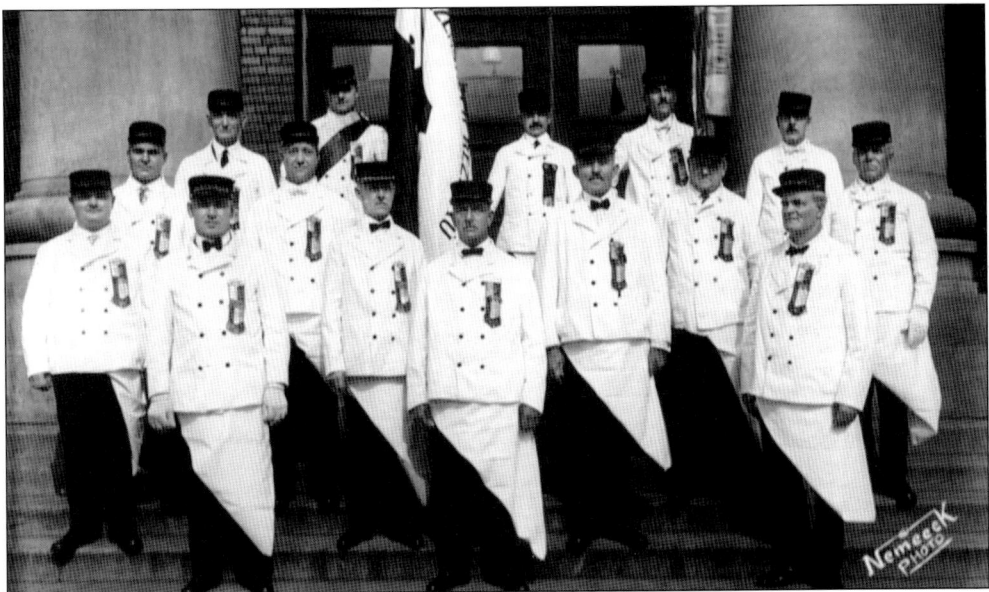

The Pilsen Butchers' association was begun in 1886 as a benevolent and supportive society to help Czech butchers and their families. One of the oldest protective societies in Chicago, the Pilsen Butcher's Association is still in operation, sponsoring charitable events and giving back to the Czech community. This early picture of its membership exhibits the pride of trade among these men. (Courtesy Czechoslovak Society of America, Museum and Library; photograph by E. F. Macha.)

John Louis Mensik was naturalized as a U.S. citizen at the age of 30 in 1927. He settled in the Pilsen neighborhood. He made his way well in his new home. His daughter Jean is active in the Moravian Cultural Society and along with her siblings contributes profoundly to the life of the Czech American community. (Courtesy Jean Mensik.)

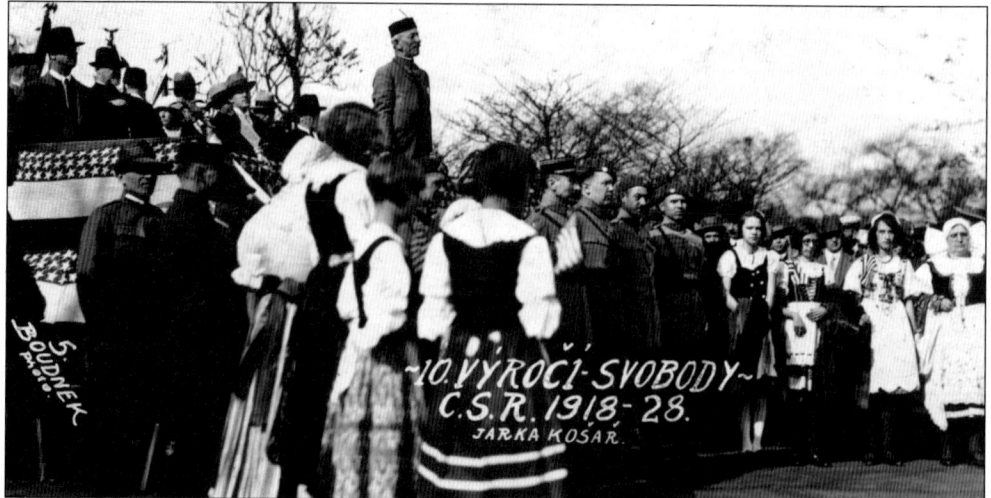

This image is from Chicago's 1928 celebration of Czechoslovakia's decade as an independent nation-state. The etched caption on the photograph reads, "10th anniversary of freedom. Č.S.R. (Czecho-Slovak Republic) 1918-1928." Jarka Košař, one of the Czech community's most important leaders, a Sokol organizer and a writer, is shown here addressing the assembled crowd; he is flanked by Czech legionnaires and servicemen from World War I and women in traditional national costume, or *kroje*. (Courtesy University of Chicago, Archive of Czechs and Slovaks Abroad; photograph by Frank Boudnek.)

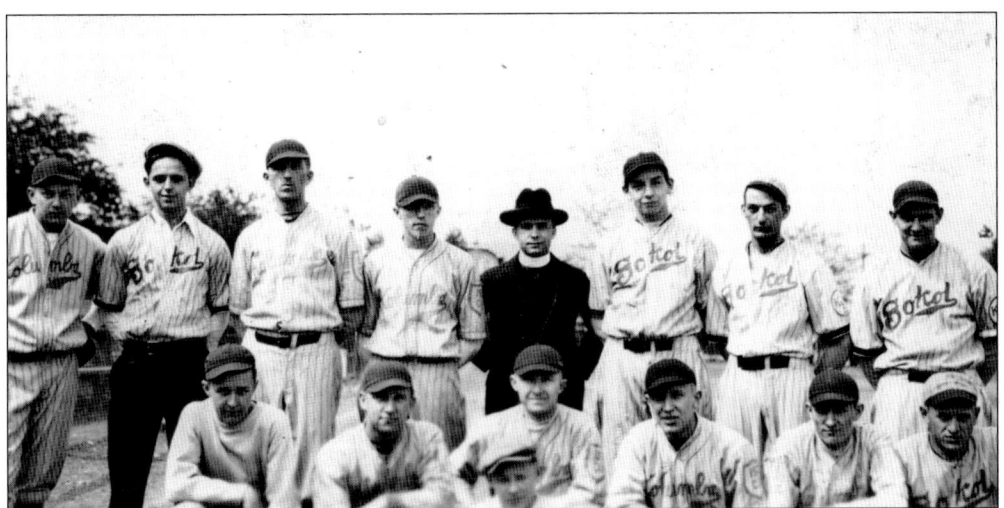

Baseball was a very popular sport among Czech American athletes, and indoor baseball dominated the scene until the 1920s, when it gradually became known as an outdoor sport. This photograph of the lineup of Blessed Agnes's baseball team from 1928 shows how important baseball was to all organizations as a sport that brought the community together in competition and camaraderie. (Courtesy Chicago Public Library, Special Collections and Preservation Division, LCCC 1-67.)

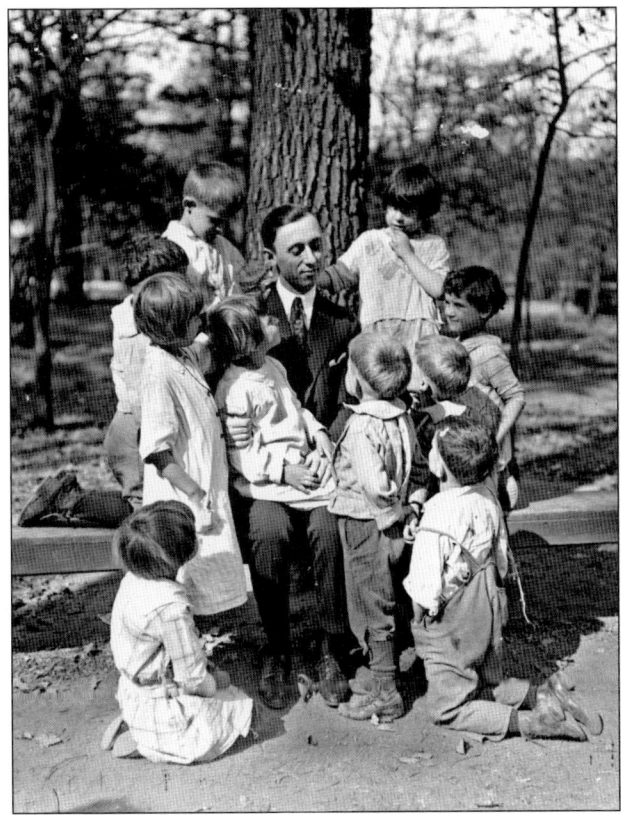

Popular Czech alderman James Otto Kostner is here surrounded by children of the Bohemian Orphanage, a community home that had been established under the auspices of the Bohemian National Cemetery. Kostner was a formidable rival to Antonín Čermák's plans to consolidate power. In true poetic justice, the avenue named for him runs perpendicular to the road named for his compatriot and political rival, Čermák. (Chicago History Museum, DN-0072465.)

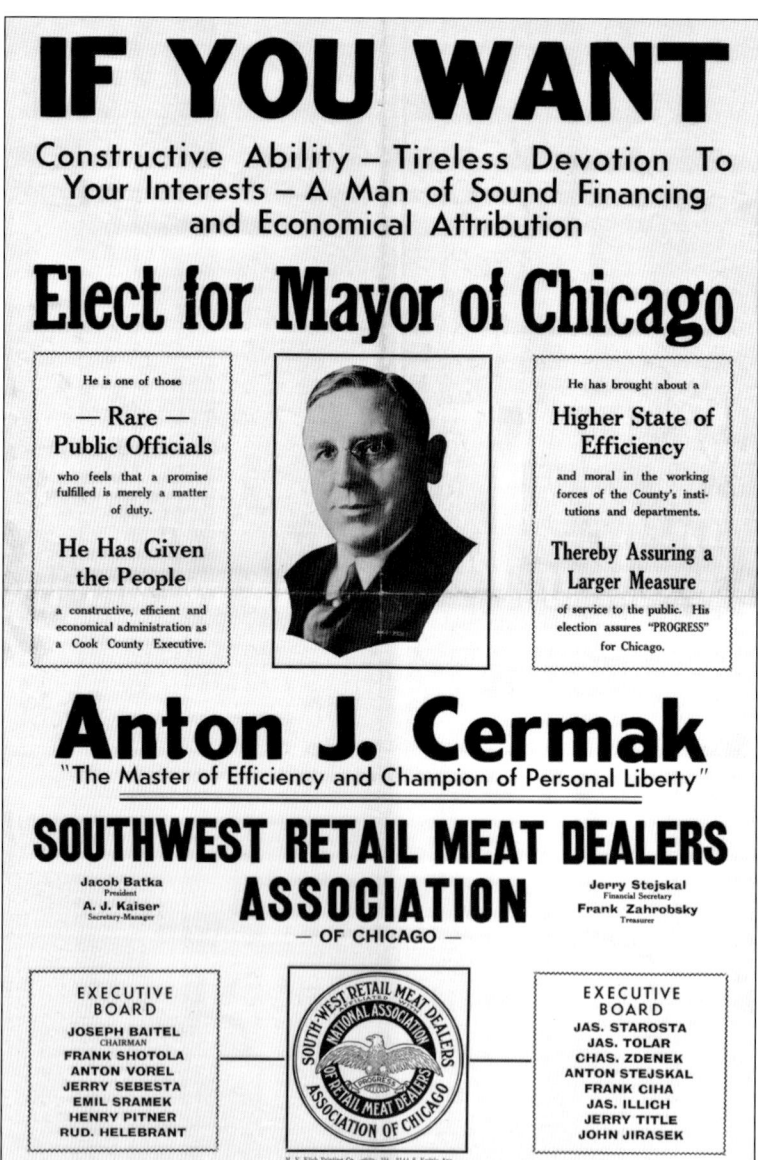

Born in 1873 in the coal town of Kladno, in the Czech lands of Austro-Hungary, Antonín Čermák was barely a year old when his family emigrated to the United States. They first settled in Chicago's Pilsen neighborhood, but soon moved to work in the coal town of Braidwood. The family returned to Chicago when Antonín was a teenager. This time, they put down their roots in the more affluent Czech California, on Millard Avenue. When he ran for mayor in 1931 against the openly anti-immigrant William Hale "Big Bill" Thompson, Čermák was victorious, becoming Chicago's first "ethnic" mayor. Thompson and his handlers slurred Čermák, with jingles like "I won't take a back seat to that Bohunk, Chairmock, Chermack or whatever his name is./Tony, Tony, where's your pushcart at?/Can you picture a World's Fair mayor?/With a name like that?" Čermák's campaign against the Thompson machine electrified Chicago's immigrants, including the growing African American population, for the first time into a strong voting block. The turn out on election day was enormous, as was the importance of Čermák's victory. (Courtesy CSA.)

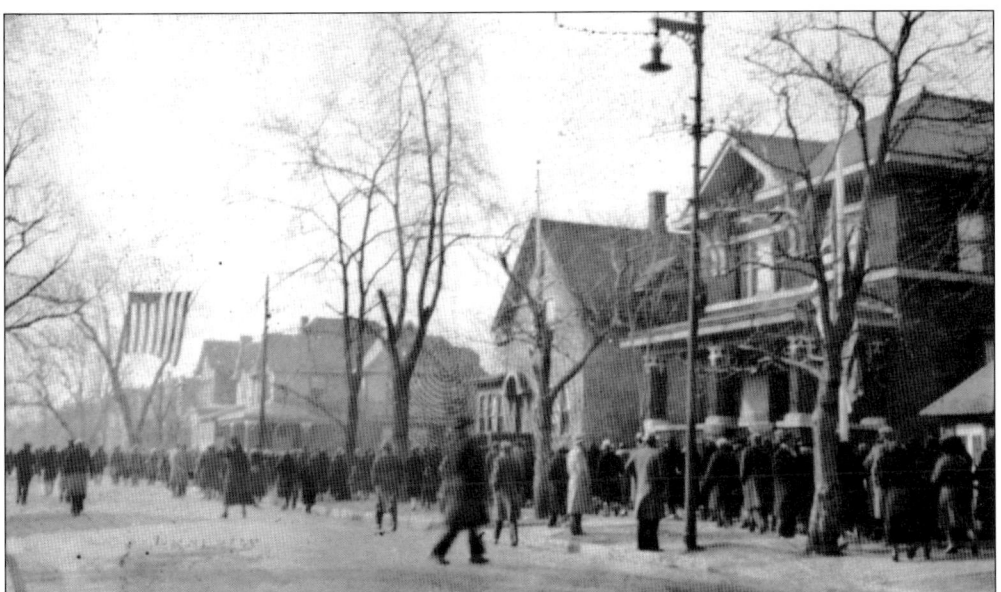

On February 15, 1933, while traveling in a motorcade with Pres. Franklin Roosevelt in Miami, Mayor Čermák was shot by Giuseppe Zangara. Crowds came to mourn outside Čermák's home on Millard Avenue in the days after the news came of the incident. Theories abound as to who was the real target of the assassination, but many now believe Čermák was the intended victim. On March 10, 1933, four days after his death from wounds sustained, Čermák's coffin was carried by a police-escorted horse-drawn wagon through Chicago's downtown. City leaders made up the funeral procession as Chicago's citizens looked on. The entire city—whether they had been supporters or critics of the mayor—mourned Čermák's passing, united in grief. (Chicago Historical Society, DN-0010530; photograph by Chicago Daily News.)

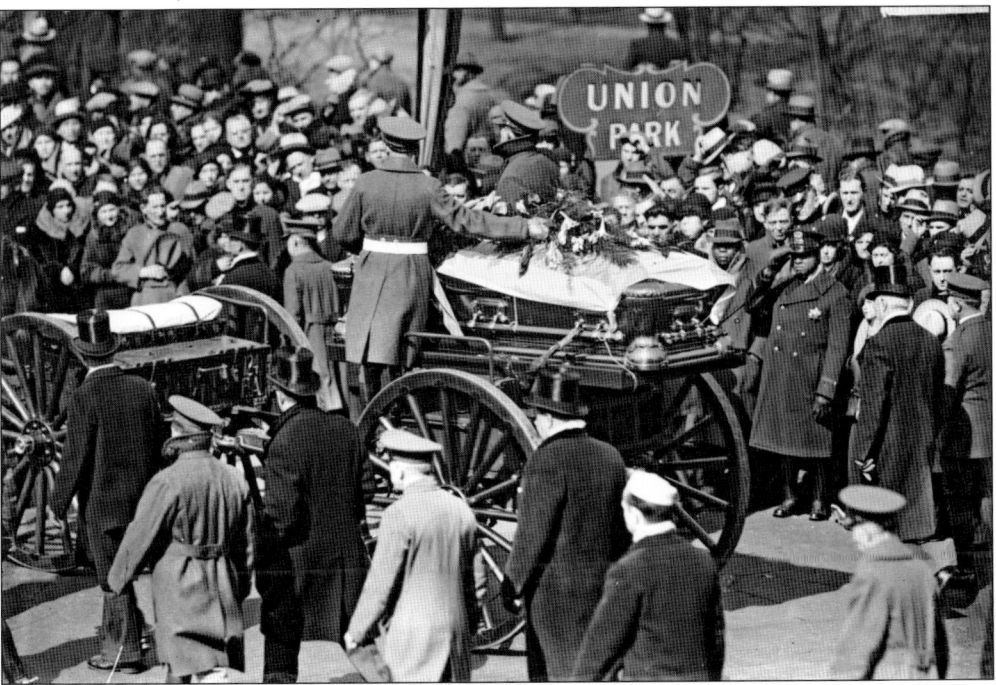

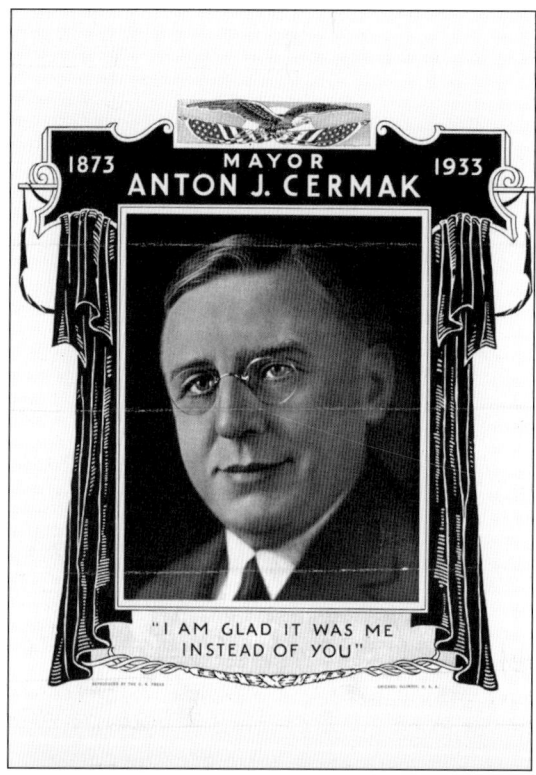

"I'm glad it was me instead of you" were the apocryphal dying words of Antonín Čermák to Pres. Franklin Roosevelt. The belief that Mayor Čermák intentionally "took the bullet" meant for President Roosevelt as they rode in a motorcade in Miami, Florida, has been long held by many a Chicagoan. But the theory that the phrase was likely concocted by reporters has just as many adherents, and these believe that Čermák, and Čermák alone, because of the enemies he had made among organized crime in Chicago, was the target of the assassin's bullet. The Čermák memorial train was organized also to honor the man who had made history in the city, breaking the Lace Curtain Irish machine and forging new possibilities for the emigrant working class in the city. (Courtesy CSA.)

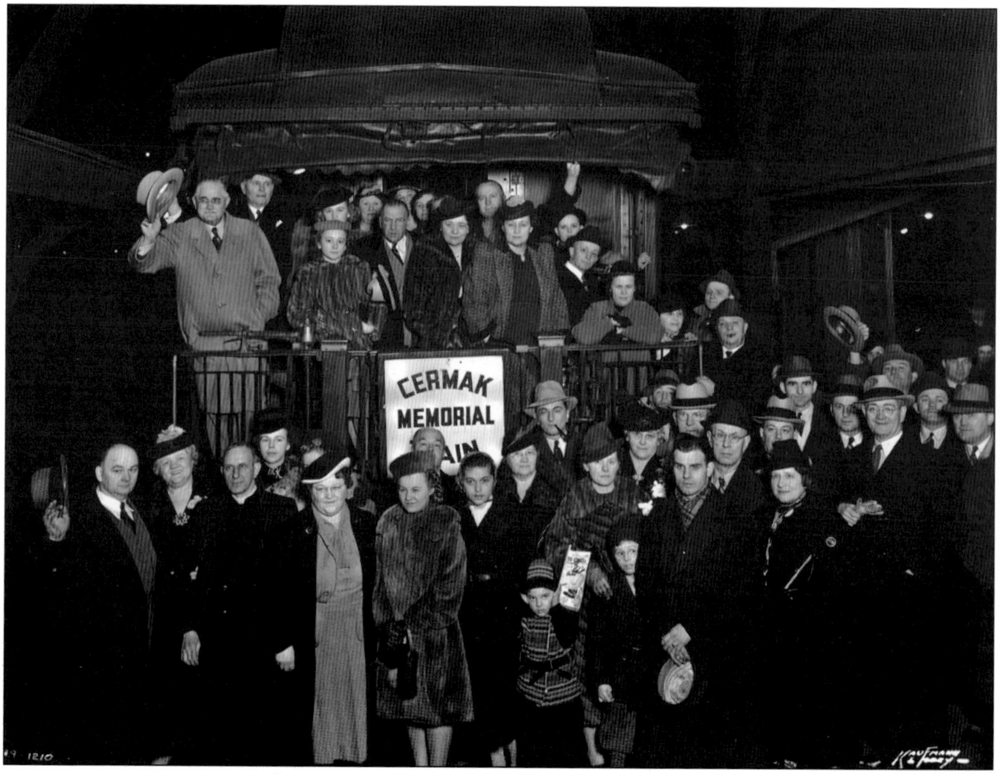

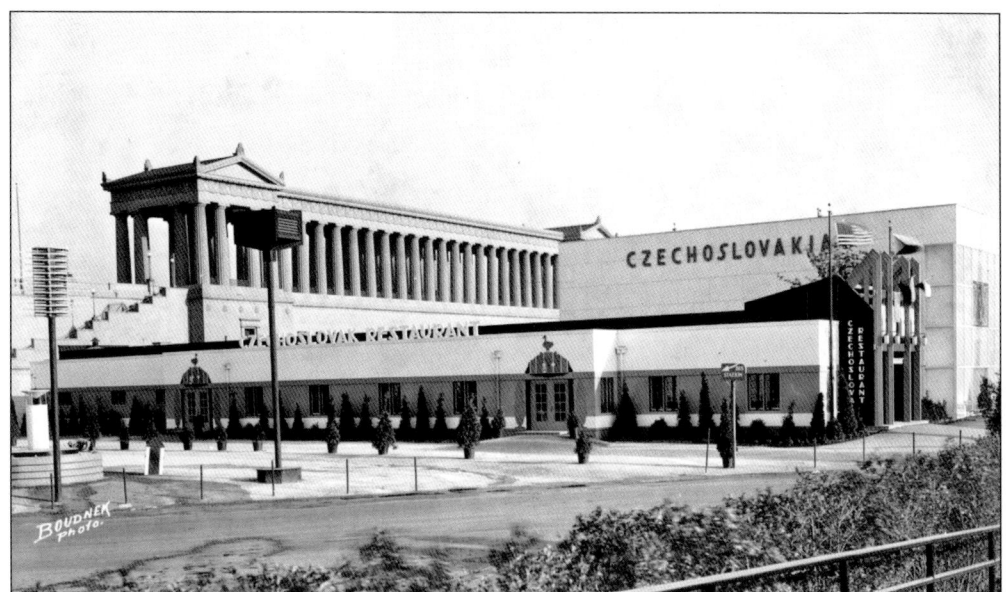

The state-of-the-art Czechoslovak pavilion at the 1933–1934 Chicago Century of Progress world's fair showcased Czech culture and highlighted the achievements of the 15-year-old First Czechoslovak Republic. The pavilion had special sponsorship in its Czech-born mayor, Antonín Čermák. It must have been one of his most satisfying assignments during his tenure as mayor to preside over the highly successful world's fair. (Courtesy CSA.)

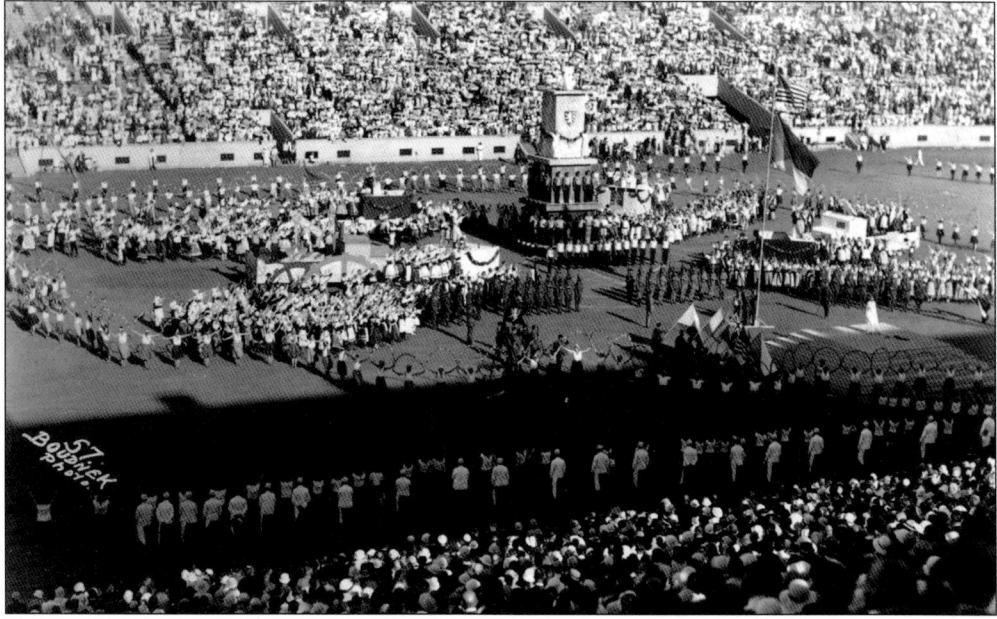

In the midst of the Chicago's world's fair, a showcase of Chicago's 100 years of industrial, technological, and civic development, a day was set aside to celebrate the achievements of one of the city's most loyal ethnic groups; Czech (and Slovak) Day in Chicago was an extravaganza of native costume, Sokol performances, and dance and music. The celebration of Czech day culminated with a spectacle of Czech culture staged in the city's grandest stadium, Soldier Field. (Courtesy CSA.)

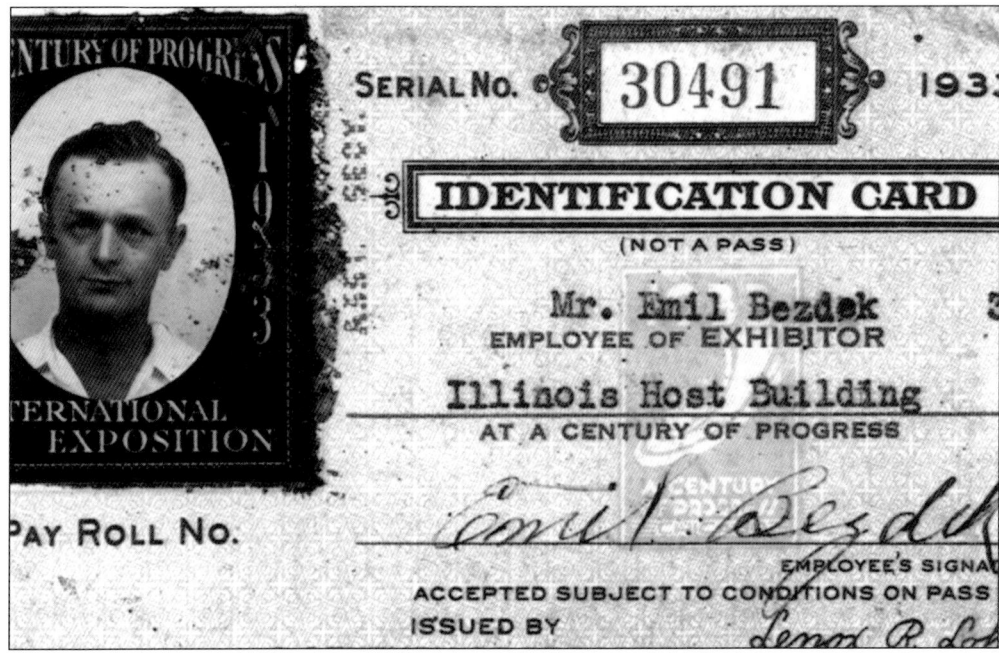

Seen is Emil Bezděk's identification card for the Chicago Century of Progress world's fair, 1933–1934. The fair was a major success for Chicago, financially and in terms of public relations. The fair was also considerably gainful for Chicago's working class, which was able to find extra work as fairground employees. (Courtesy Matthew and Ray Mulac.)

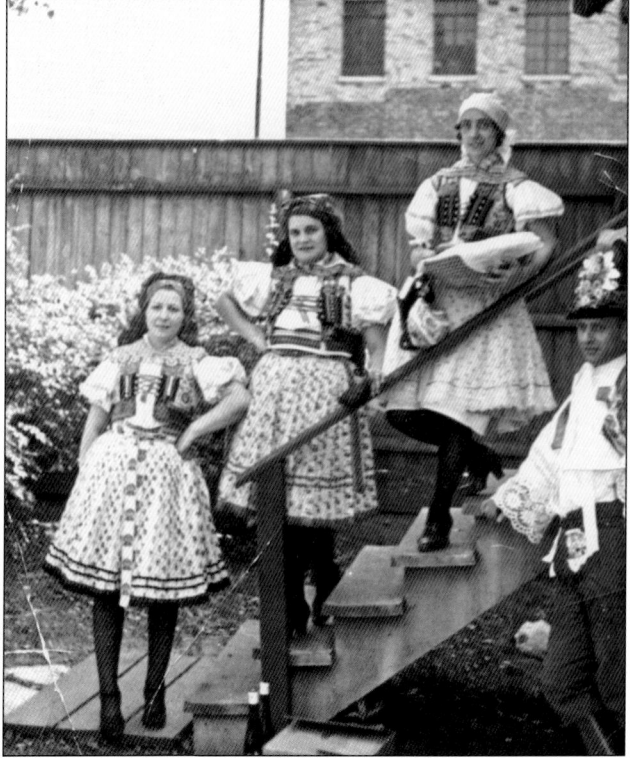

To this today, Chicago annually celebrates Moravian heritage with Moravská den, or Moravian day, which gives Czechs of Moravian heritage a chance to observe their particular traditions. In this 1939 image, Moravian wedding folk dresses are displayed with due pride. (Courtesy CSA.)

Enrique Stanko Vráz was a Czech-born writer, photographer, zoologist, and explorer. He founded the Czech-American National Council, in Chicago in 1910. Other metropolitan Czechs leaders, including Rudolph Pšenka of *Svornost*; Jarka Košař, a Sokol leader; Joseph Triner Sr.; Charles Vopička; Jaroslav J. Zmrhal, superintendent of Chicago schools; and Dr. Ludvík Fisher, all worked for a free Czech nation-state. It is no exaggeration to say that were it not for the dedication of these Czech Chicagoans, the First Czechoslovak Republic may not have come to fruition. The Czech-American National Council, especially its executive section, pictured here, was a bold attempt to unify the Chicago Czech community, culling leaders from various factions. The council established Czech-language teaching in Chicago public schools and organized lectures on the situation of the Czech lands under Austrian rule. (Courtesy University of Chicago, Archive of Czechs and Slovaks Abroad.)

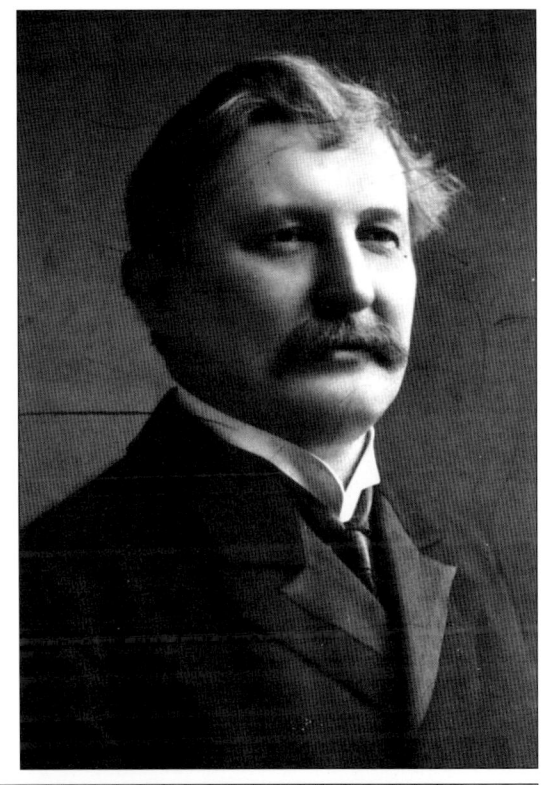

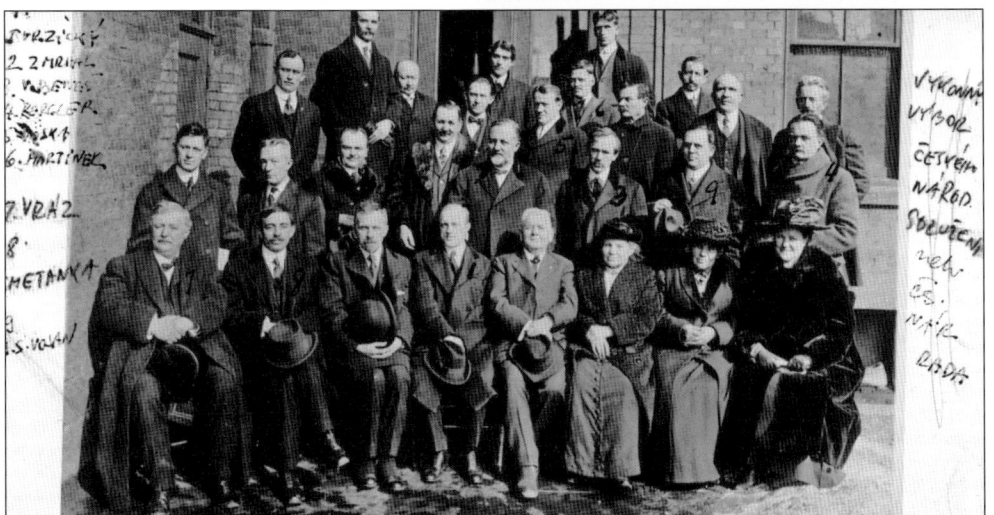

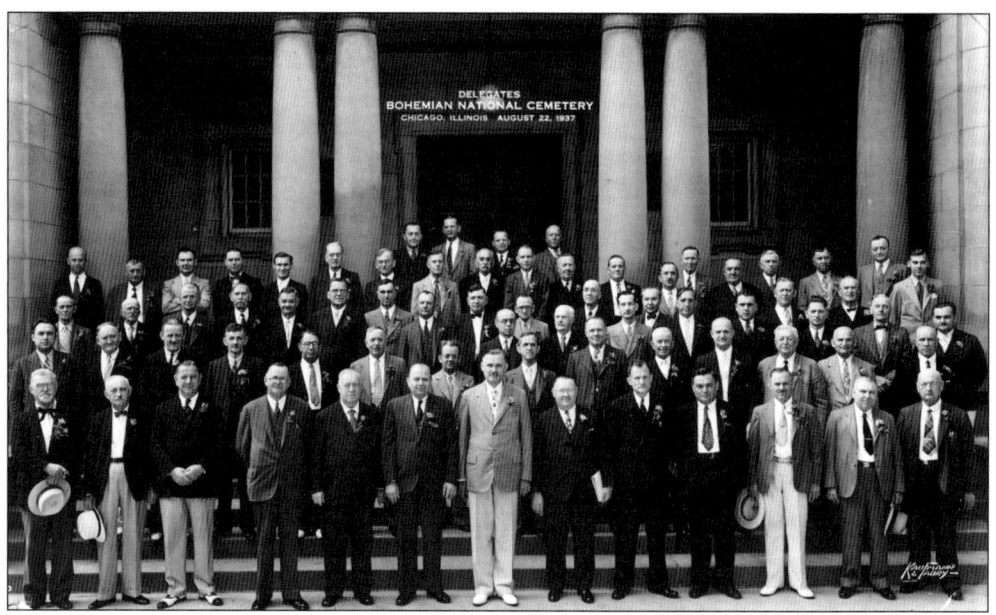

Delegates of the Bohemian National Cemetery (BNC) delegates stand before its main offices in 1937. The treasure of funerary art and architecture and historical relevance that is the BNC has recently been acknowledged with a generous (and competitive) grant. (Courtesy CSA.)

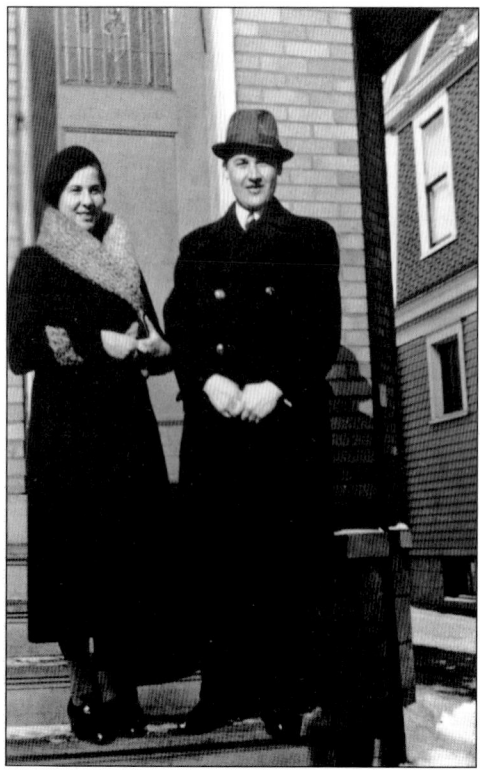

Chicagoland's Czech community enabled the escape of many Czech citizens, who might otherwise have been the victims of Adolf Hitler's death camps. In particular, the University of Chicago—the institution so instrumental in giving a forum to Tomáš Garrigue Masaryk's views of the need for Czech independence—was able to place many Czech "refugee scholars," like sociologist Antonín Obrdlík, pictured here with his wife, in positions not just in its departments but in universities throughout the United States. (Courtesy University of Chicago, Special Collections.)

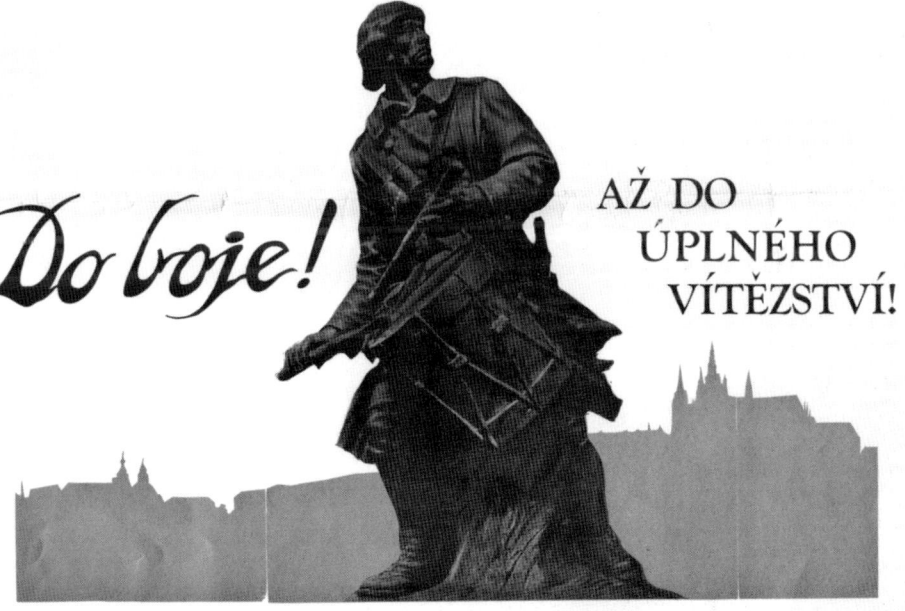

Hitler's 1938–1939 invasion of Czechoslovakia was "legitimized" by the Nazi irredentist claim that the so-called Sudentenland belonged to Germany. Hitler's claim was allowed by the United Kingdom and France, and it quickly turned into a full-scale occupation of the entire nation. One of the most ignominious moments came when Hitler occupied the seat of Czech power, the Hradčany, or castle grounds, and proclaimed his victory over Prague from the symbolic sanctuary of Czech princes and emperors. The Czechs of Chicagoland did all within their power to make the urgency of aiding the Czechslovaks primary in the mind-set of U.S. citizens. (Courtesy CSA.)

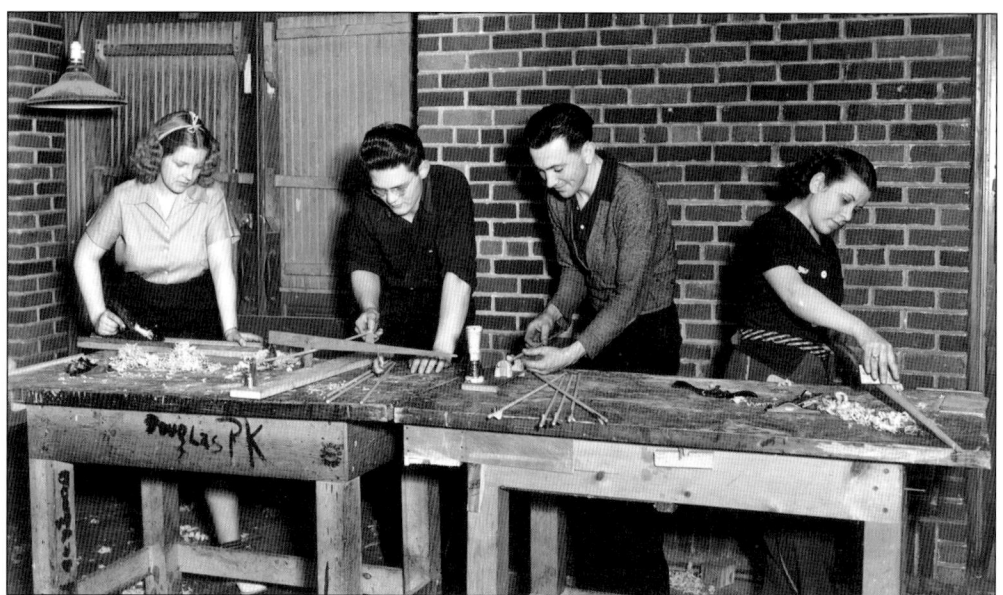

The Czechs of Czech California made the most of what the city had to offer by way of its park district programs in arts and crafts, dance, and athletics, especially those programs designed specifically for children and teenagers. This photograph from 1938 of the Douglas Park archery workshop includes boys and girls of Czech heritage. "Testing the arrow" is Gus Yirsa, "trimming feathers" is John Strnad, and "scraping the bow" is Miriam Peurye. (By permission and courtesy of the Chicago Park District Special Collections.)

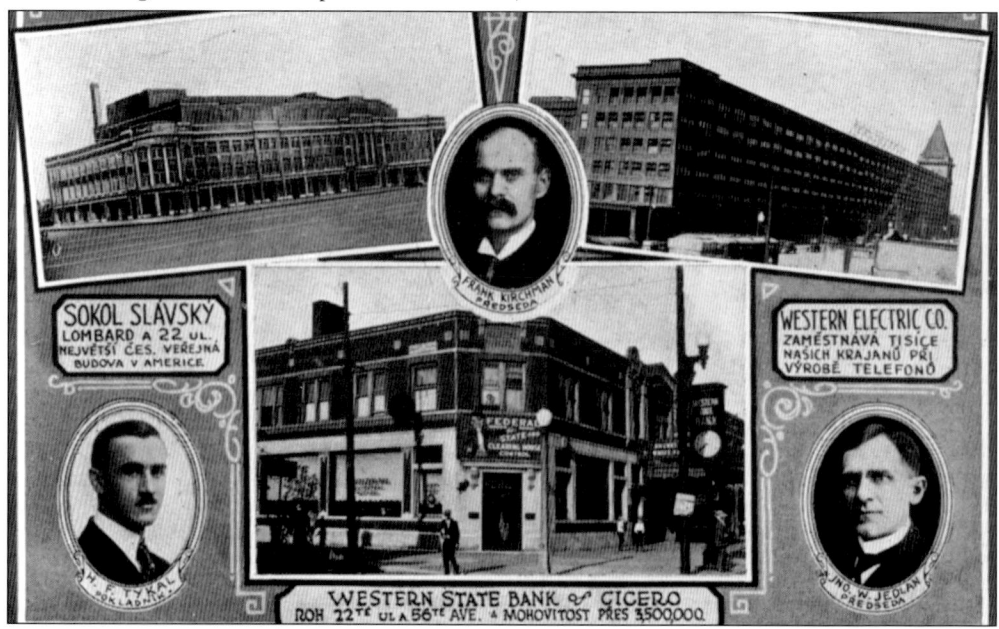

This chapter ends with a Macha montage from 1925, this time of three of the largest and most significant structures and businesses in the life of Czech Chicagoland: the Western Electric's Hawthorne Plant, described as "the employer of thousands of our countrymen and women in the manufacture of telephones"; Western State Bank of Cicero, with subsidies at near $500,000 in 1925; and Sokol Slávský, the "largest Czech public building in America." (Courtesy CSA.)

Four
CICERO AND BERWYN

Immigration outward from the neighborhoods of Chicago into the towns of Cicero and Berwyn was a natural outgrowth of the Czechs' westward movement—and upward mobility—in the years before World War II.

Founded in the 19th century, Cicero came into its own when the Galena and Chicago Union Railroad linked it with the city. It soon became a commercial hub, with many small businesses and major manufacturing industries. The influx of Czechs helped to grow the population of Cicero three times over in the 1930s. Not long after the settlement of Cicero, the town of Berwyn to its west became another center for the Czech community.

When in 1939 Czechoslovakia was sacrificed to appease Adolf Hitler, the Czechs of Chicagoland made every effort to help those in their ancestral homeland. Many Czech Chicago families sent their sons to fight and their daughters to work for the American Red Cross. It was in Cicero and Berwyn that the majority of Chicagoland's Czechs weathered the storms of World War II and where they awaited the return of their loved ones from the European and Pacific theaters. Among the young men who fought bravely was navy lieutenant Frank Jirka, member of the elite underwater demolition force responsible in large part for the U.S. victory at Iwo Jima. The Allied victory was sweet, but the Czechs of Chicagoland were soon faced with the 1948 Communist coup and the 1968 Warsaw Pact invasion, and thus once again in a position to rally for Czechoslovakia.

It could be argued that the suburban decentralization of the Czech community contributed to a diffuse sense of identity. But it is more accurate to say that the protests that occurred against the Soviet-controlled Communist government now took the tenor of a greater Chicago voice: the Czechs were now fully Chicagoans.

In the 1970s and 1980s, Czechs moved farther west again, a world away from the humble roots their ancestors put down in Pilsen. New immigrants joined their ranks, attracted by Chicagoland's reputation as a Czech center. In 1972, there was finally something to celebrate: astronaut Eugene Cernan, commander of *Apollo 17*, born in 1934 in Chicago to a Czech mother and Slovak father, was one of the last men to walk on the moon.

In the 1970s and 1980s, Cicero and Berwyn replaced central European cadences with Latino American ones and many Czech Americans dispersed to suburbs further afield.

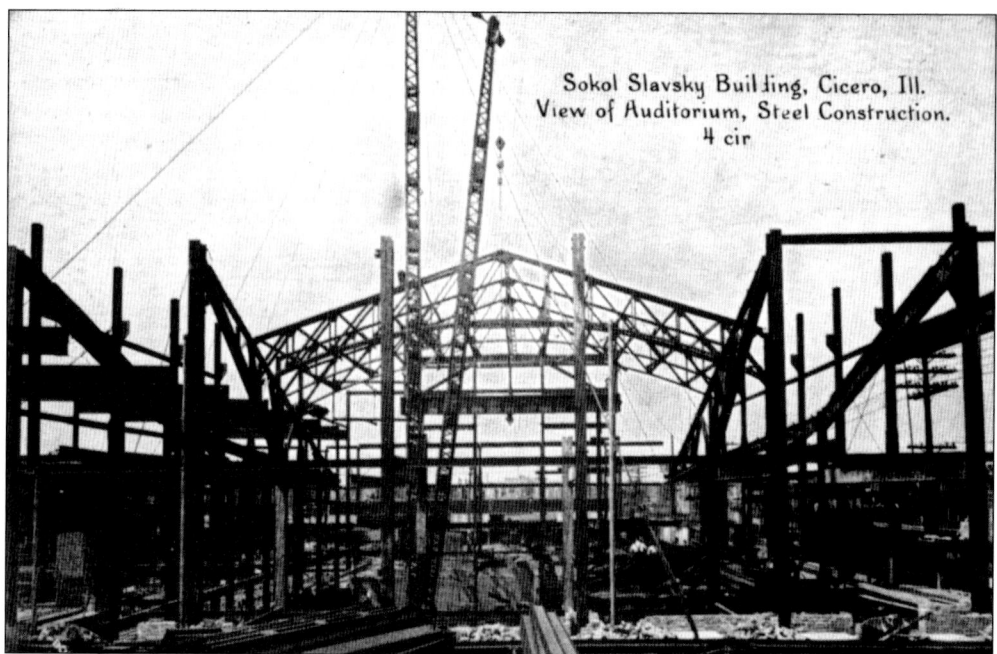

When the Czechs began colonizing Cicero and Berwyn, the community had a chance to build a truly grand meeting place. The Sokol Slávský building, boasting a ballroom, theater, restaurant, indoor gymnastic facilities, and an Olympic-sized swimming pool, came to be the most important Czech building in Chicagoland. Its opening in the mid-1920s was a feted affair. The result of the merger of Sokol Slávský in Pilsen with Sokol Berwyn, the new Sokol Slávský occupied an entire town block at Lombard and Twenty-second Streets. It laid claim to being the largest Sokol and the largest Czech public building in America. Although the Czech contingent has long since moved, the building still stands and spells out its Czech heritage on its facade. (Courtesy Frank Magallon.)

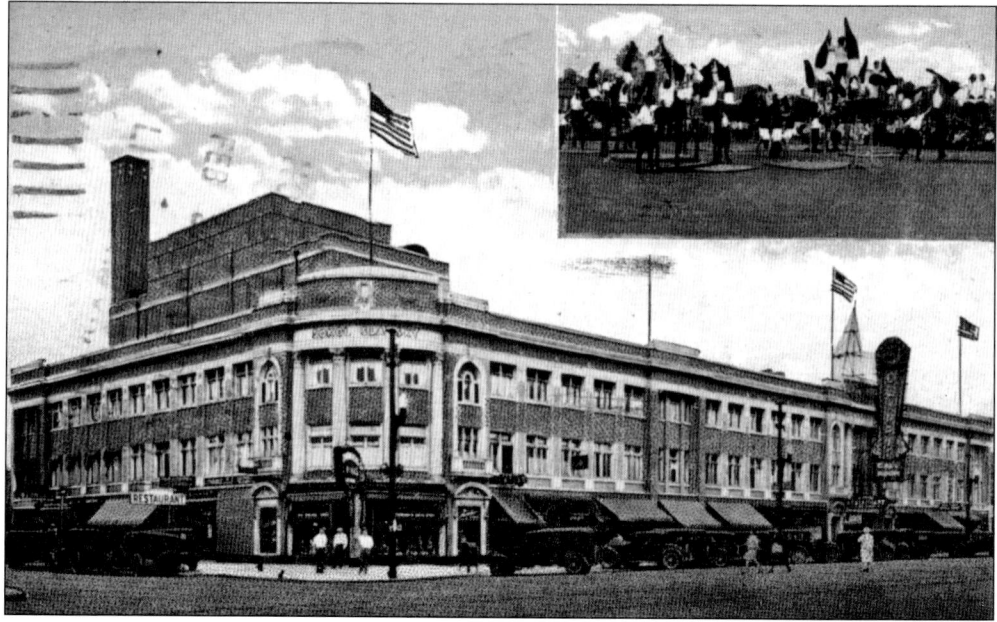

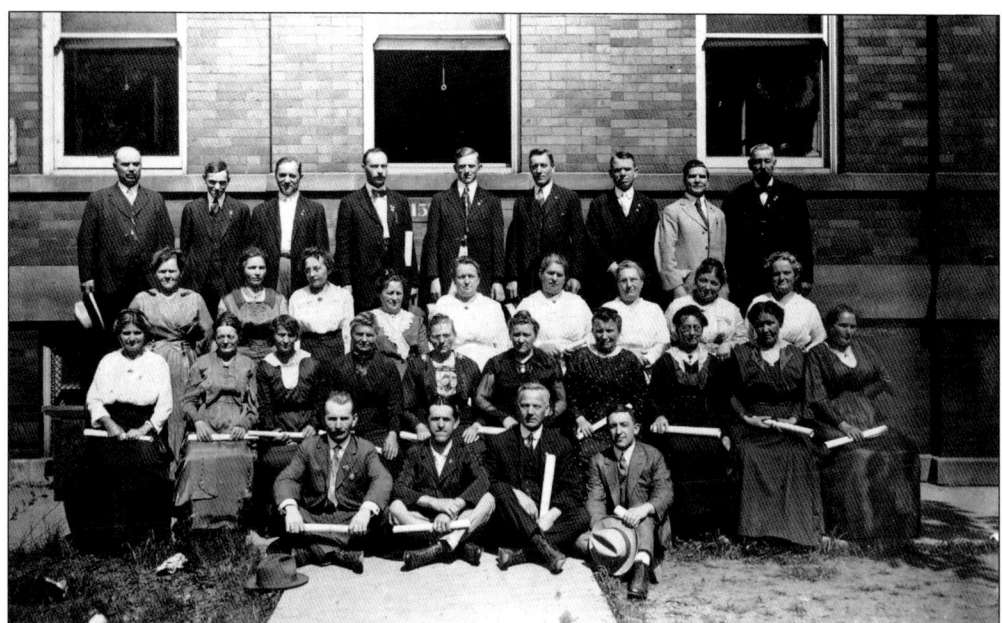

The adult students of the Palacký School on Karlov Avenue in Cicero stand in front of the school building for their class photograph in 1919. The school, named after the 19th-century Czech national revivalist and scholar, was located, according to the information on the photograph, at 1902 South Forty-ninth Avenue. (Courtesy Czechoslovak Society of America, Museum and Library; Donated by Stanley Loula; photograph by E. F. Macha.)

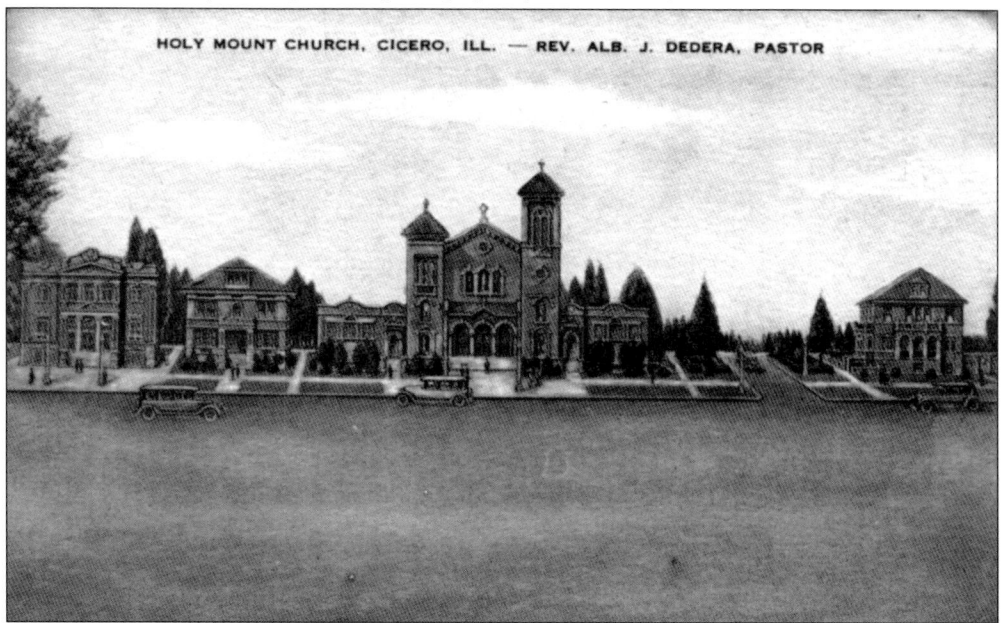

Our Lady of the Holy Mount was established in Cicero in 1919 by Czech émigrés who arrived in Chicago around the end of World War I to serve the ever-expanding population of Czech Catholic faithful moving westward into the suburbs. The name of the church is taken from a hill in Bohemia where in 1849–1850 three young girls reported to have seen visions of the Virgin Mary, and other apparitions have been reported since. (Courtesy Frank Magallon.)

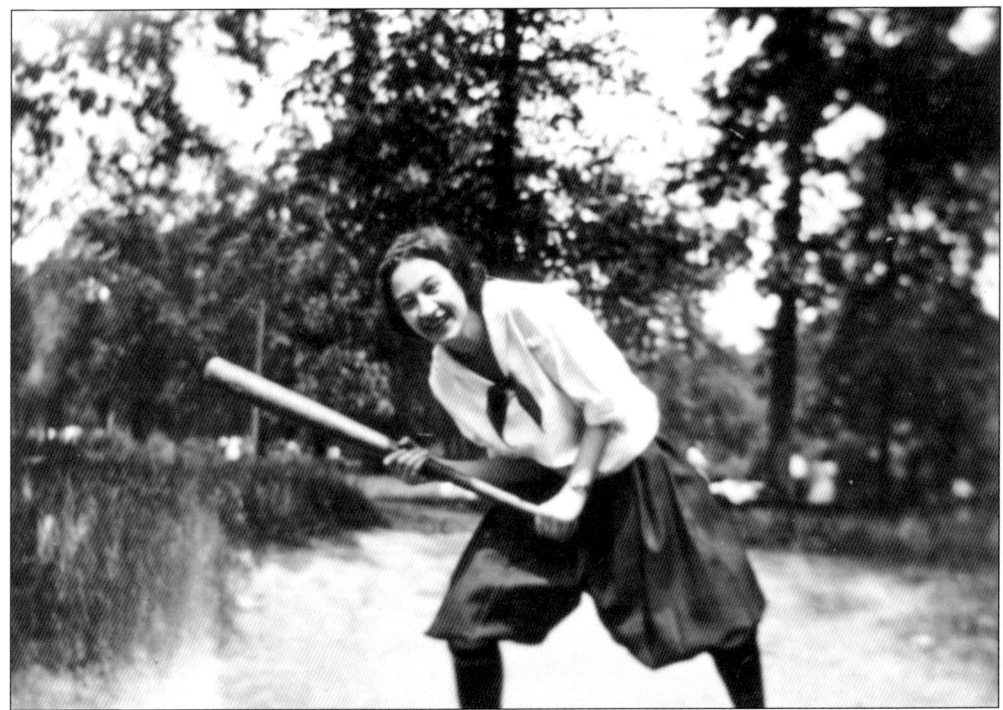

Athleticism was by no means restricted to Czech boys, Czech Sokol girls were also very active in sports. In this 1922 picture taken in Riverside, another Czech-dominated western suburb near Cicero and Berwyn, a Sokolice poses in a batting stance. (Courtesy CSA.)

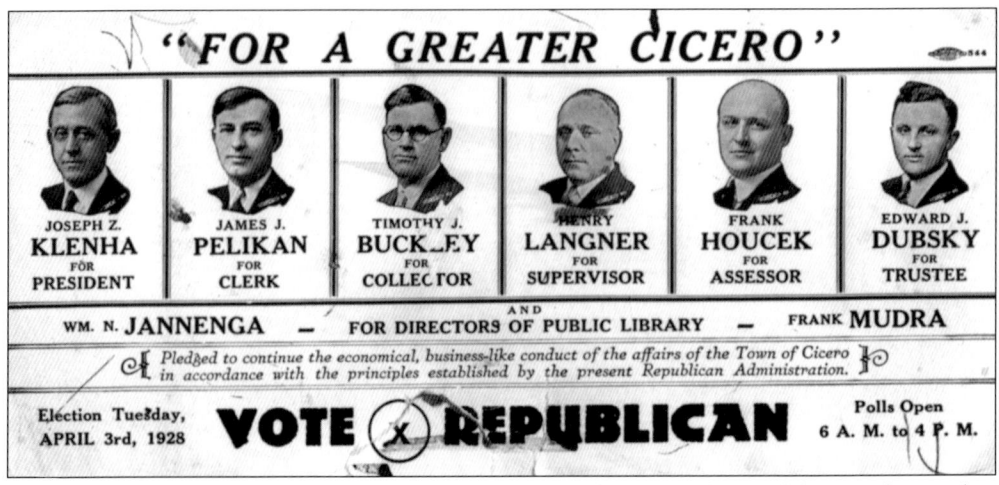

Czech Chicagoans historically have tended to vote on the basis of a candidate's values rather than his or her party affiliations. Chicagoland Czechs with political aspirations have been drawn equally to the Democratic and Republican Parties. This blotting card was a common give-away during political campaigns of the 1920s. Here the Czech dominance of Cicero politics is clear from the many Czech names on Cicero's Republican slate. (Courtesy Frank Magallon.)

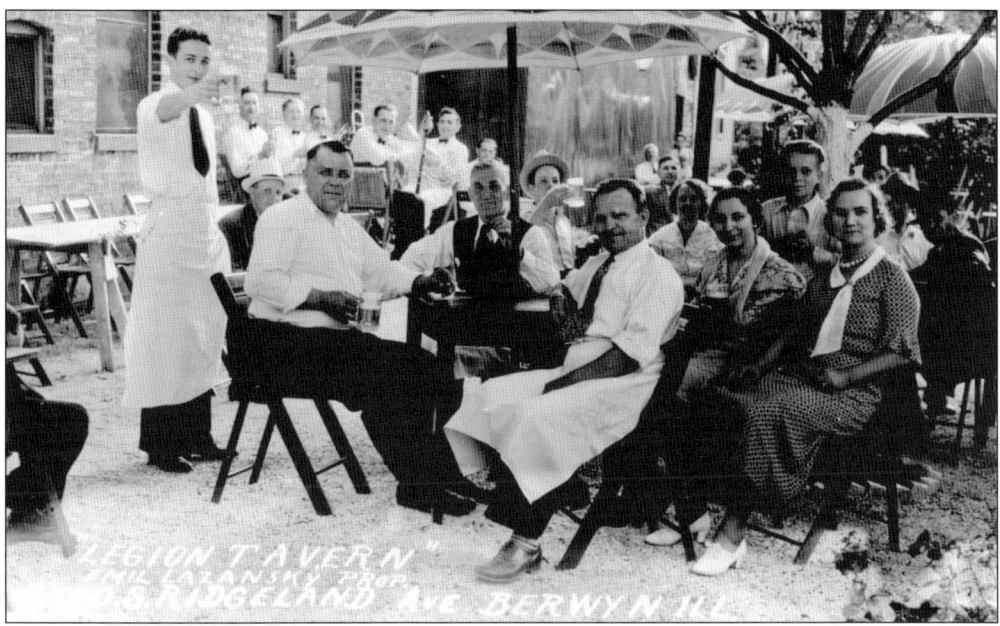

The Legion Tavern, run by Emil Lazanský and located on South Ridgeland Avenue, was a center of activity in the newly colonized suburb of Berwyn. This photograph was probably taken just before Prohibition went into effect in 1920. The organized crime that built up around the illicit sale of alcohol was headquartered in Cicero and Berwyn under the rule of one Al Capone. (Courtesy Frank Magallon.)

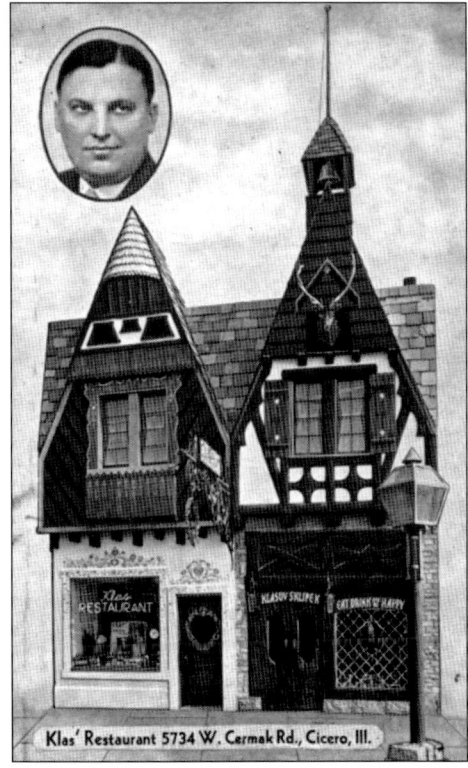

Klas restaurant was established in 1922 in Cicero by Bohemian Jew Adolph Klas, who meticulously designed it to be as authentically Bohemian as possible. Through the years, even as the Czech community moved into outlying suburbs, Klas has remained in Cicero and been the choice meeting place of Czech American families, organizations (like the Bohemian Lawyers' Association), and dignitaries, presidents, and ambassadors alike. Today it is the country's largest Czech restaurant. (Courtesy CSA.)

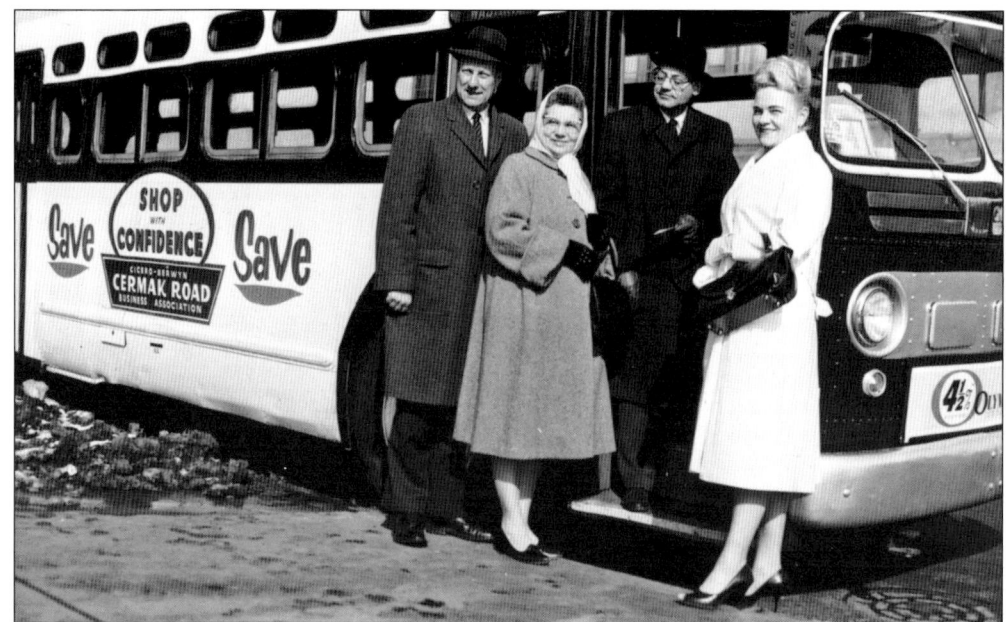

William and Lillian Baar were pillars in the Czech community. William was a Sokol member of Česká Beseda; he maintained the language of his parents and served in the U.S. Army Air Corps. William and Lillian ran a successful real estate company in Berwyn and raised their daughter Judy, best known for her statewide political achievements, in a household with strong Czech and American values. (Courtesy CSA.)

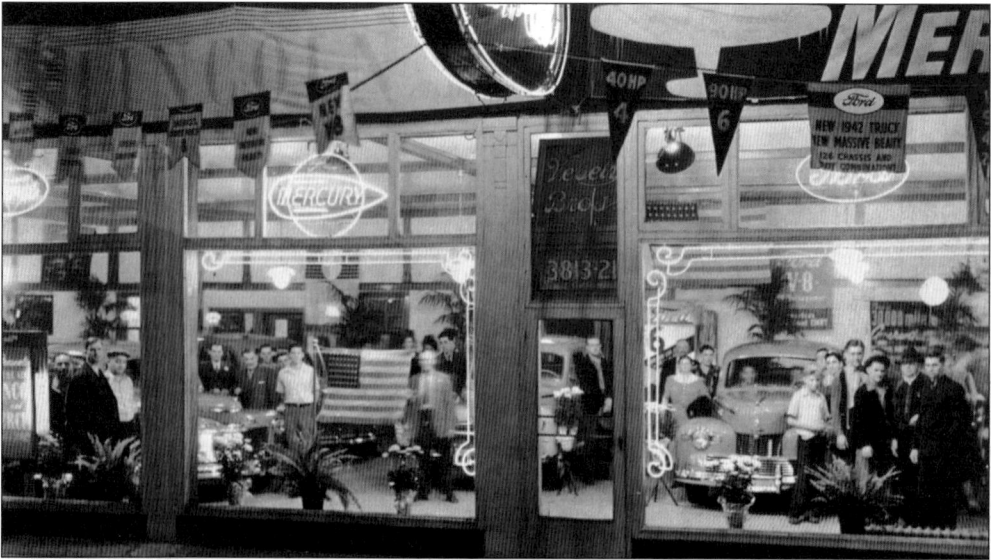

As the Czech community grew wealthier and more stable, Czechs moved into more comfortable work that also bore witness to the increased affluence of the community and to the general development of the postwar U.S. economy. Car dealerships, Vesely Ford, for instance, owned and operated by Czechs, sprang up in Czech California, Berwyn, and Cicero and thrived on healthy competition with one another. Czech Americans to this day can recall which dealership was where and which were preferred. (Courtesy Czechoslovak Society of America, Museum and Library; photograph by E. F. Macha.)

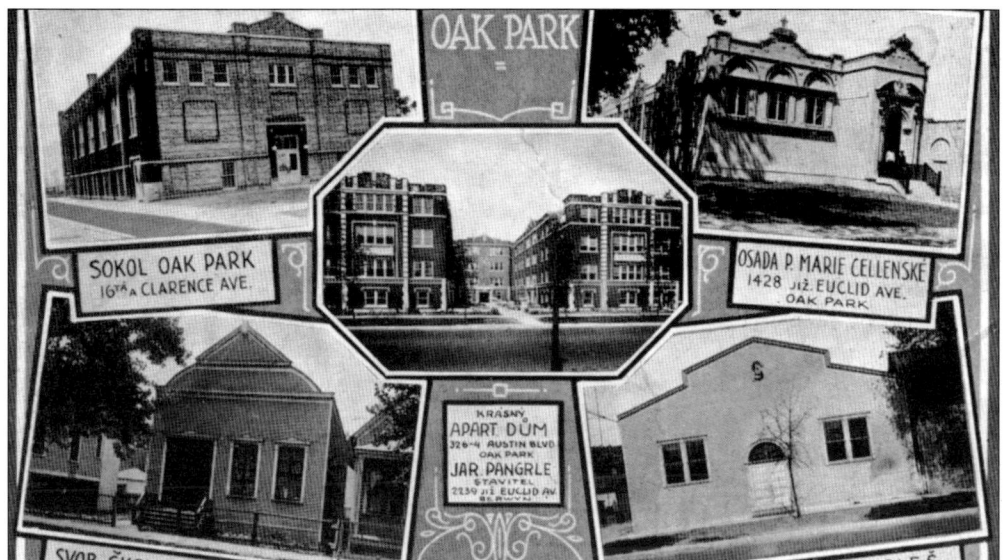

Officially part of the township of Cicero until 1902, Oak Park was another popular destination for Czech Chicagoans. The village prided itself on its decent and upright citizenry (the village was dry from 1872 to 1972). Many affluent Czechs were born and bred in the community, including Ray Kroc, owner of the McDonald's restaurant corporation. That Oak Park, a community not predominantly Czech, could sustain so many Czech-specific institutions is testimony to the ethnic group's resilience. (Courtesy Czechoslovak Society of America, Museum and Library; photograph by E. F. Macha.)

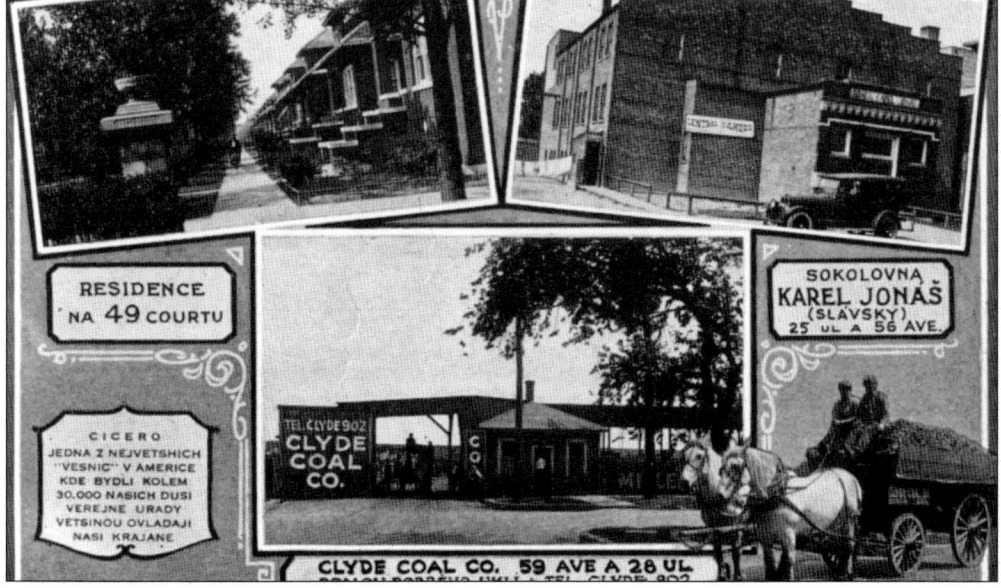

Macha's 1925 postcard series says of Cicero "it is one of the largest 'villages' in America where around 30,000 of our souls live [with] public offices held in the majority by our countrymen." Images of the bungalow-style homes, the Sokol Karel Jonáš (Slávský) building, and the Clyde Coal Company, the "home of good coal," co-owned by Czechs C. A Nádherný and J. C. Nový, afford insight into the prosperity of Czech Cicero. (Courtesy Czechoslovak Society of America, Museum and Library; photograph by E. F. Macha.)

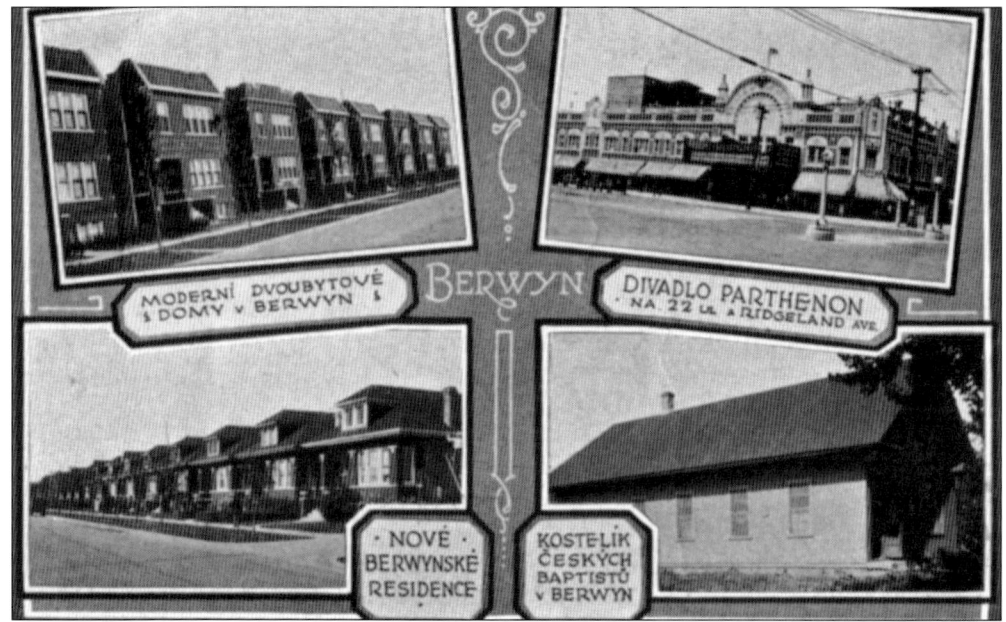

Macha's views of Czech Berwyn show the Parthenon Theatre at Twenty-second Street and Ridgeland Avenue, site of many a first and second date for young Czech couples; the chapel of the Czech Baptists in Berwyn below it; "new Berwyn residences" to the chapel's left; and above this image, the modern "duplex homes in Berwyn." (Courtesy Czechoslovak Society of America, Museum and Library; photograph by E. F. Macha.)

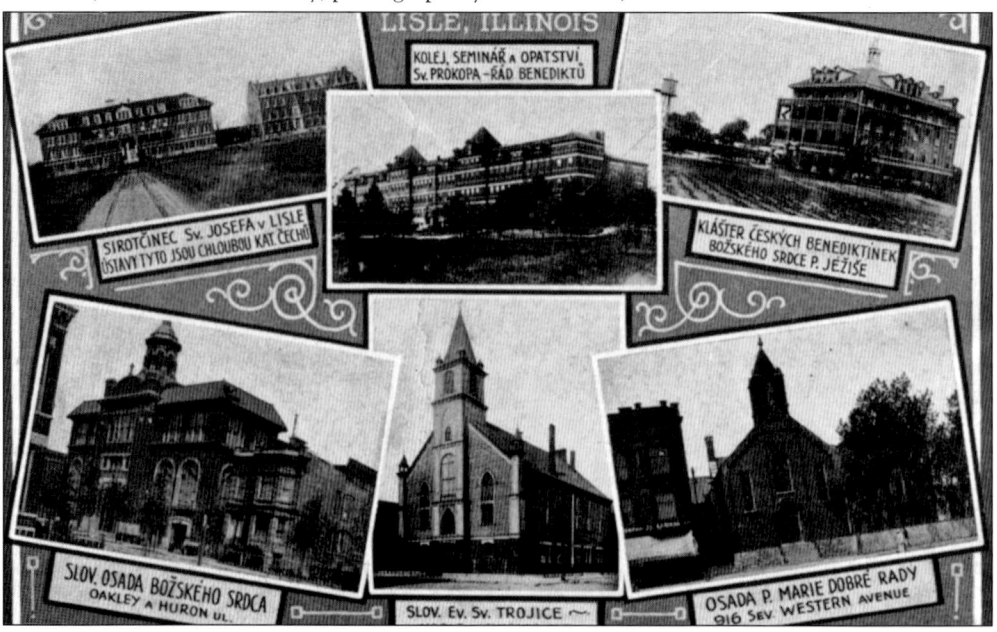

With the number of Czech Catholics growing, the Benedictines were invited to minister the congregation of St. Procopius in Pilsen in the 19th century, and soon thereafter a Czech college, the first of its kind in the United States, was founded. The College of St. Procopius in Chicago soon outgrew its city home and in 1901 moved to Lisle, where it still operates today. (Courtesy CSA; photograph by E. F. Macha.)

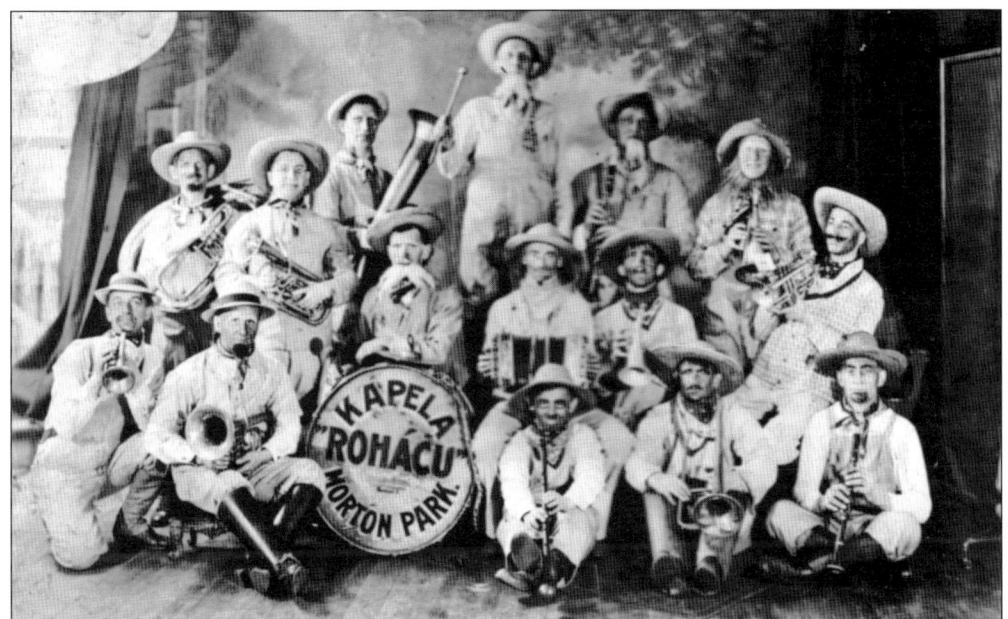

The singing group named the Stag-Beetle Band (Kapela roháčů) formed in Morton Park early in the second decade of the 20th century and are assembled in a group photograph dated from 1914. Singing groups were immensely popular among Czechs, and folk songs and popular music—in Czech and English—cohered the community in a deep way; song and dance for Czechs is a strong performance of their ethnic identity. (Courtesy CSA.)

As Czechs moved up in social status and out to the suburbs, many Sokol lodges found it best to merge and combine efforts and memberships into one new lodge located in the western suburbs of Cicero and Berwyn, where their members now lived. (Courtesy CSA.)

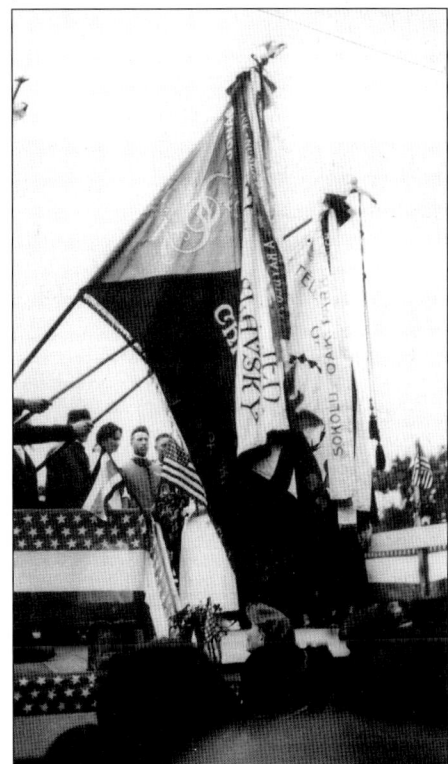

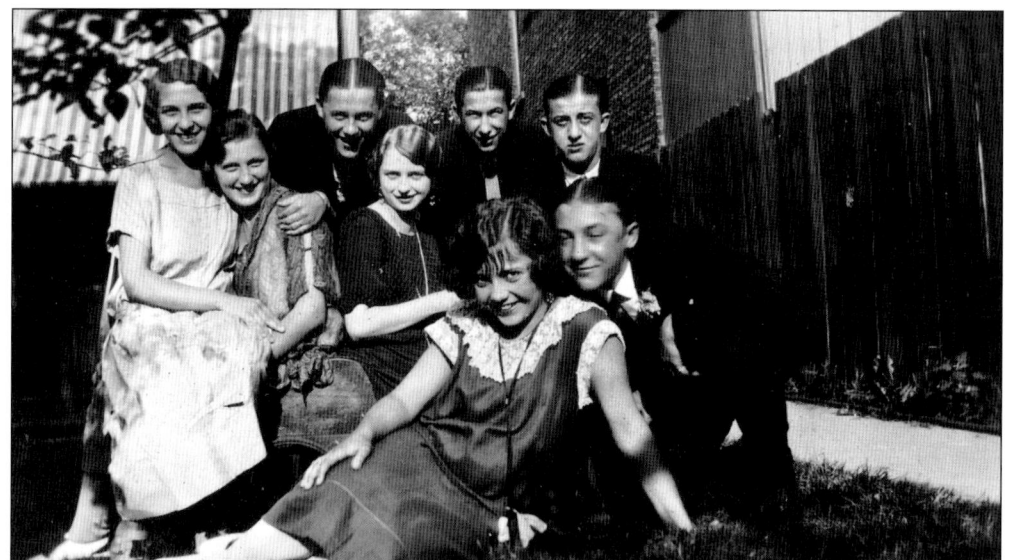

Czech Chicagoans, now fully at ease in their American environment and often with Czech and English both as their native languages, increasingly made up sizable portions of the city's west side high schools like Farragut, Harrison, and Crane Technical. Blanche Straka's Harrison High School memory book contains this snapshot of a lawn party, giving a special glimpse into the life of a teenager of Czech heritage in the 1920s and 1930s. (Courtesy CSA.)

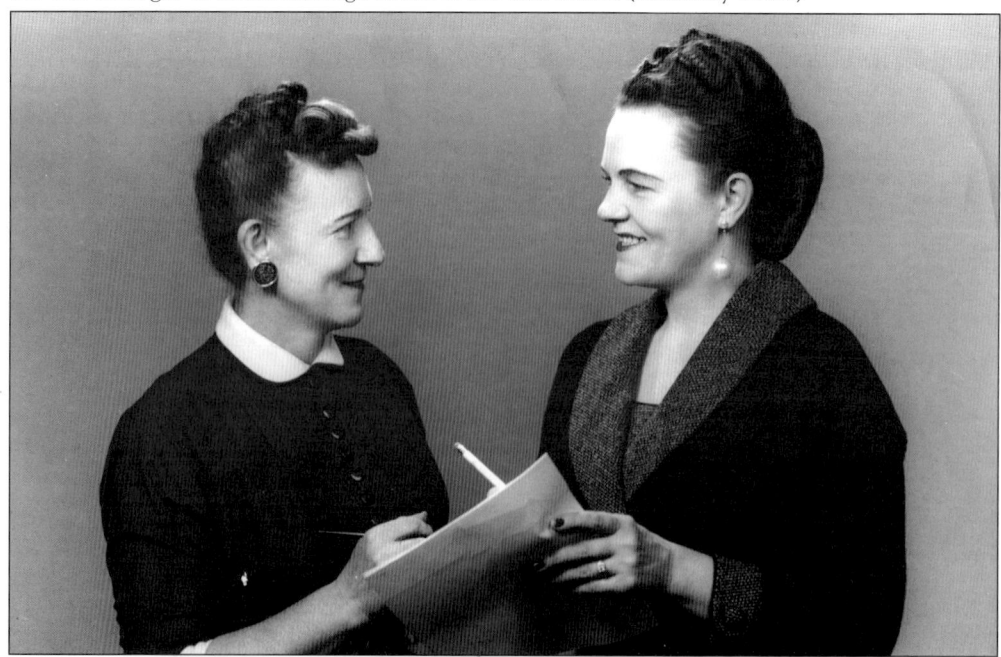

In the 1940s and 1950s, Czechs constituted enough of the total population of Chicagoland for regular Czech radio shows to be aired. On Sundays mornings WHFC hosted sing-along radio lessons, Czech songs that helped to teach the Czech language to an ever more Americanized community. Rev. Ernest Zizka, Anie Albrecht, and Julian Baar (the latter two pictured here) were stars of Chicagoland Czech radio. (Courtesy Czechoslovak Society of America, Museum and Library; photograph by Bessenbill-Kolar Photographers.)

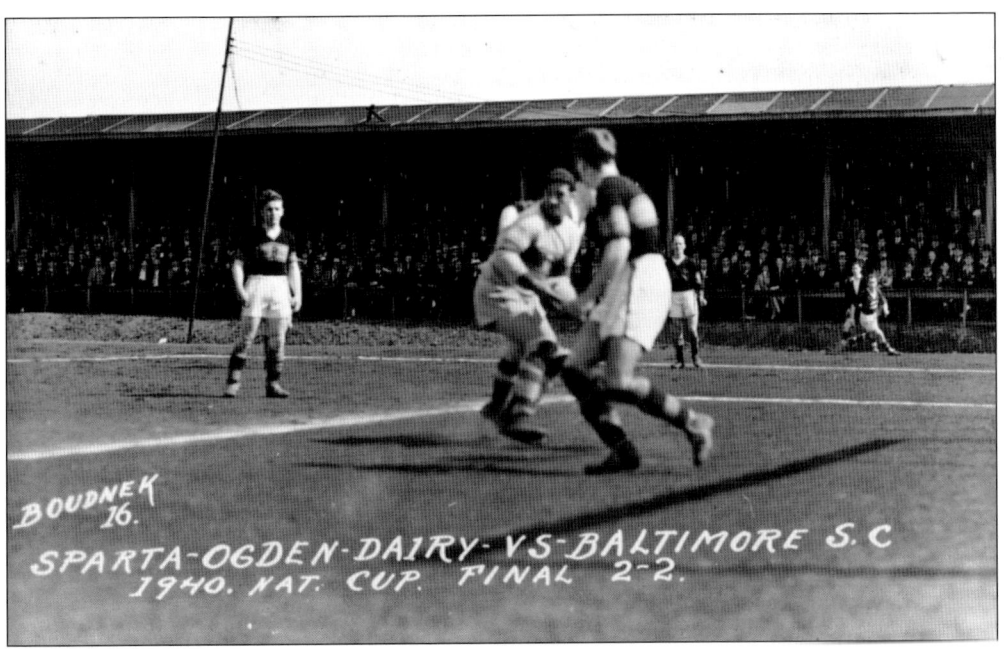

In the 1940s, Sparta Athletic and Benevolent Association was a powerhouse soccer team. Comprised of those of Czech ancestry, its winning record is witness again to the Czechs' natural athleticism. Sparta Athletic Benevolent Association was also an association organized for the greater good of its players and their families. Here Sparta, sponsored by Chicago's Ogden Dairy, hosts Baltimore Soccer Club in the 1940 national championship game. The game ended in a tie (2-2). (Courtesy University of Chicago, Archive of Czechs and Slovaks Abroad.)

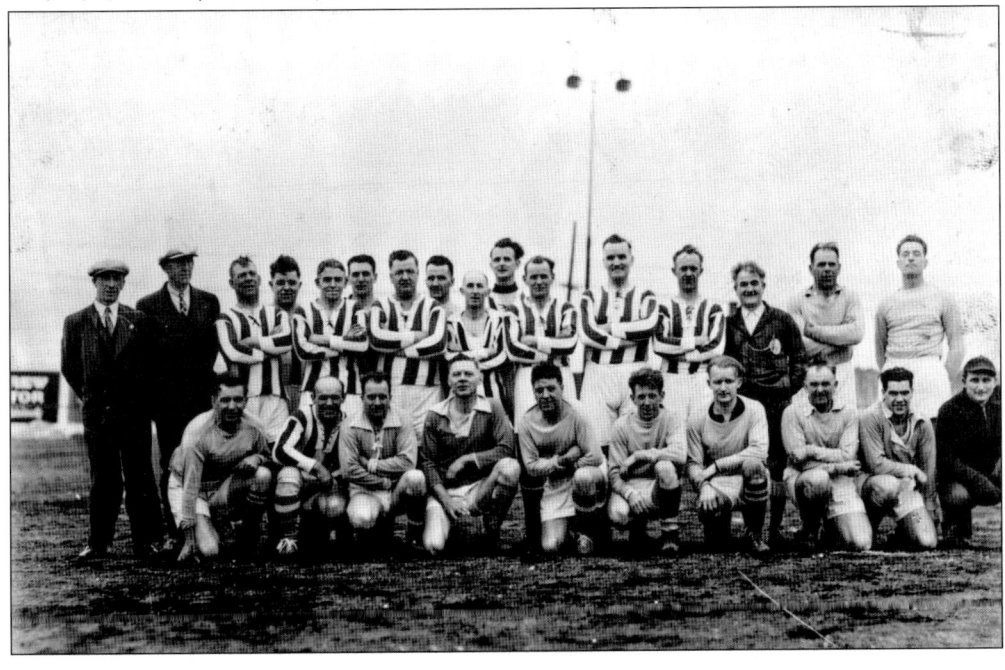

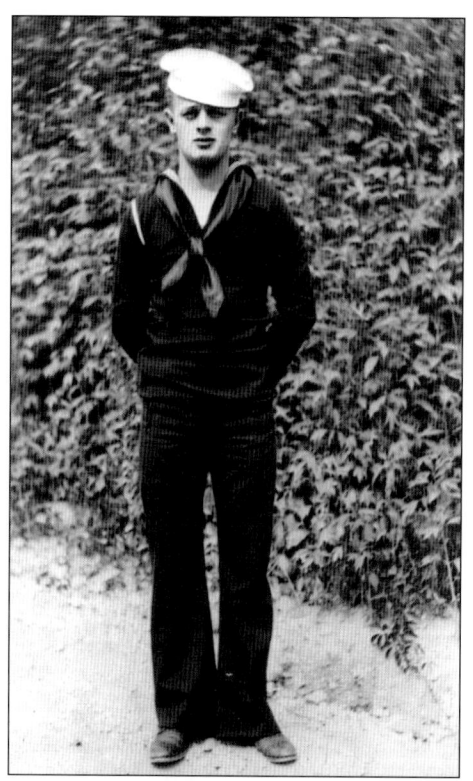

Picking up the trace of the story of the Palma and Bezděk families again here, Emil Bezděk is seen during World War II in the navy uniform of his adopted homeland. He did his training in San Diego and, like many Czech Americans, fought bravely for his country. He was assigned to the storied USS *Oklahoma*. After the war, he returned safely to his sweetheart, Rose Palma, and they began their life together back again in Chicago. (Courtesy Ray and Matthew Mulac.)

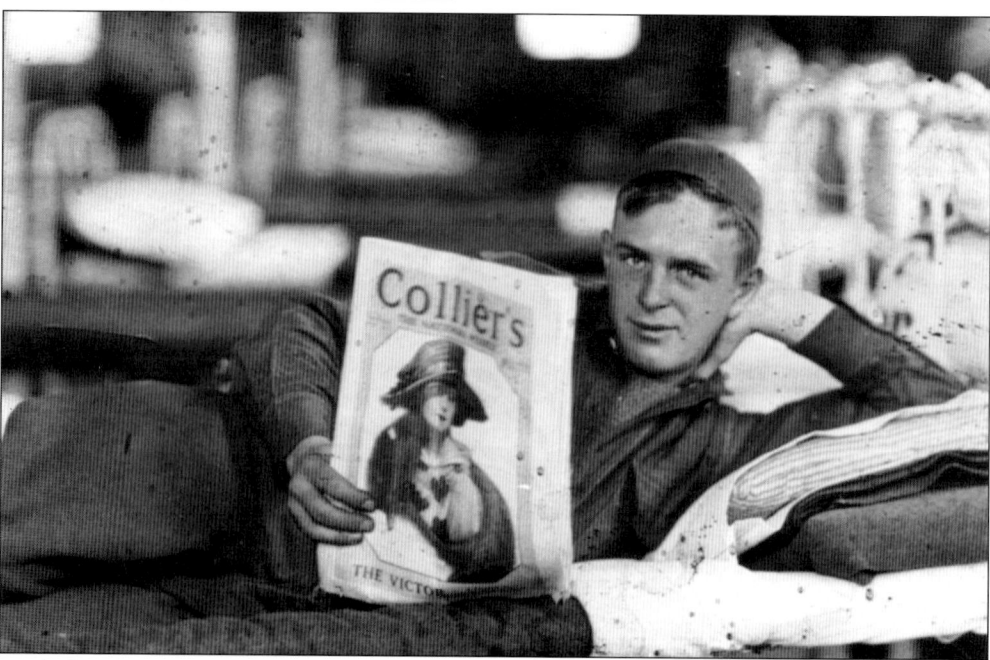

Emil's brother Edward also enrolled as a serviceman during World War II. Here he is pictured in the U.S. Army cavalry barracks. All the Bezděk boys served their country in the war and, in doing so, also served as liberators of their ancestral homeland. (Courtesy Ray and Matthew Mulac.)

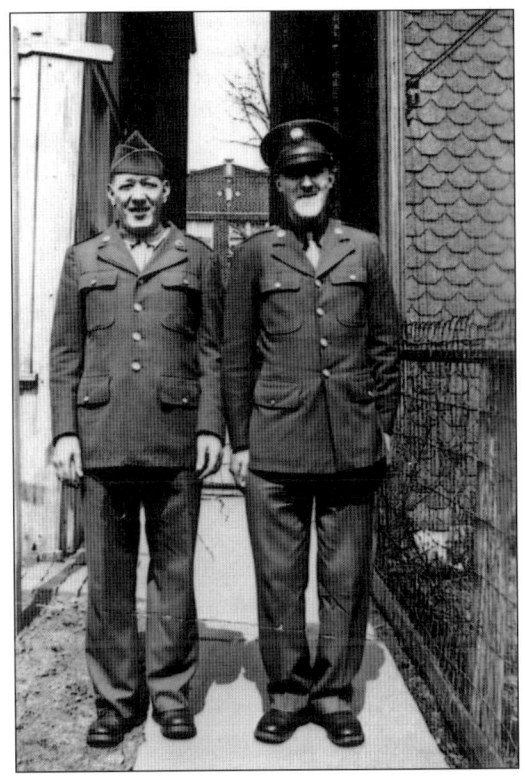

The Palma brothers, James and John, Rose's brothers, also served their country. Here they are pictured on leave dressed in their uniforms. They would both serve bravely and make it back to Chicago, returning to their civilian jobs in the automotive and railroad trades. (Courtesy Ray and Matthew Mulac.)

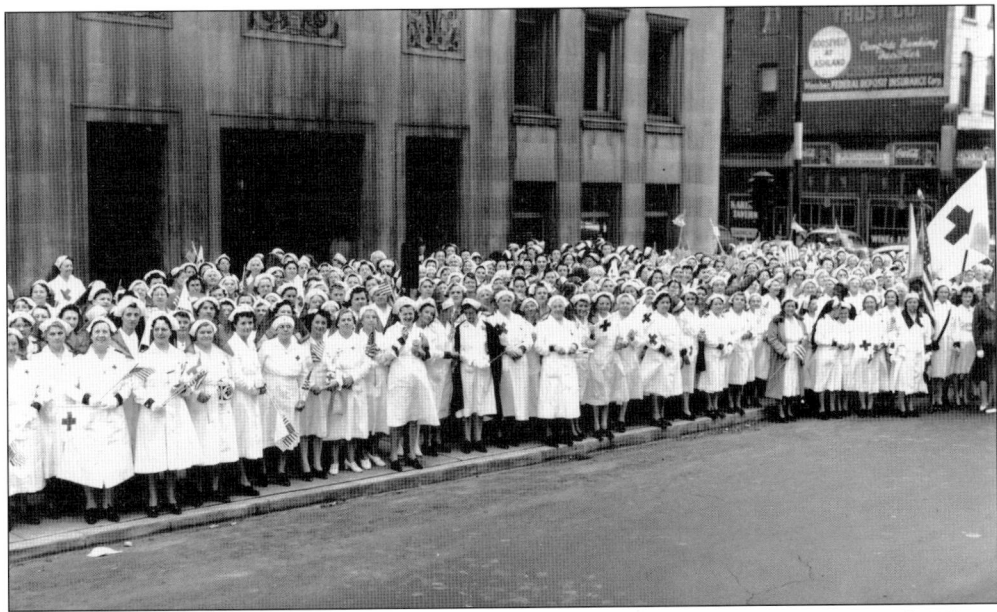

It was in Chicago that the Czechoslovak Red Cross was established by Betka Papánek, Vlasta Vráz, and Dr. Alice Masaryk, daughter of the president T. G. Masaryk. Over 2,000 Czech Chicagoans worked on the home front gathering medical supplies, raising funds, and running blood drives, through the auspices of the Czech National Alliance, an organization that was reorganized to meet the Nazi threat. (Courtesy CSA.)

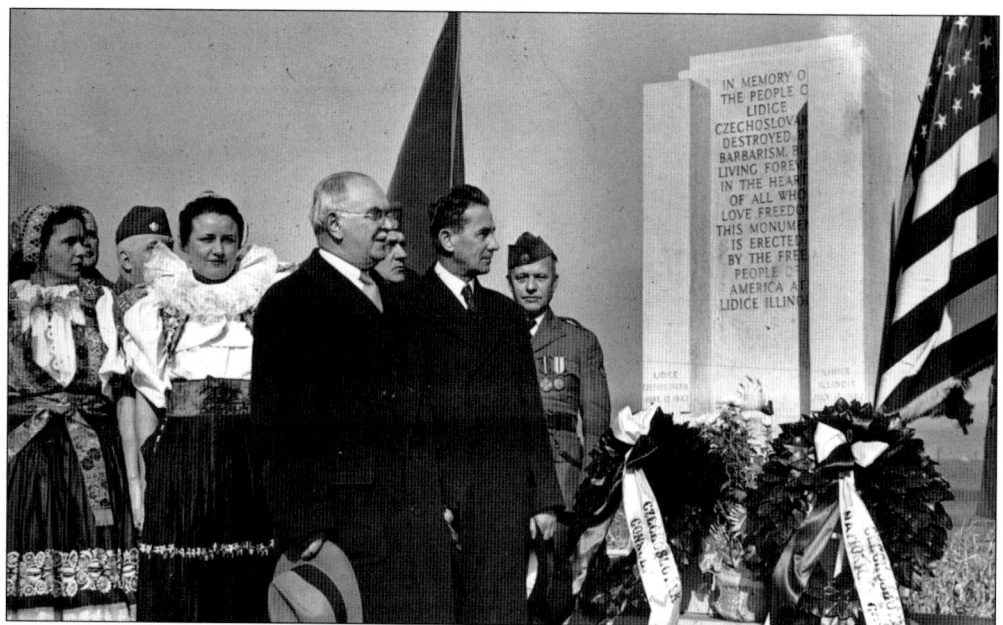

The 1942 assassination of Reinhard Heydrich resulted in two Nazi atrocities: the towns of Lidice and Ležáky were razed, their men shot and their women and children hauled to concentration camps. In response, towns around the world renamed themselves Lidice. First among them was Illinois' Crest Hill, and in a ceremony attended by Edvard Beneš, Czechoslovak president in exile, the town dedicated a monument to Lidice. (Courtesy University of Chicago, Archive of Czechs and Slovaks Abroad.)

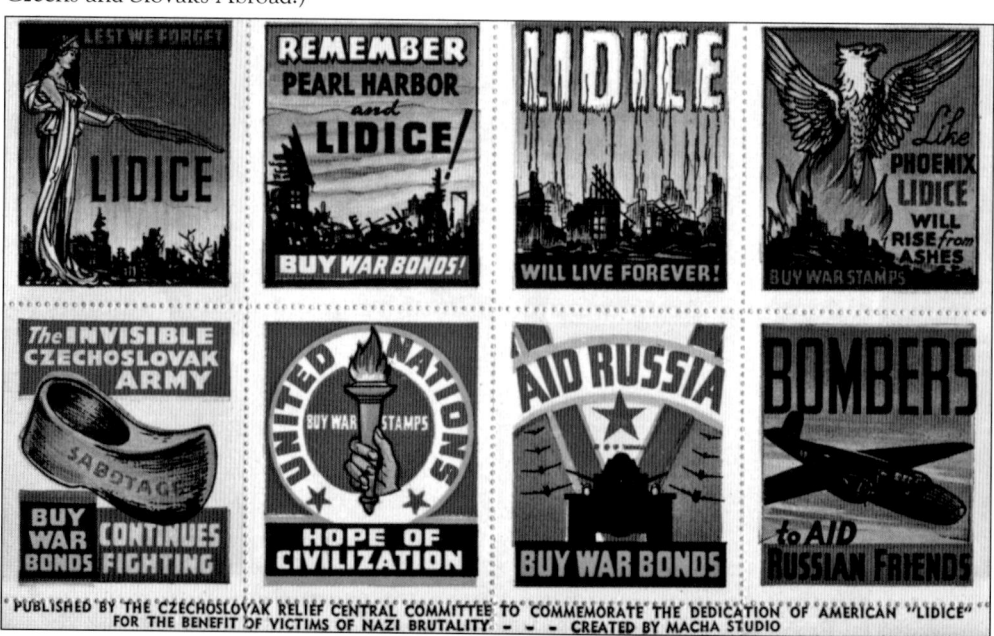

These stamps honoring the memory of the victims of Lidice were issued from Chicago to raise funds and awareness for the atrocities the Czechs were facing at the hands of their Nazi occupiers. The stamps describe in brilliant colors and moving, urgent messages the devastation of World War II. (Courtesy CSA.)

In 1949, Dorothy Bezděk married Joseph Mulac, of Croatian ancestry. Here they are pictured a few weeks before their wedding day, on Easter Sunday 1949. (Courtesy Ray and Matthew Mulac.)

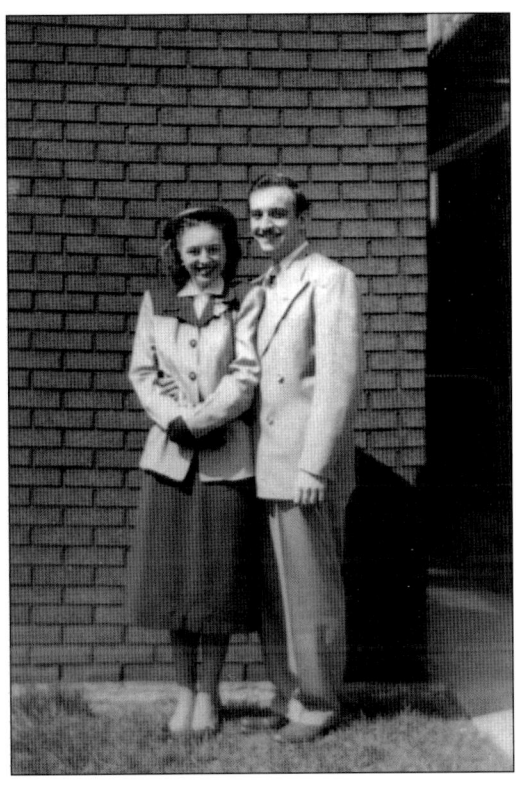

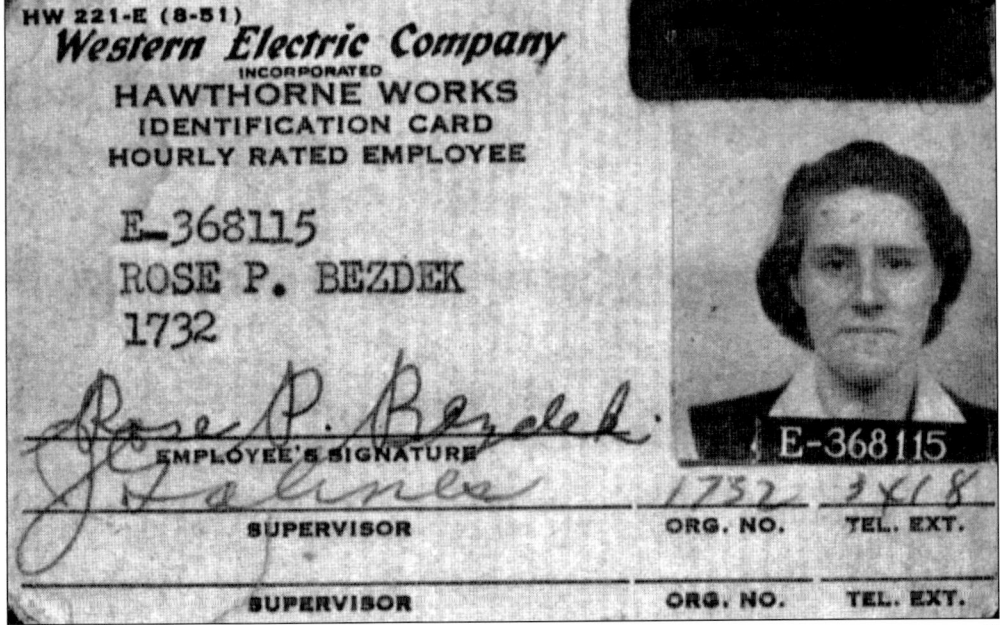

During and after the war, Dorothy's mother, Rose Bezděk, like so many Czech Americans, still worked for the Western Electric Company. Her employee identification from the 1950s gives insight into the vastness of the company even postwar. (Courtesy Ray and Matthew Mulac.)

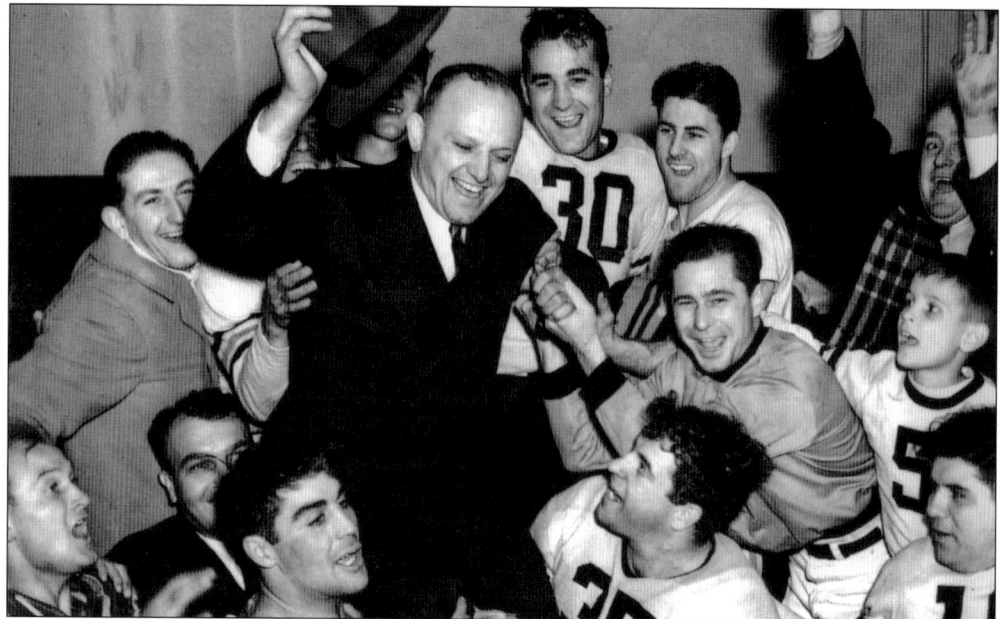

After graduating from the University of Illinois, where he played football, the boy who narrowly escaped the *Eastland* disaster was hired to manage the Decatur Staleys football team. In 1922, George Halas bought the team for a reported $100 and, since they played in Wrigley Field, renamed them the Chicago Bears, in a nod to the Cubs. Halas coached the Bears from 1921 until 1967 and led them to eight NFL championships. (Author's collection.)

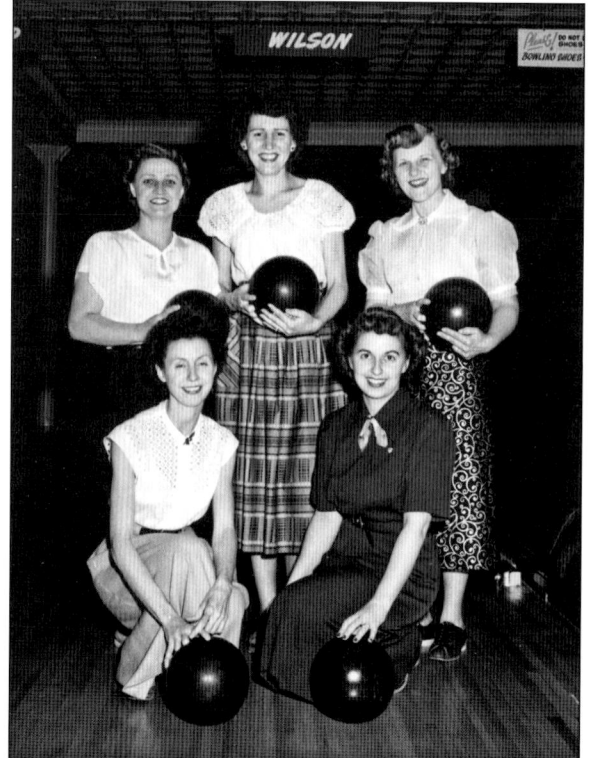

Bowling leagues were another way to keep the more widely dispersed Czech community together, and these leagues were often tethered in turn to a larger organization, such as the CSA, Sokol, or benevolent societies. (Courtesy CSA.)

Albín Polášek emigrated to the United States at the age of 22 and in 1916 was offered the chair of the Department of Sculpture at the Art Institute of Chicago. His sculptures can be found throughout the United States. In 1955, to honor the man who made Czech independence possible, the Czech community commissioned Polášek to sculpt a memorial to Tomáš Garrigue Masaryk. The statue was placed on Midway Plaisance on the campus of the University of Chicago, where Masaryk had taught in the early 1900s. Polášek experimented with several designs until he settled on this one of a Blaník Knight. Czech folklore has it that when the Czechs are beset by enemies, the Knights of Blaník Mountain will awake to save and unify the Czech people. (By permission and courtesy of the Chicago Park District Special Collections.)

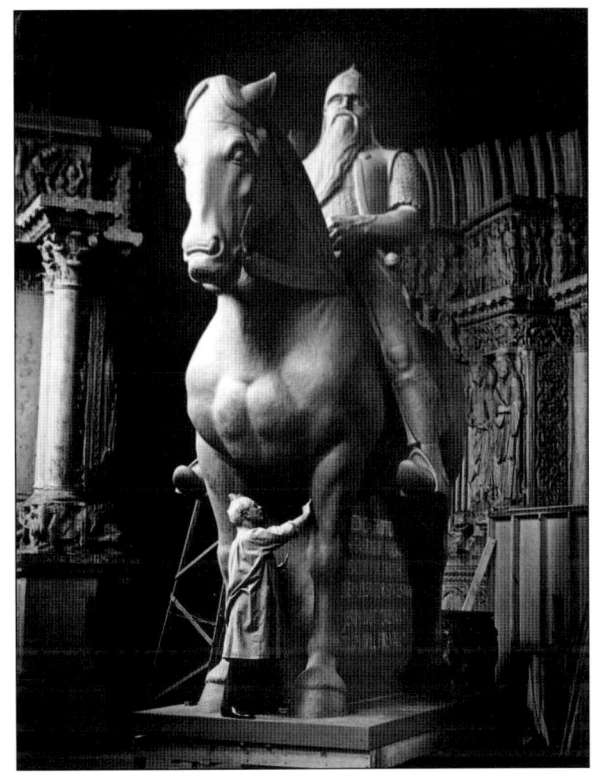

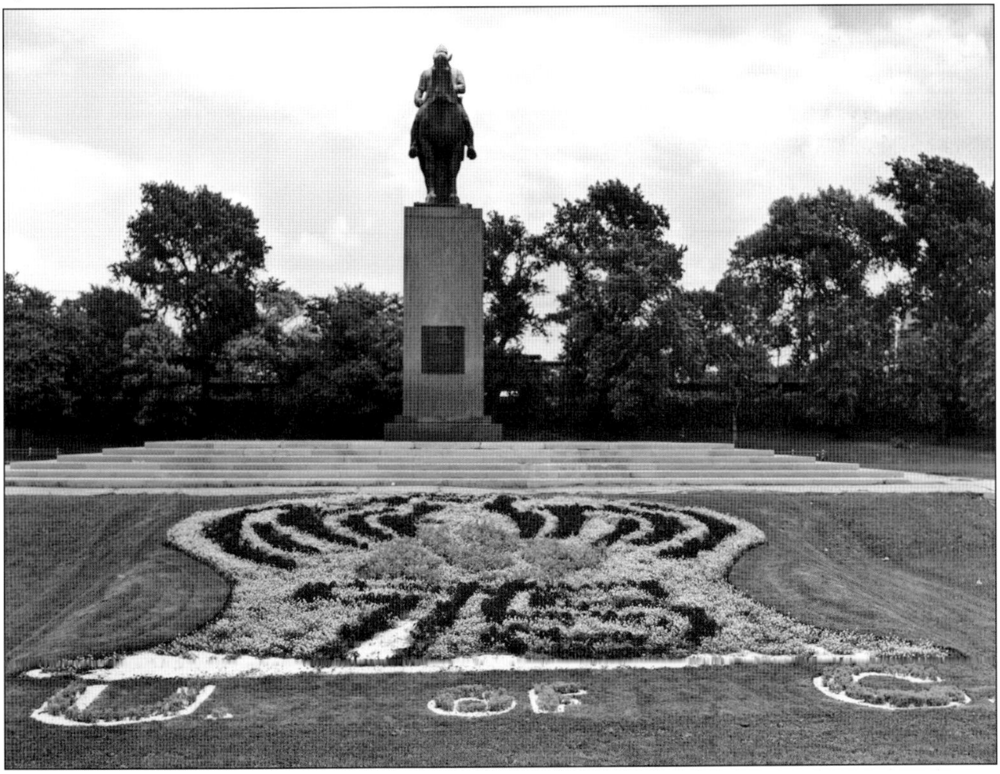

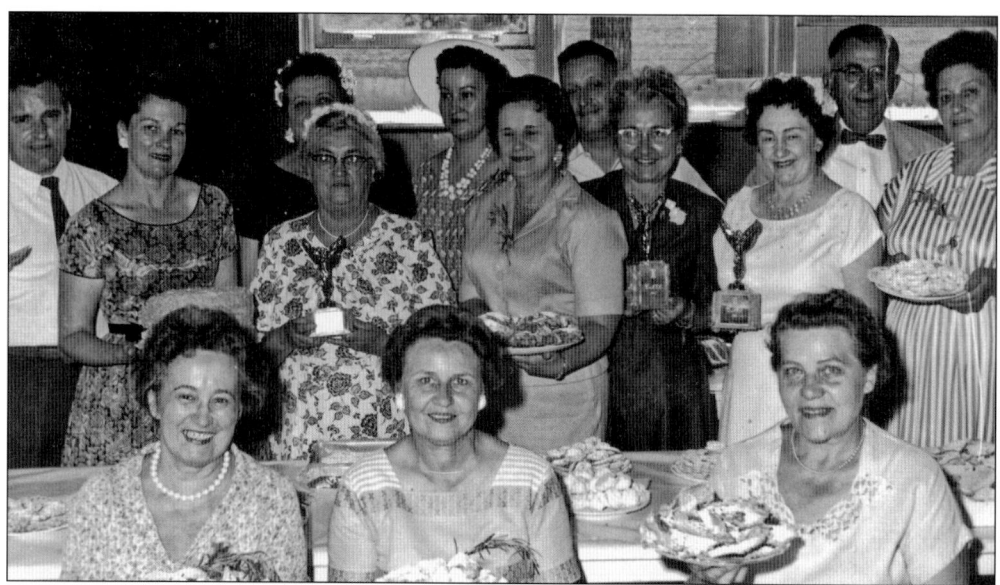

Baking and bazaars are another Czech American custom. Czech baked goods are so famed for their tastiness that many cookbooks emerged from this tradition and are passed down from generation to generation, occasionally even being published. Bazaars and bake sales also help to fund community causes, and as the Czechs moved farther from the city, such events became more common as the community felt the need to draw together from its dispersal in the suburbs. (Courtesy CSA.)

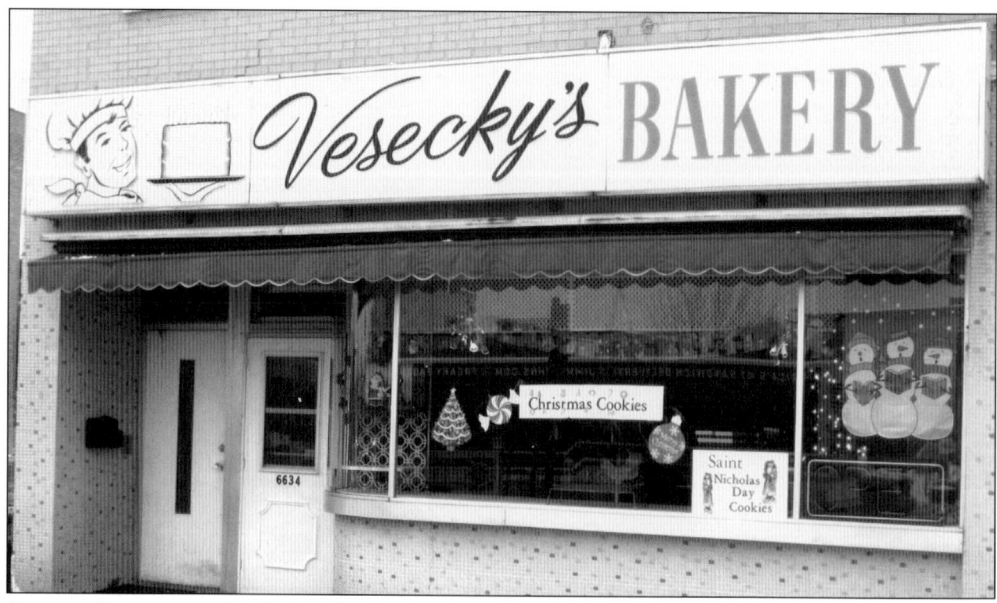

Outstanding among the Czech businesses of Berwyn is an institution that wins accolades year after year. Vesecký's Bakery on Cermak in the town of Berwyn opened in the early 1930s and continues to bake its celebrated *housky*, traditional Czech rye breads, and *koláčky* fresh daily. As a tribute to its exceptional food and authentic Czech hospitality, *Savuer* magazine's October 2007 issue counts Vesecký's as one of Chicago's finest eating establishments. (Author's collection; photograph by Thomas Gaulkin.)

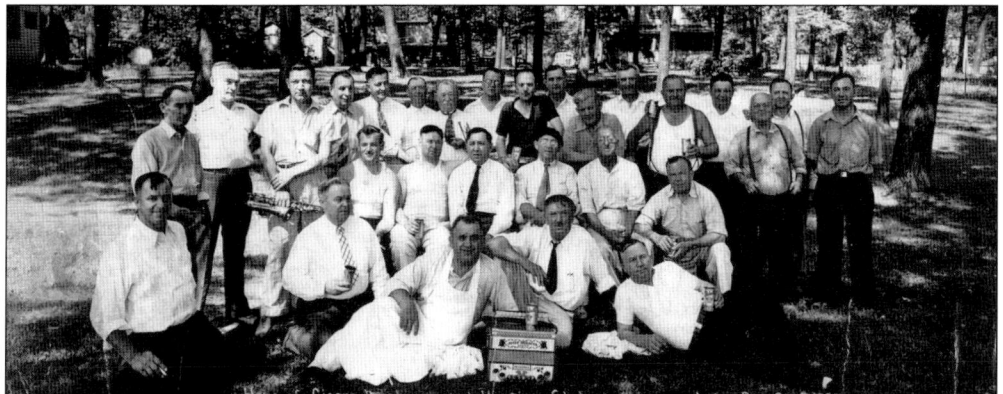

This group portrait of the Cicero Mushroom and Hunting Club on an outing in Antioch was taken on Labor Day 1938. Mushrooming is a great sport among Czechs, who take their mushroom foraging as serious fun. Note here also the role that the concertina plays in Czech outings—this one is Czech-made by the Josef Hlaváček company. (Courtesy CSA.)

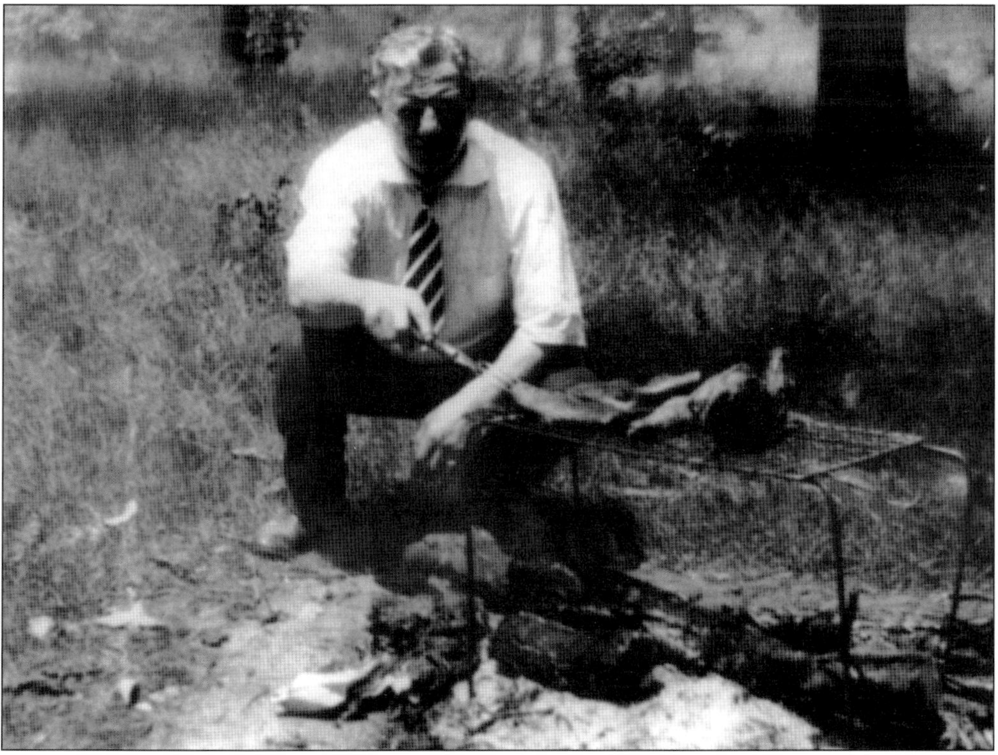

Dolores Beneš Duy recalls how her grandfather Karel Beneš and her family "used to go on picnics in the summer time," it was the only place, she recalls, where all of his children and grandchildren could congregate at one time together. Like many Czech families, they "chose many different picnic grounds" in the western suburbs and outlying towns of Chicago, where green spaces and forest preserves re-created in many ways the atmosphere of the Bohemian countryside. (Courtesy Dorothy Benes Duy.)

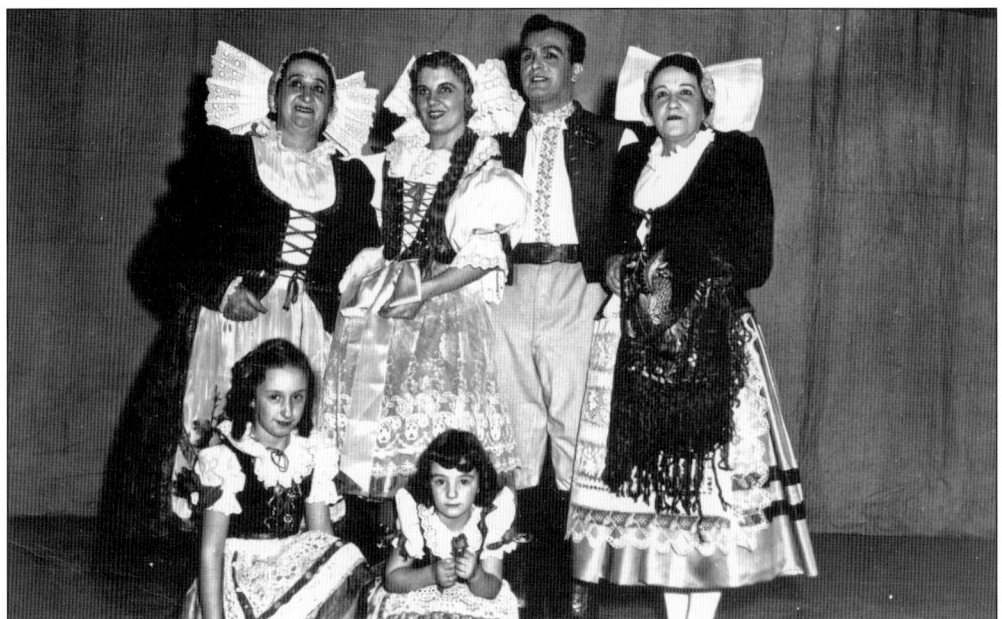

As the community moved to the near western suburbs, the schools and colleges of Cicero and Berwyn filled with Czech students. Evelyn Fergl (née Křenek), an alumna of Morton West High School who grew up in Berwyn and now lives in the Detroit area, recalls that at least 60 percent of the student body was of Czech ancestry. Here Morton West stages the famous Czech comic opera *The Bartered Bride*. (Courtesy CSA.)

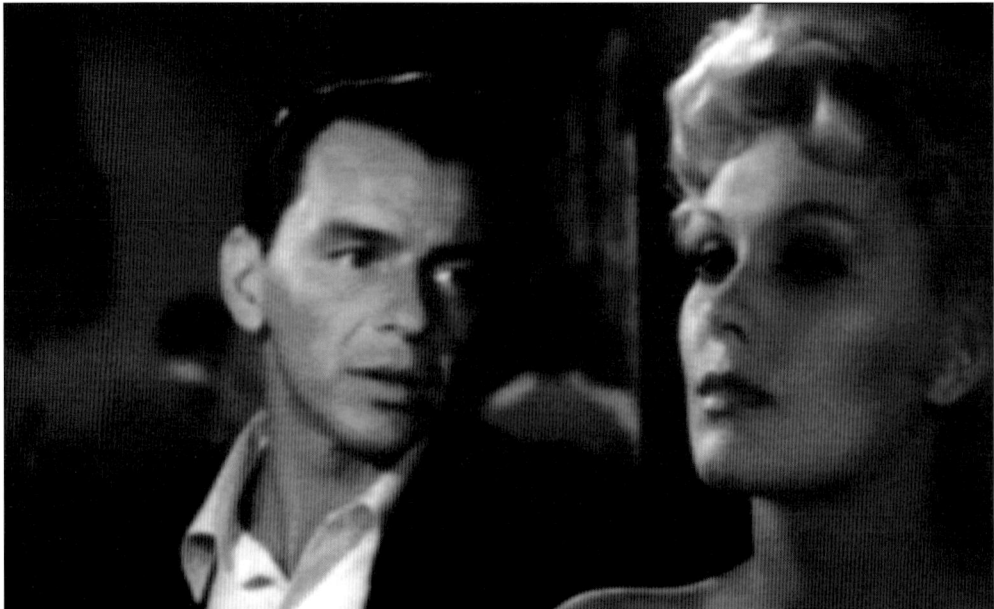

Born Marilyn Novák in 1933 into the Chicago Czech community, Novak would skyrocket to fame in Hollywood. Here she stars opposite Frank Sinatra the film *The Man with the Golden Arm*. Interviewed in 1996, Novak was asked about the pressure to change her name to one less "ethnic"; studio bosses told her "Well, nobody's going to go see a girl with a Polack name." She said, "Well, I'm Czech, but Polish, Czech, no matter, it's my name."

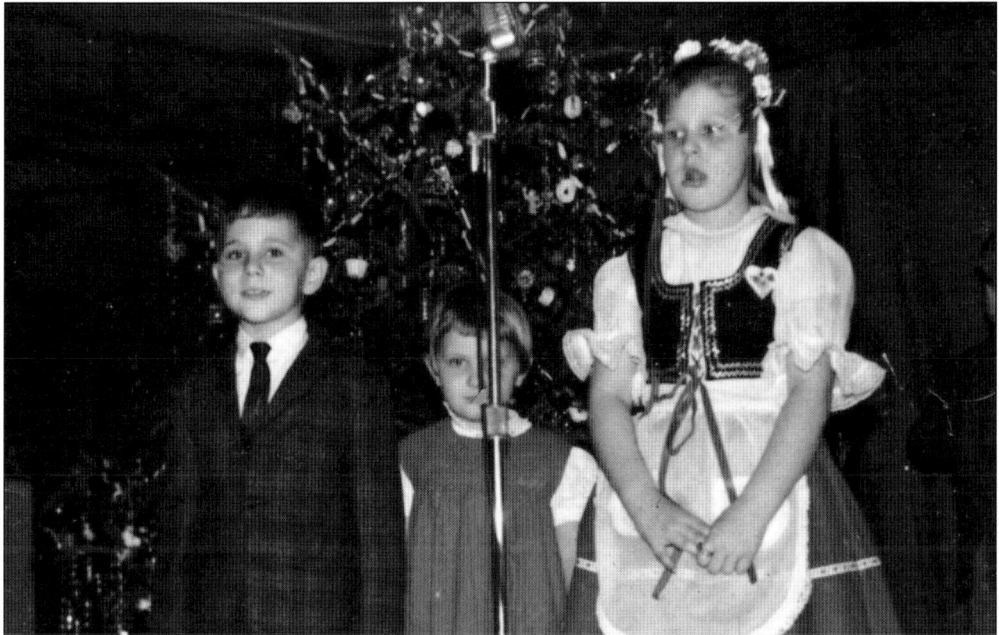

The 1963 Czech-inflected Christmas bazaar in Berwyn featured Joe, Jane, and Rosemary Pritasil, three of Joseph and Rose Pritasil's children. All grown up, another Pritasil, John, and others tend to the traditional Czech Christmas tree at Chicago's annual Christmas Around the World these days. (Courtesy Pritasil family.)

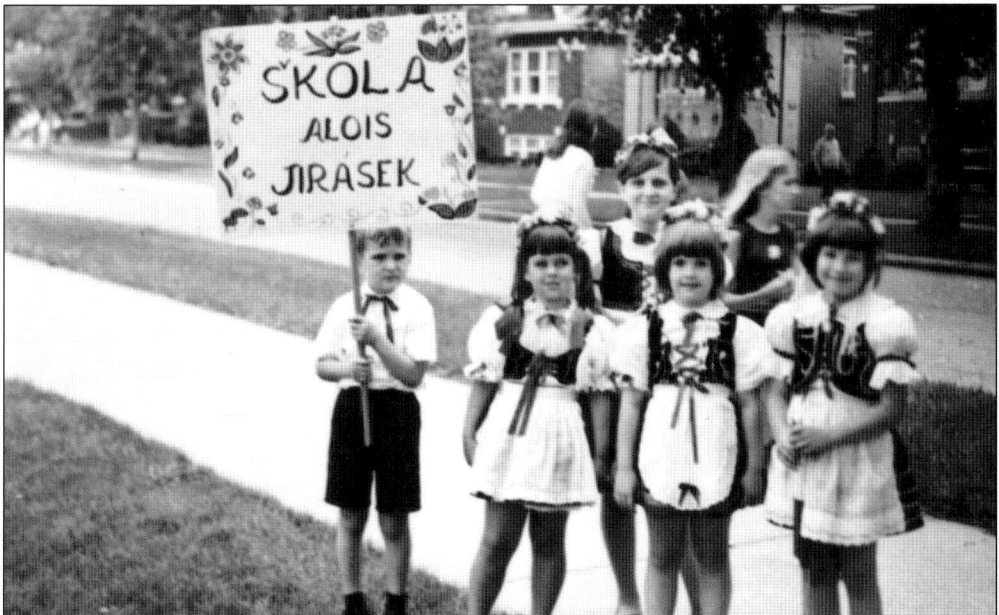

John Pritasil, in an image from the 1960s, holds a sign lovingly made by his mother, Rose, that reads, "School of Alois Jirásek." John's father, Joseph, was born in the Czech lands, emigrating with his family to the United States. John's maternal grandmother came to the United States at the tender age of 14, and his mother grew up in Czech California before the family moved to the western suburbs. (Courtesy John Pritasil.)

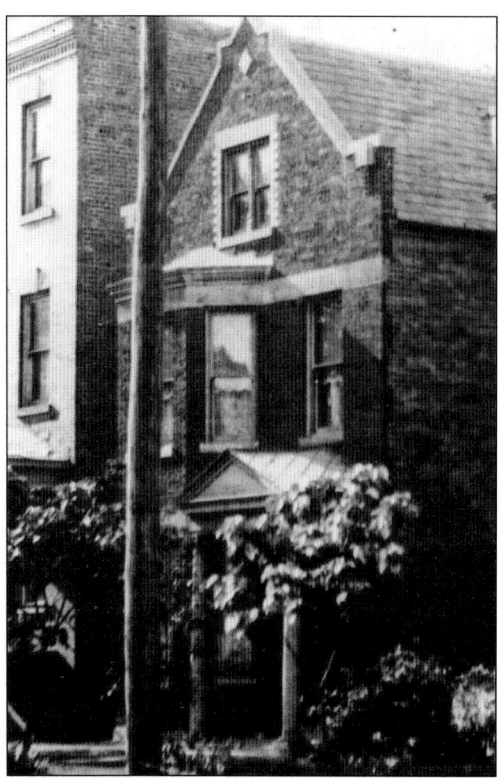

James and Emma Palma moved from the city to the western suburb of Cicero like so many of their Czech compatriots. They purchased this home and lived out their lives there. In true Czech fashion, the house is still in the family today, home to their great-grandsons Ray and Matthew, whose generosity has made the story of the Bezděks and the Palmas available to here. (Courtesy Ray and Matthew Mulac.)

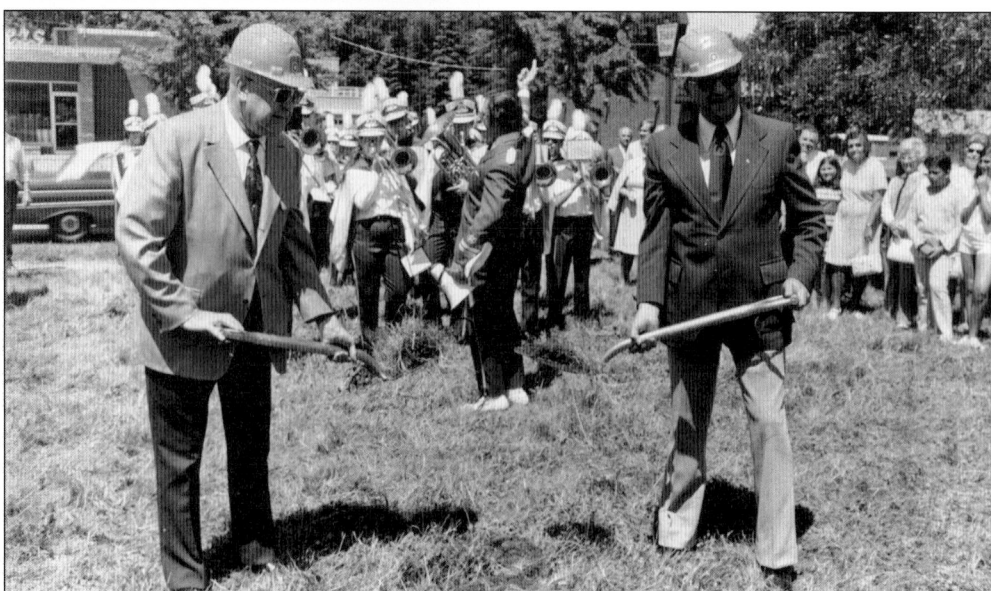

As late as the mid-1970s, Berwyn was still considered the home of the Czech community in Chicagoland. In 1974, one of the cornerstones of the Czech community, the Czechoslovak Society of America, an evolution of the Czechoslovak Protective Society, a fraternal benefit society initiated in 1854, cut the ribbon to its new headquarters in Berwyn. It was here that it established a Czechoslovak Heritage Museum, library, and archives open to the public. (Courtesy CSA.)

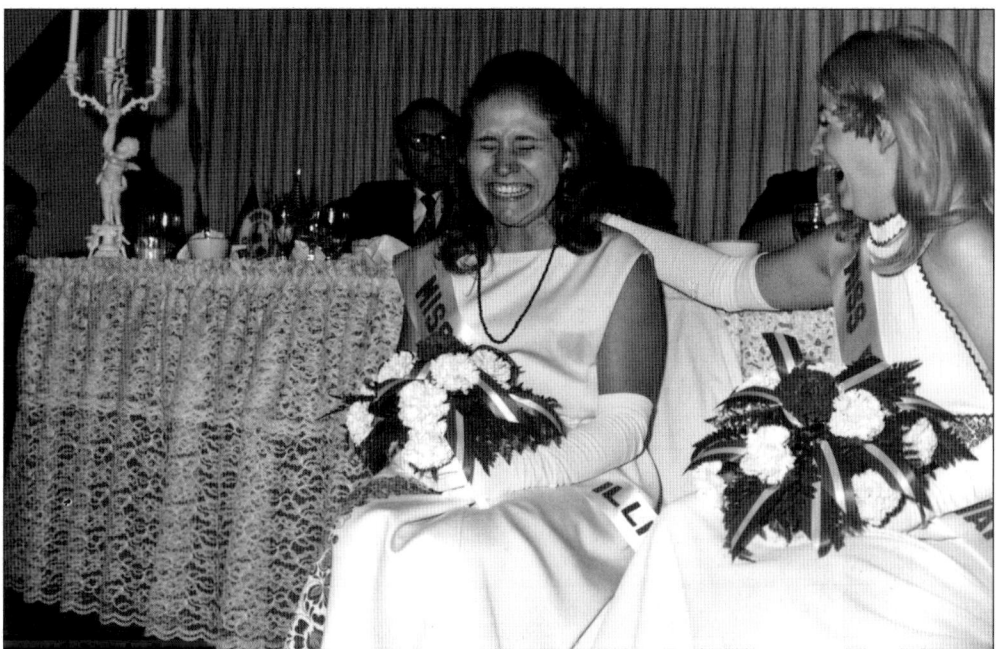

Vera Wilt remembers the excitement of this moment when she won the title of CSA America queen in 1972, and with it the title of Houby Festival queen. After her reign as CSA queen, she served as a member of the board of the CSA and is active today in the Sionilli CSA Lodge of Brookfield and an inspiring community leader. (Courtesy Vera Wilt.)

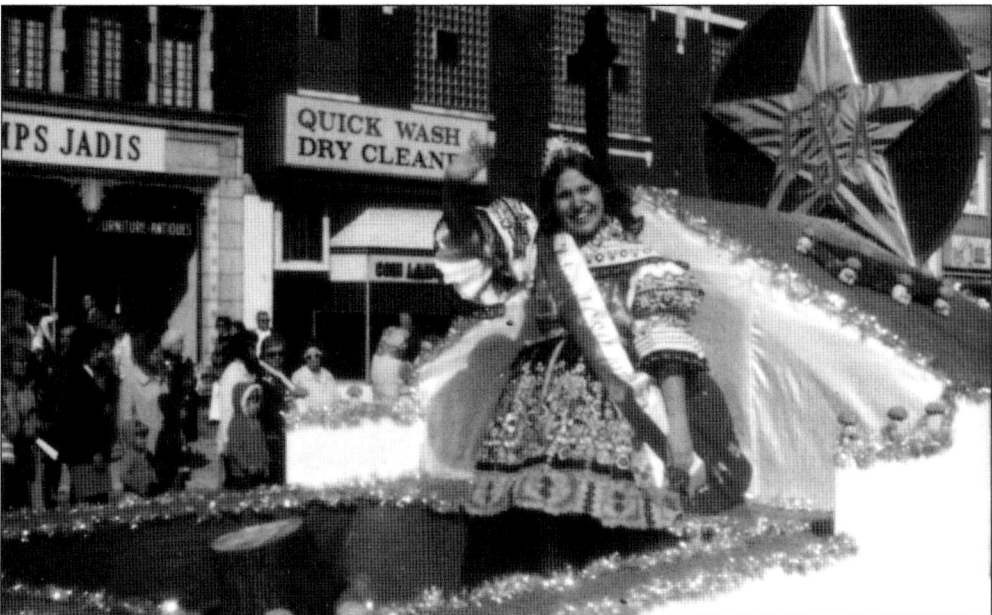

In 1968, a Czech Chicagoland tradition got its start in Berwyn. The International Houby, or Mushroom, Festival celebrated its 39th anniversary in October 2007. Mushroom foraging is a time-honored custom among Czechs, and the fact that the Houby Festival has survived these many years and grown to engage the now predominantly Latino residents of Cicero and Berwyn is evidence of the appeal of Bohemian celebrations. (Courtesy CSA.)

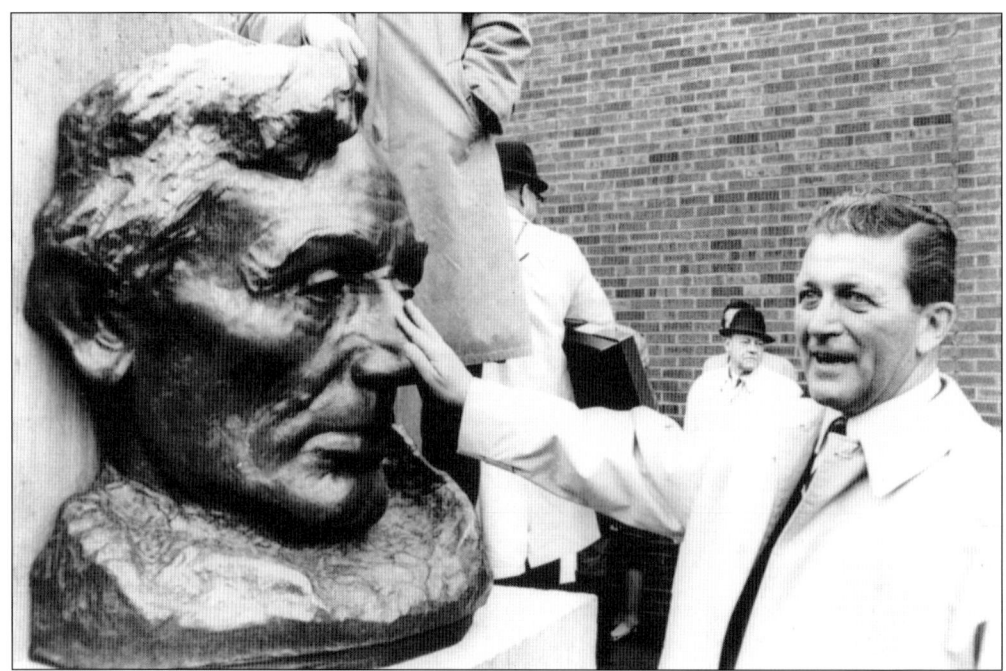

Otto Kerner Jr., 33rd governor of Illinois from 1960 to 1968, participates in an Illinois political ritual, the rubbing of Abraham Lincoln's nose for luck. Kerner Jr. married into another important political family when he wed Helena Čermák, Antonín Čermák's daughter, in 1934. In 1968 Kerner Jr. followed in his father's footsteps and served as a judge on the Seventh Circuit U.S. Court of Appeals. (Author's collection; photograph by Roger Higgins.)

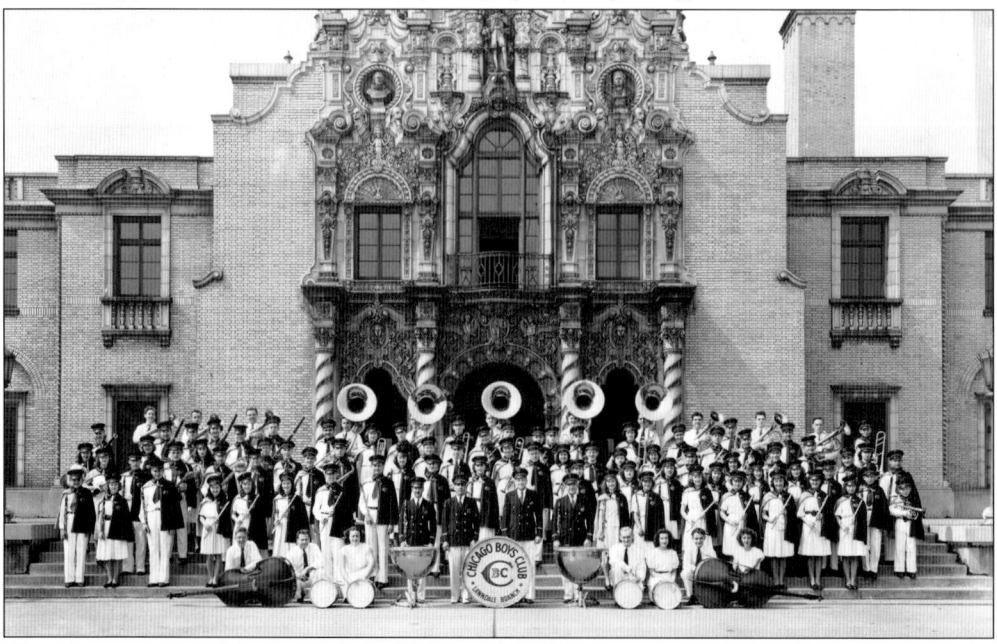

The Chicago Boys Club Concert Band, directed by John Sovinec and organized in 1921 at the Lawndale Club, was renowned for its skill, proof again of the Czech love and gift of musicality. (Courtesy Angela Bultas.)

Five

CZECHS IN CHICAGOLAND TODAY

By the 1970s, with its hard work, native frugality, and business acumen, the Czech community in Chicagoland had a strong and successful reputation. Czechs began settling now in suburbs and towns like Stickney, Oakbrook, Riverside, La Grange Park, and Brookfield further afield of the city. Neighborhoods in the northwest of the city too are now a hub for Czech American business; in Montclare, Café Prague is a vibrant site for Czech culture in the city; in Portage Park, Club Euro offers an authentic European nightclub experience.

More difficult now, dispersed as they are, to call any one public space definitively Czech, the resourcefulness of the Czech spirit makes itself felt in communal get-togethers such as picnics and in organizations, like the acclaimed Moravian Cultural Society. Sokol lodges are still extremely active in Chicagoland, due in large part to the energies of leaders like Jean Hruby. American Sokol has its new headquarters in Brookfield. The Czechoslovak Society of America, or CSA Fraternal Life, with due pride celebrated its 150th year of service in 2004. And literally up the road from these institutions stands another Czech-affiliated organization's world headquarters: McDonald's. Without the intervention of Oak Park–born Czech Chicagoan Ray Kroc, McDonald's may still be a California-based burger joint with a just a few local outlets.

Czech radio and television also have become important mediators for a more dispersed ethnic community. *Czech American TV in Chicago* has a weekly show on Sundays on Channel 41 that has been broadcasting since 2004 to a wide audience; and Czech radio has its weekly slot also on Sunday mornings on WCEV AM 1450.

The connections between Chicago and the Czech lands are profound. The Chicago-Prague sister cities program established in 1990, a year after the Czechs had peaceably regained their independence, galvanized the already strong relationship that has existed between Chicago and the Czech lands, a relationship that in the summer of 2007 was celebrated with the city's Czech-Chicago Days.

Despite rhetoric about the Czechs' overzealous assimilation into U.S. culture, Czech Chicagoland is still a lively and very self-assuredly Czech community. The Czech desire to become model U.S. citizens goes hand in hand with a deep pride in their roots and a well-developed consciousness of their ethnic identity.

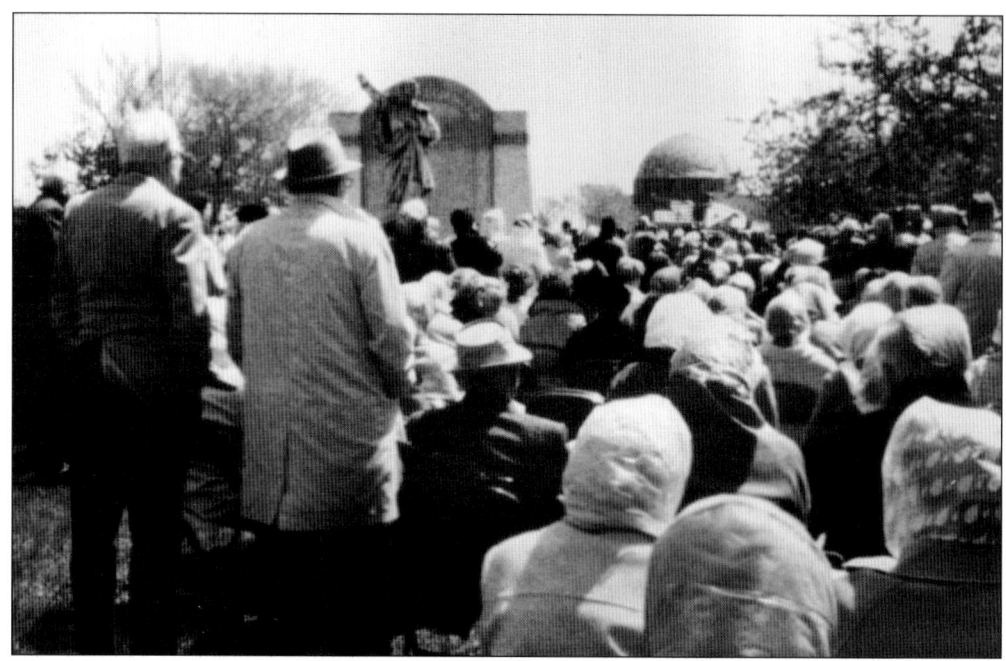

In 1983, the statue of Czech poet and patriot Karel Havlíček Borovský sculpted by Joseph Strachouský was moved from its original home in Douglas Park in the city's North Lawndale community—once central to the Czech community—to the lakefront, in a prized location near the Adler Planetarium. (Courtesy CSA.)

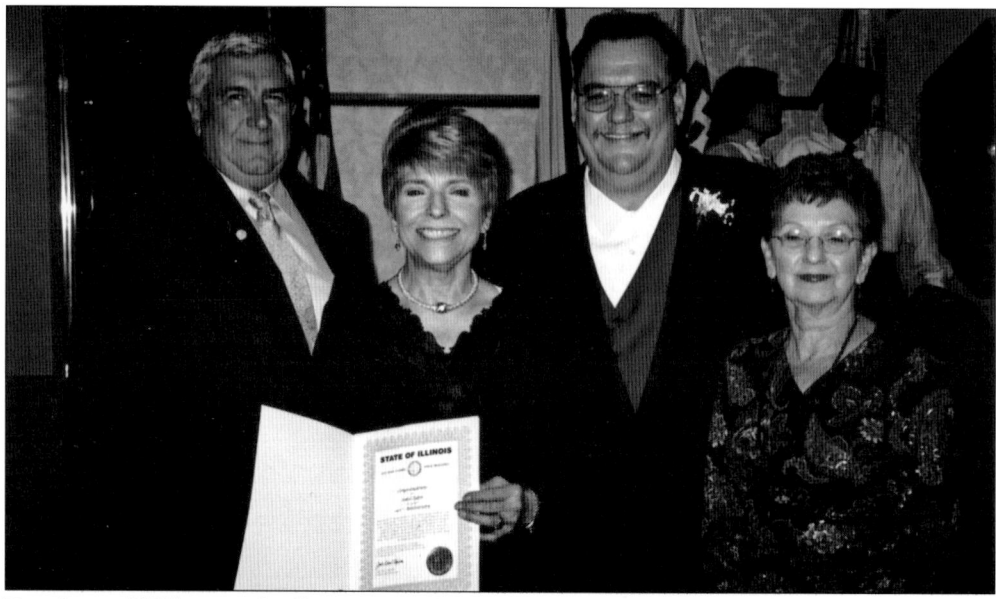

Daughter of William and Lillian Baar, Judy Baar Topinka was born and raised in the Chicago suburb of Riverside. After holding key positions in Illinois government, in 1994 she became Illinois state treasurer. In 2002, she was appointed chair of the Republican Committee of Illinois and in 2006 won her party's nomination for the gubernatorial election. Although she lost the campaign, Baar Topinka continues to be an active member of the Republican Party in Illinois and an important voice in the Czech Chicagoland community. (Courtesy CSA.)

Facets Multimedia has been an important Chicago cultural establishment and a nationally recognized center for artistically important films since the mid-1970s. Czech-born Miloš Štehlík, who founded and runs Facets Multimedia, has an international reputation for his film expertise. Here world-famous Czech director Jan Němec, who made Chicago his home in exile in the 1970s and 1980s, is shown in the Facets theater. (Courtesy Miloš Štehlík/Facets Multimedia.)

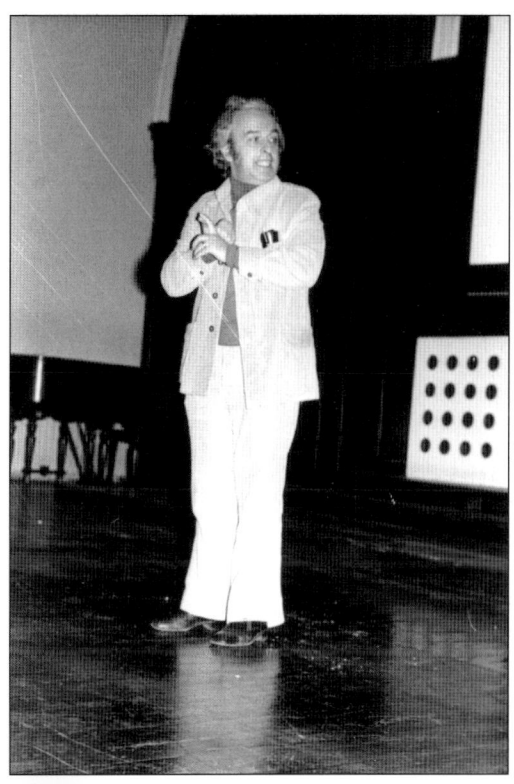

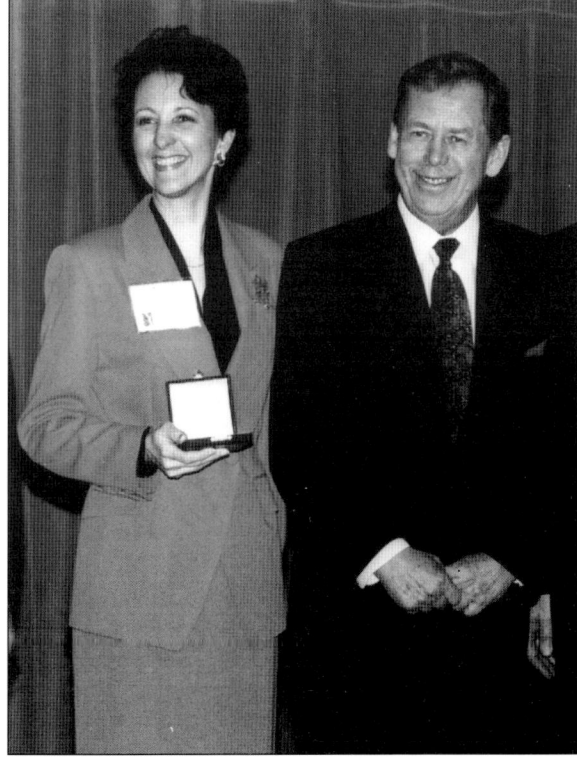

It was Chicago that one-time dissident writer Václav Havel, duly elected president of then Czechoslovakia, made a priority destination in his tour of the United States to discuss postcommunist reparations. This photograph from 1999 shows Havel with then vice president of the CSA Deborah Zeman. Havel has just bestowed Zeman with the Presidential Medal of Honor in recognition of the CSA's immense contributions to the Czech nation. (Courtesy CSA.)

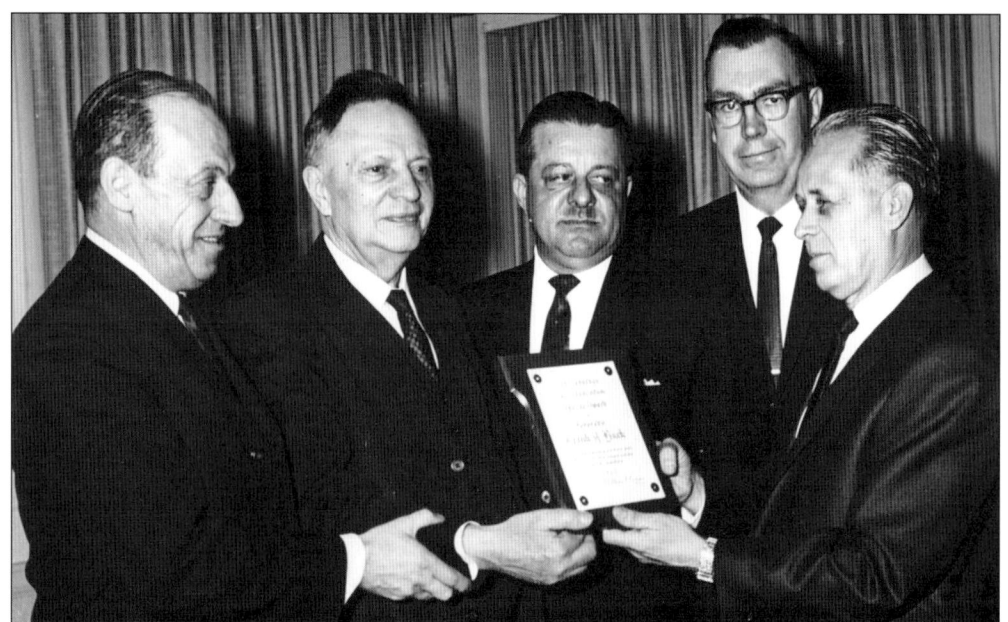

Frank Bicek, a founder of the Bohemian Lawyer's Association, the oldest ethnic bar association in the country, accepts the West Suburban Bar Association award in this image from the 1960s. Bicek was a highly decorated and successful judge in Cook County. He and his wife, Sylvie, have left as legacy a scholarship in their name, for exceptional students of political science at Benedictine University in Lisle. The association turns 100 in 2011. (Courtesy CSA.)

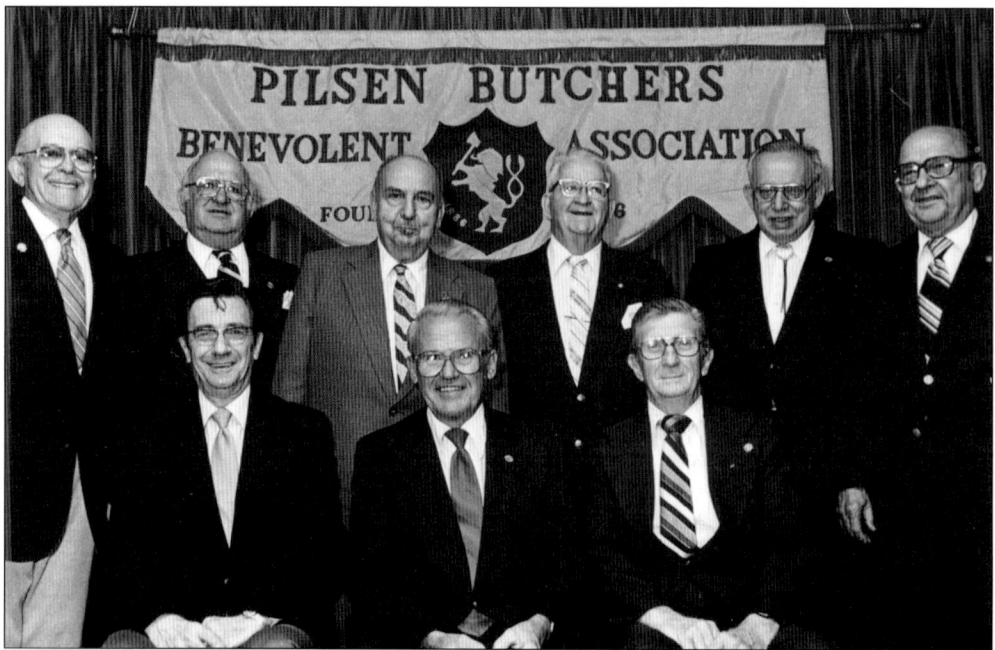

In 1986, the Pilsen Butcher's Association celebrated its 100th year of service. Although few of the butchers in the benevolent society today work in the neighborhood where the organization began, their commitment to the fraternal ideals and sodality of the organization are stronger than ever. (Courtesy CSA.)

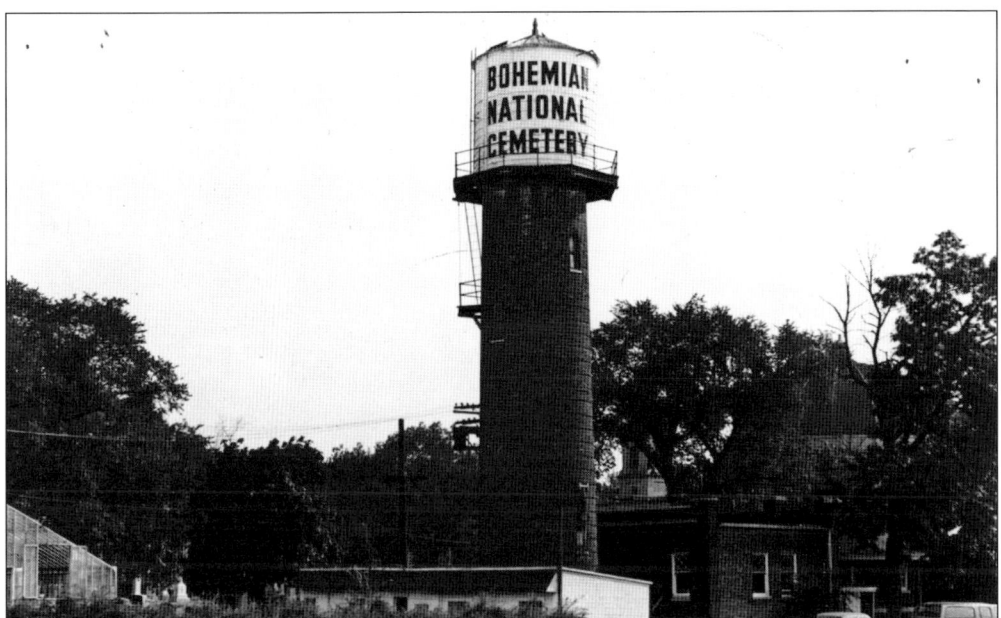

The Bohemian National Cemetery (BNC)—after much work on the part of Angela Bultas and other Friends of the BNC—was designated a national historic place in 2006. In 2007, it won a restoration grant in a campaign spearheaded by Marge Sladek Stueckemann. The BNC testifies to the enduring spirit of Czech Americans to preserve their cultural achievements and share these with a wider audience. (Courtesy Marge Sladek Stueckemann.)

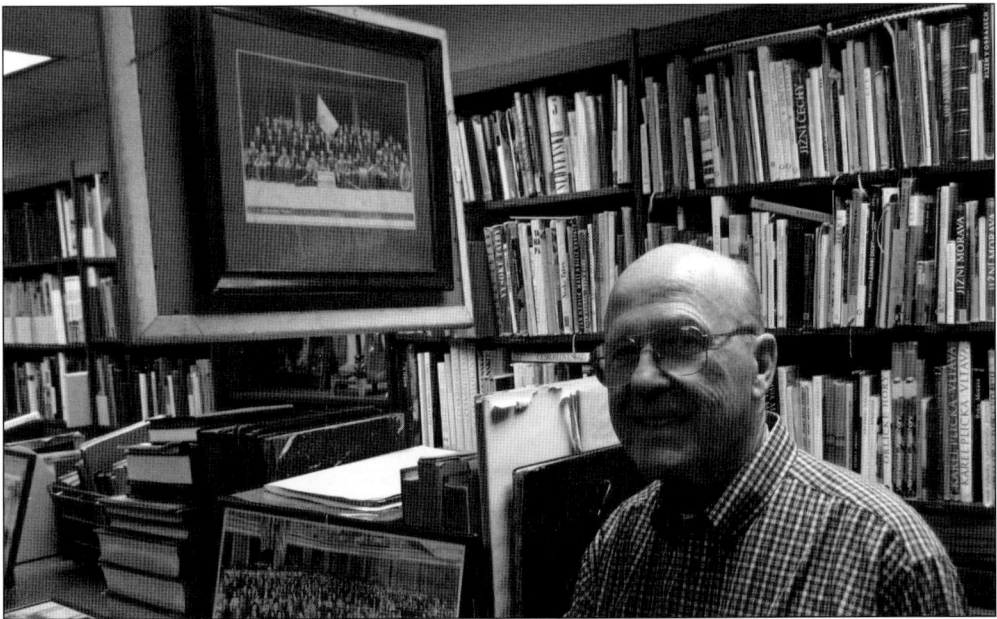

Paul Němeček, pictured above with photographs by his grandfather Francis D. Němeček, is an acclaimed Czech genealogist and archivist of Czech culture in the United States. The setting for the photograph above is the library of the CSA in Oakbrook, an archive that Paul, along with several other dedicated individuals of Czech heritage through the years, has been instrumental in preserving and maintaining. (Author's collection; photograph by Thomas Gaulkin.)

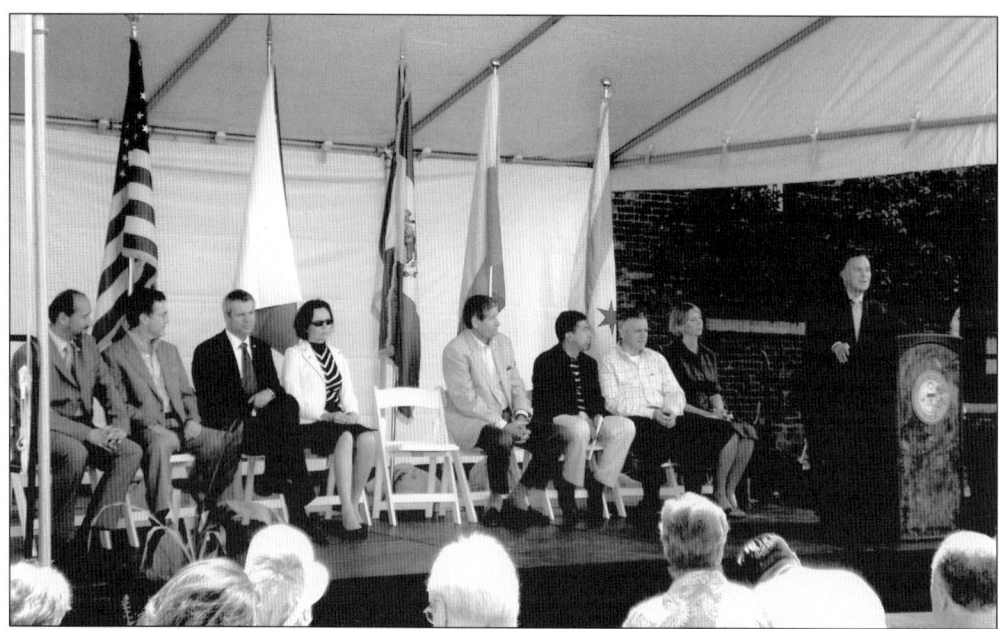

The year 2007 was a banner year for the Czechs of Chicagoland. In June, Prague Days, a celebration of Chicago's Czech cultural life, was launched. The celebration offered a variety of Czech artistic and musical attractions. On June 30, Cermak Road, named in honor of the Czech-born mayor of Chicago, was rededicated by Mayor Richard M. Daley with Czech ambassador to the United States Petr Kolář in attendance. (Courtesy Czech Consulate in Chicago.)

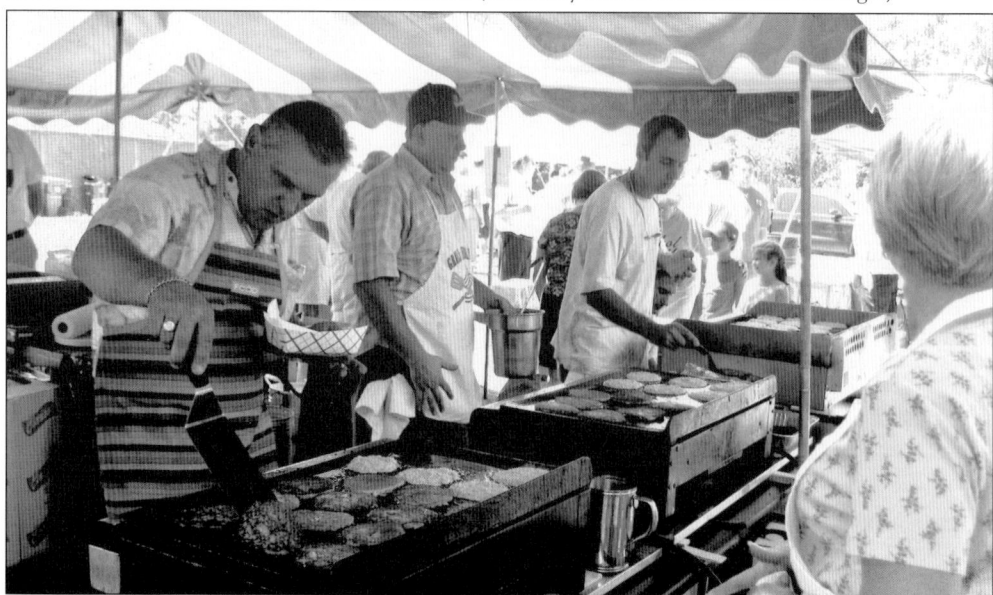

Czechs have a long tradition of the picnic as a favorite social pastime, and they are held regularly in Chicagoland's clement months (like this one in August 2007). The picnics usually take place in the cooler forest preserves near the western suburbs of the city, and people of all ethnic backgrounds are welcome, but, as the author now knows, it takes a real Czech to fry up potato pancakes in the heat of a Chicagoland summer. (Author's collection; photograph by Thomas Gaulkin.)

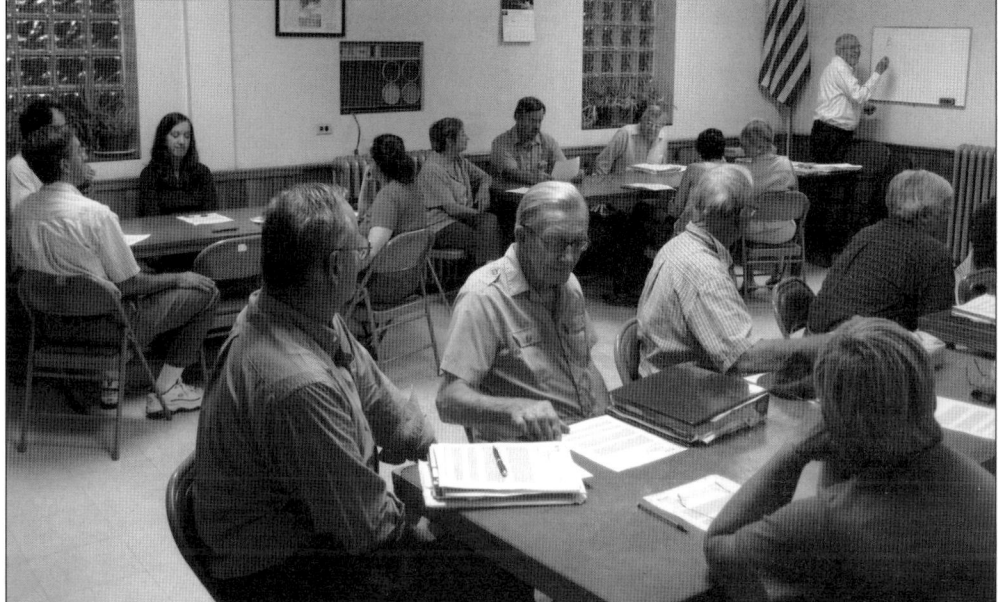

Cicero's Masaryk School opened in 1921, the same year an international Sokol slet was held in the city. Czechoslovak Sokol leader Jan Havránek proclaimed, "as long as they are building Sokol halls and Czech schools, there is no need for concern about the life of the American branch of the Czechoslovak nation." Today inspiring teachers, like Bob Baumruch pictured here, continue to teach Czech. (Author's collection; photograph by Thomas Gaulkin.)

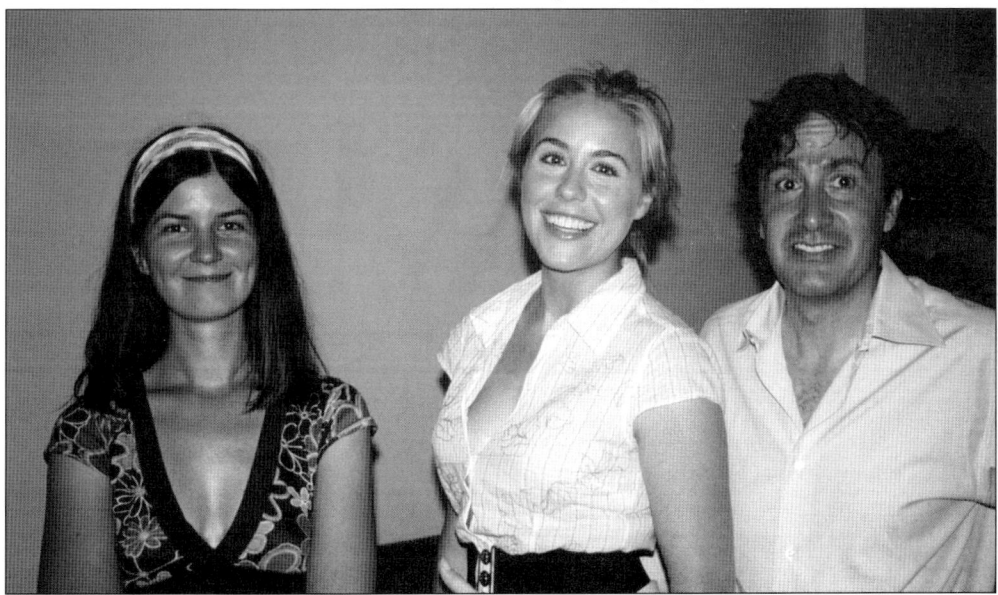

Lenka Dolanová, Czech native and art critic who worked in Chicago on a project called "It's fun to be Bohemian," is pictured above with Katrina Walker and her partner Giuseppe Burlando. Walker and Burlando's passion for the restoration of Pilsen's Thalia theater has reinvigorated interest in the Czech beginnings of the neighborhood. The building, now 115 years old, is already showing its art nouveau inspirations once again in the many beautifully painted glass doors. (Author's collection; photograph by Thomas Gaulkin.)

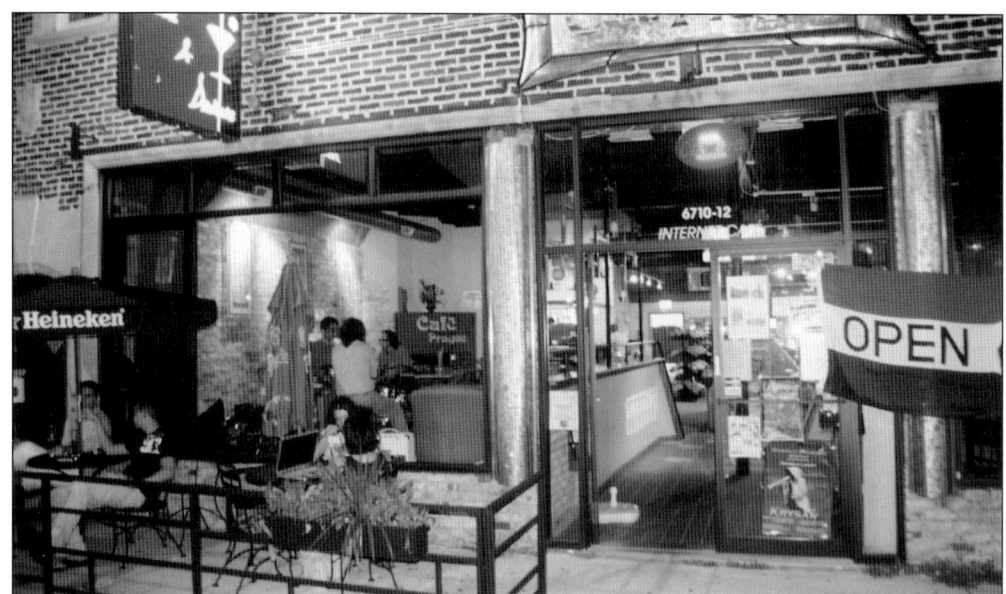

Café Prague in Montclare is a restaurant, bar, and café, where patrons are not only allowed to sit for hours sipping their coffee or imported Moravian wine, but are encouraged to. The café, owned and operated by Czech-born Milada Chlubnová, also sells Czech books, magazines, CDs, DVDs, and other Czech imports. This picture from a Sunday evening blues performance gives some sense of the special Czech life and spirit of Café Prague. (Author's collection; photograph by Thomas Gaulkin.)

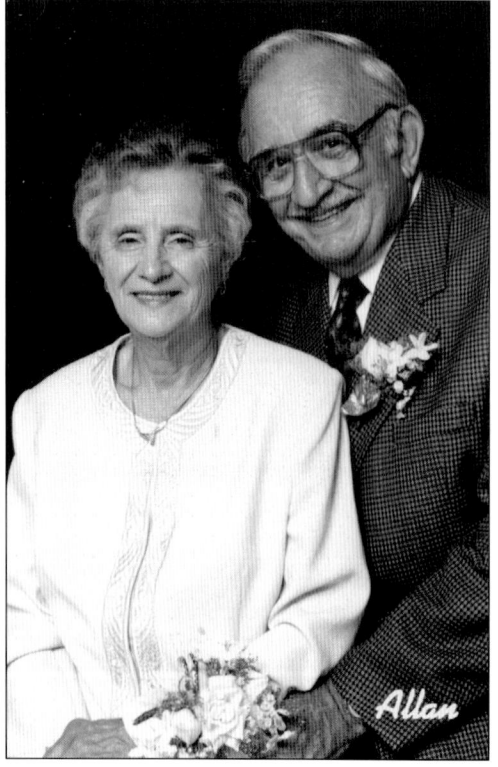

This story of the family of Dorothy (Bezděk) Mulac culminates in this picture taken on the occasion of her 50th wedding anniversary. She and her husband had seven children: Carolyn, Joseph, Jacqueline, Mary Christine, Gregory, Raymond, and Matthew. She dedicated the memory book, which the author has been given the gracious permission to share, to them. (Courtesy Ray and Matthew Mulac.)

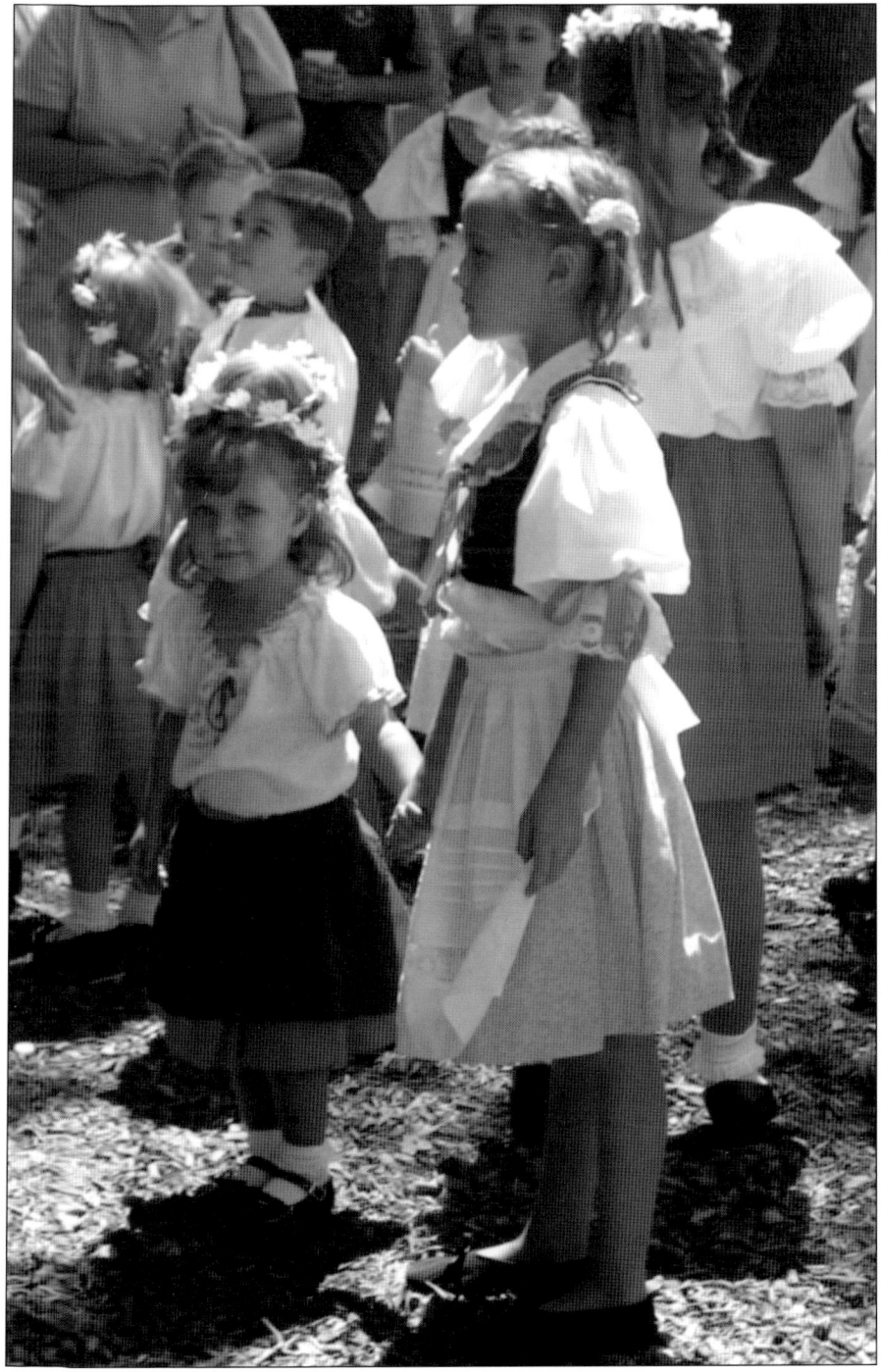
Czech national consciousness and ethnic pride are manifest in the many annual festivals the Czech American community stages. Here children from the United Moravian Society, Madeline Fisette (left) and Olivia Lata, are dressed in kroje. These traditional folk costumes, often family heirlooms, hold a place of pride in Czech homes throughout Chicagoland. (Author's collection; photograph by Thomas Gaulkin.)

Across America, People are Discovering Something Wonderful. Their Heritage.

Arcadia Publishing is the leading local history publisher in the United States. With more than 3,000 titles in print and hundreds of new titles released every year, Arcadia has extensive specialized experience chronicling the history of communities and celebrating America's hidden stories, bringing to life the people, places, and events from the past. To discover the history of other communities across the nation, please visit:

www.arcadiapublishing.com

Customized search tools allow you to find regional history books about the town where you grew up, the cities where your friends and family live, the town where your parents met, or even that retirement spot you've been dreaming about.

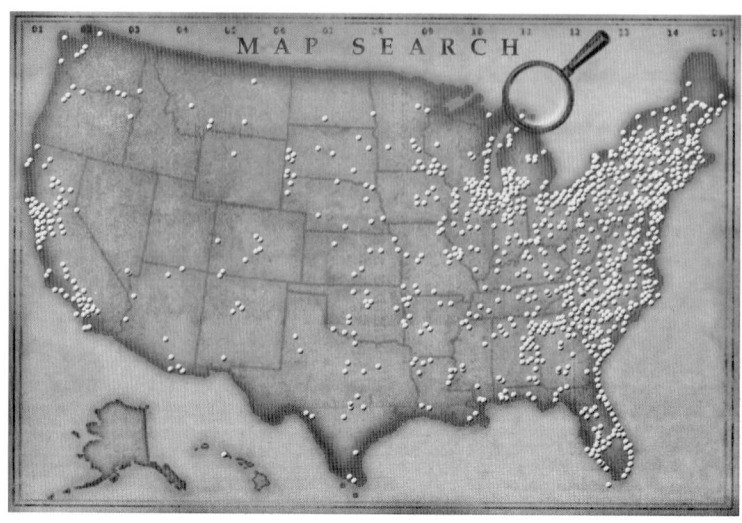